HUNGER AND FURY

D1263185

JASMIN MUJANOVIĆ

Hunger and Fury

The Crisis of Democracy
in the Balkans

OXFORD
UNIVERSITY PRESS

Oxford University Press is a department of the
University of Oxford. It furthers the University's objective
of excellence in research, scholarship, and education
by publishing worldwide.

Oxford New York

Auckland Cape Town Dar es Salaam Hong Kong Karachi
Kuala Lumpur Madrid Melbourne Mexico City Nairobi
New Delhi Shanghai Taipei Toronto

With offices in

Argentina Austria Brazil Chile Czech Republic France Greece
Guatemala Hungary Italy Japan Poland Portugal Singapore
South Korea Switzerland Thailand Turkey Ukraine Vietnam

Oxford is a registered trade mark of Oxford University Press
in the UK and certain other countries.

Published in the United States of America by
Oxford University Press
198 Madison Avenue, New York, NY 10016

© Jasmin Mujanović, 2018

Library of Congress Cataloging-in-Publication Data is available
Jasmin Mujanović
Hunger and Fury: The Crisis of Democracy in the Balkans
ISBN: 978-0-19087-739-2
Printed in the United Kingdom by Bell & Bain Ltd, Glasgow

For my grandparents, the revolutionaries

CONTENTS

ACKNOWLEDGEMENTS

The completion of this book is only partially the result of my own efforts. In fact, it is mostly the product of the support, patience, and mentorship of a constellation of people who have navigated me through this journey. As large segments of this text first saw the light of day as a dissertation at York University, my sincere thanks go first and foremost to Terry Maley, Daphne N. Winland, and Robert Latham for their intellectual and scholarly guidance, accommodation, and vigour. Each of them read my original project through a different lens and each of them improved it infinitely as a result. Their generosity in supporting my, at times, rather unorthodox ruminations made the entire endeavour of obtaining a PhD a rewarding challenge rather than a punishing trial, for which I am genuinely grateful. And they likewise deserve credit for allowing me to craft an academic treatise that has lent itself relatively easily to reanimation as a text for a wider audience.

I am also indebted to a broader community of scholars and experts who have significantly improved my analytical capacities through their mentorship and friendship. Dejan Guzina and Amila Buturovic were key to the original phase of the project at York, while Adis Merdzanovic and Kurt Bassuener showered early drafts of the book version with generous and much needed critique. For his part, Eric Gordy has been a patient counsellor and, like Dr Maley, Dr Winland, and Dr Latham, a still more patient letter writer. I am also obliged to thank Toby Vogel, an incisive analyst in his own right, for making the initial introductions with Michael Dwyer. Mr Dwyer, in turn, has afforded me the greatest courtesy in putting together this work, and his team at Hurst Publishers has been professional and supportive throughout.

There is also a broader universe of folk whose friendship (and vulgarity) has sustained me for the past two decades. In Vancouver, these are Dejan Preradović, Nikola Mitrović, Ognjen Đukić, and Nenad Knežević. In Sarajevo, they are Emir Efendić, Gorana Dedić, Emin Eminagić, and Damir Imamović. Strewn across the rest of the world are also Dario Čepo, Kole Kilibarda, Tea Hadžiristić, and Francisco de Borja Lasheras.

The role my parents and family have played in this undertaking is difficult to encapsulate, no less so the significance of its completion in their eyes. My parents' eternal dedication, bravery, and sacrifice for their family is something I have only grown more awed and humbled by with age. I am especially blessed by my sister, to whom I have scarcely often enough expressed gratitude for her friendship and affection, and my niece Ayna. Though still the littlest member of our tribe, she has shown outsized courage and wisdom in her young life already.

It has been from Elise Wang, however, that I have learnt the finer points of functioning personhood. Where I middle at opining, she is the true scholar. And though her every accomplishment fills me with immeasurable pride, I still hold that she deserves more than the world has to offer. Above all, she is my friend, always, an exhausting feat for which I am eternally in her debt.

Because I am graced by them all, the reader will recall that all errors, typos, and gross generalizations in this text are solely my own.

March 2017

ABBREVIATIONS

BiH – Bosnia and Herzegovina

CPY – Communist Party of Yugoslavia

EAEU – Eurasian Economic Union

ECHR – European Court of Human Rights

EEC – European Economic Community

FBiH – Federation of Bosnia and Herzegovina

FRJ – Federal Republic of Yugoslavia

FPRJ – Federal People's Republic of Yugoslavia

HDZ – Croatian Democratic Union

ICTY – International Tribunal for the Former Yugoslavia

JNA – Yugoslav National Army

LCY – League of Communists of Yugoslavia

NATO – North Atlantic Treaty Organization

NOP/NOB – National Liberation Movement

NRS – People's Radical Party

OHR – Office of the High Representative

OSCE – Organization for Security and Co-operation in Europe

RS – Republika Srpska

SDA – Party of Democratic Action

SDP – Social Democratic Party

SDS – Serb Democratic Party

SDSM – Social Democratic Union of Macedonia

SFRJ – Socialist Federal Republic of Yugoslavia

SNSD – Alliance of Independent Social Democrats

UAE – United Arab Emirates

UK – United Kingdom

US – United States of America

VMRO-DPMNE – Internal Macedonian Revolutionary Organization-Democratic Party for Macedonian National Unity

WB6 – Western Balkan Six

ZL – United Left

INTRODUCTION

The parliamentary regimes of southeastern Europe are in crisis. Left to teeter and wobble much longer, these regimes will dissolve entirely and, with them, the tenuous peace that has held the Balkans together since the conclusion of the Yugoslav Wars (1991–2001). With Greece still on the brink of financial catastrophe, and Turkey in a headlong rush towards outright autocracy, all that stands between the prosperous, stable core of Europe and the chaos of Syria and Iraq is a string of economically stagnant and politically volatile polities wedged between the Adriatic and the Bosphorus. However, the heart of my argument – both geographically and thematically – concerns the specific crisis of democracy in the states of the former Yugoslavia. The accession of Slovenia and Croatia to the European Union (EU) in 2004 and 2013 respectively has been celebrated by policymakers in Brussels and Washington as definitive proof of the region's fundamental transformation. Indeed, missives from the Union regularly remind the leaders of the region's remaining prospective member states that the EU is the "only game in town". On both points, this book contends otherwise.

The process of Euro-Atlantic integration (i.e. EU and NATO membership) in the Balkans has not significantly altered the structural dimensions of the region's prevailing political and economic dynamics. Politically, the post-Yugoslav Balkan elite are still a band of oligarchs. They are survivors of the collapse of one-party rule and decidedly

1

authoritarian in orientation, despite the proliferation of nominally competitive multiparty elections and parliamentary institutional arrangements across the region. Their economic policies, meanwhile, remain rooted in clientelism, corruption, and dispossession: a system that has elsewhere been referred to as "kleptocracy".[1] The coercive power of the state is still the primary means of accumulation for Balkan elites, allowing them to continue to govern as warlords even in an era of peace. Since 2012, however, in reaction to both the bankruptcy of Western democratization efforts and the retreat of local elites from even nominal commitments to accountable and responsive democratic governance, a wave of new grassroots social movements – from Slovenia to Bosnia-Herzegovina (BiH) to Macedonia – has dramatically realigned politics in the former Yugoslavia. In their wake the essential cleavage of contemporary Balkan politics has become the determined attempt by insurgent mass movements to topple the entrenched, oligarchic elites of the region, who alone in the sea of former communist regimes in Europe successfully navigated the collapse of the Cold War order without ever actually losing power.

I refer to this combination of oligarchy and criminality – a central feature of the region's general historical development – as "elastic authoritarianism": the process of persistent ideological mutation contrasted with static political and economic patterns, through which local elites have deliberately stunted social transformation processes in the Balkans since the nineteenth century. As a result, the basic contention of this book holds that Western[2] democratization policy in the former Yugoslavia was and remains fatally flawed in its reliance on the willingness of local leaders to abandon authoritarian and clientelistic patterns of rule, patterns that have kept them, their predecessors, and their peers in power for generations. Instead, genuine democratic transformation depends on the ability of popular, grassroots social movements to contest, challenge, and eventually topple recalcitrant authoritarian regimes or regime elements.

In the Western Balkans,[3] such movements with such power have only begun to appear in the last four or five years.[4] The belated appearance of these social ruptures, however, is not merely the result of the violent dissolution of Yugoslavia but is instead rooted in the aforementioned generational patterns of state formation and dissolution in the region. As a result, we are only now, at the tail end of the second decade of the twenty-first century, witnessing the kinds of social confrontations that have elsewhere in Europe marked the end of authoritarian rule.[5] Accordingly, and in contrast to the majority of the academic, policy, and popular analyses of post-Yugoslav politics, this book contends that democratization, in any meaningful sense of the term, has yet to occur. Ultimately, this work suggests that unless "regime change" is a local, bottom-up exercise, driven by organic social mobilizations, it is unlikely to be decisive or lasting, or to occur at all.

By insisting on a grassroots, participatory conception of democratization, this work rejects both the institutional and elite-focused approaches of preceding studies and accounts of post-war politics in the former Yugoslavia. Their concentration on the shibboleth of Euro-Atlantic integration has left them unable to process the recent crisis of governance in the region's EU and non-EU member states alike and their intimate relationship, in turn, to the origins of the state form (and its elastically authoritarian bent) in the Balkans as a whole. Moreover, this narrow focus has largely blinded them to the fact that the Balkans are no longer a site of active Western democratization efforts. Instead, the EU and United States (US) are increasingly being eclipsed in influence by resurgent authoritarian regimes, with Russia chief among these. For their part, local elites have eagerly embraced this exchange of benefactors. After all, in place of Western "conditionality" – the exchange of financial and development aid for political and economic reforms – Moscow, Beijing, and Ankara (among others) in fact prefer and actively encourage the recalcitrant authoritarian tendencies of local leaders.

The Balkans are thus not merely a passive terrain for the clash of empires, or a swamp of "ancient ethnic hatreds", as Robert Kaplan notoriously characterized them in his 1993 bestseller, *Balkan Ghosts*.[6] Instead, this book contends that the region is a vibrant space of social and political contestation in which substantive democratization processes are just beginning. And as much as it is an area of geopolitical confrontation, it is also a space of agency, in which local struggles will have global consequences. Therefore, rather than being peripheral or marginal to our thinking about the changing tides of European and global affairs, the Balkans and their history are in fact central to both.

And in this moment of historic geopolitical realignment, this book intends to harness the incredible explanatory power of two lines of striking graffiti to make sense of events in Europe's neglected corner and thereby in the continent in its entirety. Still scrawled on the walls of BiH's central government complex in downtown Sarajevo more than three years after the buildings were ransacked and torched by disgruntled masses of citizens, the words read simply: "sow hunger, reap fury". Like the revolutionary slogans of previous eras, while the hunger is local, the reach of the fury is wider, far wider.

Before we proceed, it bears explaining specifically what the terms "democracy" and "the state" mean in the context of this book, as these concepts are so often misunderstood, especially in the Balkans. This explanation will also make clear why the historical outlook of this book must be relatively long, even as the primary focus remains the contemporary crisis of democracy in the region.

On Democracy and the State

To begin with, there is the matter of certain archaic terms that are peppered through this text (i.e. "demos", "plebes", "polis", and "agora"). The use of these lynchpin concepts in democratic political theory in this context may seem somewhat peculiar since one of the central claims of this text is that state and political development in southeastern Europe has been differently constituted from the development of these institutions and norms in the West. Does it even make sense to speak of the demos in the Balkans if, as this book claims, a substantive sense of democratic citizenship remains unrealized in the region? The aim here is not to provide for a theory of citizenship in southeastern Europe, however, and in any case that task has already been undertaken more ably elsewhere.[7] Nor is the aim to deviate very far from the established understandings of these terms as proposed by other democratic theorists. Martin Breaugh, for instance, suggests a definition of "plebes" that is both refined and functional: "'The plebes' is the name of an experience, that of achieving human dignity through agency. The plebes designates neither a social category nor an identity but rather a fundamental event: the passage from a subpolitical status to one of a full-fledged political subject".[8] Breaugh argues that the plebes are not like the demos because the former has always been a pejorative term for those who were insurrectionary and revolutionary in their demands for popular power, while the demos were reformist and institutional, citizens in the most conservative sense, who sought to be granted representation by their supposedly benevolent elites.[9] Moreover, the plebes were specifically those who composed the Roman underclass but who, through a series of popular revolts, won for themselves greater rights. In the process they realized their own agency as a collective and ushered in what Breaugh refers to as a "discontinuous tradition of political freedom".[10] This is a concept akin to the political theorist Sheldon Wolin's "fugitive moments" of democracy – episodic articulations of genuine collective deliberation and agency – to which I turn in a moment. Breaugh's insistence on the crucial difference between the plebes and the demos, on the difference between the "many" as a dangerous rabble and the "people" as a refined, conservative audience, is convincing. And indeed, much of what this book proposes as a requirement for democratic renewal in the Balkans is just that: the presence of a dangerous, politically conscious rabble.

While such a radical participatory conception of democratic governance may appear functionally impossible in contemporary mass societies, it has remained a constant motif of democratic theorists: a perpetual search for perfect inclusion. More practically, for democratic theorists, who disproportionately hail from the comparatively "deeply" democratic West, citizenship remains a work in progress. It is a concept that even since the end of the Cold War, for instance, has deteriorated under the pressures of rapacious neoliberal economics and mass surveillance and is today in need of resuscitation in both Europe and the US. In this observation, there is a point of contact with the situation as it exists presently in the Balkans and as it has developed throughout the period this book considers. Like Breaugh, Wolin, and others, this work uses the notion of the demos and plebes in an aspirational sense. And in this respect, I am less interested in a precise definition of these terms than I am concerned with a general theme: namely, conceiving of democracy as a process, as a participatory exercise that has both a life outside the parliament, a history before it, and one that ought to be intrinsic to any discussion – scholarly, policy-oriented, or for general public consumption – that concerns itself with the process of post-authoritarian or post-conflict democratization.

The use of the term "citizens" in this book, on the other hand, is more technical: the citizens of the actually existing sovereign states in the region. And in between the potential Balkan demos and the reality of what passes for citizenship in the region today, there is the "*obič.ni narod*" (ordinary people), a vulgar term perhaps within the annals of political theory but one that best approximates how the majority of the population in the former Yugoslavia think of themselves. Admittedly, the term is imbued with a certain kind of tragic pathos in the collective imagination of the region, a sentiment this work aims to actively subvert. But since this book is one invested in making legible the ideal of the plebes and the demos, of a participatory conception of democracy, I feel it is appropriate, even necessary, to use on occasion the lexicon of the people to whom I am trying to make this ideal legible in the first place.

In order to think about these Balkan citizens as emerging agents rather than victims of change, it is also necessary to situate this analysis in the context of existing debates about democracy, rather than what has elsewhere been referred to as "transitology", the seemingly unending transitions of post-communist and post-war states since the end of the Cold War. Moreover, it is necessary to move away from the massive but narrow "war literature",[11] in which one can include the bulk of current scholarship that remains primarily invested in debates about the dissolution of Yugoslavia and the various experiences of that process.[12] Both of these sets of literature have made tremendous contributions to expanding and moving studies of the Balkans beyond the essentialism of Robert Kaplan and his associates, who initially popularized the "ancient ethnic hatreds" thesis, which contended that the dissolution of Yugoslavia was inevitable because of the primitive, intractable, and almost "natural" antipathies between the various ethnic peoples of the region. But the task that remains concerns the future and not the past. While this text covers significant historical ground, it does so in order to illuminate the complex, generational structural dynamics from which contemporary democratic movements in the Balkans are struggling to emerge. In short, the book treads on some familiar historical ground but only to dislodge the traditional focus on the "national question" with an examination of the political question in the Western Balkans.

Accordingly, it is this notion of "the political" that is central to understanding the disparate succession of regimes in the Western Balkans over the past century and a half, which have nevertheless shared at least one common trait. That is, they were uniform in their attempts at preventing the emergence of an autonomous Balkan civil society able to challenge elite power – a civil society that could contest state authority, and present democratic alternatives to the uniformly exclusionary and hierarchical machinations of existing and emerging elites. While some of these regimes were categorically anti-democratic, others, like the League of Communists of Yugoslavia (LCY) and the contemporary ruling establishment, have been nominally committed to some version of electoral democracy. But to appreciate the bankruptcy of their democratic commitments it is not sufficient to merely point to frequently hypocritical, discriminatory, or otherwise inept policy decisions. A serious critique of contemporary Balkan politics, and the corresponding crisis of democracy, requires a sober examination of the foundations of these polities.

One beginning is to distinguish between the common term "politics" and the more particular notion of "the political" in the context of the Balkans. Sheldon Wolin[13] succinctly defines this difference, and clarifies its significance for any examination of democracy, in the following terms:

> I shall take the *political* to be an expression of the idea that a free society composed of diversities can nonetheless enjoy moments of commonality when, through public deliberations, collective power is used to promote or protect the well-being of the collectivity. *Politics* refers to the legitimized and public contestation, primarily by organized and unequal social powers, over access to the resources available to the public authorities of the collectivity. Politics is continuous, ceaseless and endless. In contrast, the political is episodic, rare.

> … In my understanding, democracy is a project concerned with the political potentialities of ordinary citizens, that is, with their possibilities for becoming political beings through the self-discovery of common concerns and modes of action for realizing them.[14]

What Wolin suggests is that democracy is a Janus-faced concept. It is at once the mantra of every government in the Western world and many others too, but what we understand by democracy has shifted dramatically over the centuries – with its most radical, participatory potentialities having virtually withered away completely. "Contemporary democratic governments", writes Bernard Manin, "have evolved from a political system that was conceived by its founders as opposed to democracy".[15] Today, Wolin concurs, "what is actually being measured by the claim of democratic legitimacy is not the vitality of democracy in those nations but the degree to which democracy is attenuated so as to serve other ends. The most fundamental of these is the establishment and development of the modernizing state".[16]

These accounts suggest that democracy exists in a fundamental tension with the state. The centralizing impulses of state-makers are different from the emancipatory aims of genuine democrats. And in so far as the latter can exist within the confines of the former, they can do so only through the continuous complaint, dissent, and insurrection – in the street and at the ballot box – of ordinary citizens against state-making elites who not only can imagine the state without the agora and the parliament but, indeed, would prefer it. Still, if all states sequester the political, what is significant about the particular crisis of democracy in the Balkans today and why is it necessary to take stock of the particular origins of the Balkan state? Moreover, if all states are authoritarian with regards to the question of violence – that is, as Max Weber defined it, with regard to their monopolistic claim on the legitimate use of violence in society – why do social movements and robust, autonomous civil societies persist in many other states, including those in still emerging democracies, yet have been so late to arrive in the Balkans? To answer these questions requires us to examine, at least briefly, the particular socio-economic and political histories that have shaped the emergence of the state in the Balkans.

Theorizing the State in the Balkans

While it is not my intention to argue that societies do or should have a linear or familiar path of development (i.e. that liberal democracy or capitalism is the end of history), in attempting to make the case for a democratic analysis of the state in the Balkans it is useful to follow the work of other democratic theorists who, nevertheless, focus primarily on the trials and tribulations of predominantly liberal democratic regimes. Their scholarship still offers a great deal of currency for the analysis of the development of the state and the crisis of democracy in the Balkans because, in a broad sense, the ideal of democracy has been a universal phenomenon even in societies where lived experiences of participatory governance have been few and far between.

Marx argued that "the executive of the modern state is nothing but a committee for managing the common affairs of the whole bourgeoisie".[17] That is to say, the state is a classed phenomenon and the class dimensions within the state inform its type and function. This should not be a particularly controversial thesis even if one rejects Marx's broader analysis. But as a Western-style bourgeoisie or genuinely capitalist property relations have never truly emerged in the Balkans, the regional state form has never been bourgeois either; that is, it has never genuinely incorporated bourgeois political institutions and norms. In other words, while the political is sequestered in every state, it is not equally sequestered, or for the same reasons, in all states. Correspondingly, neither are the abilities of citizens to negotiate and challenge this sequestering akin in differently constituted states. Therefore, what is in this book referred to as the elasticity of authoritarianism in the Balkans is the result of particular, local social and historical factors that should inform any serious critique of the region's contemporary politics. While contemporary Western Balkan states today broadly mimic the existence of certain liberal institutions (e.g. elected parliaments), the dominant political paradigm of these polities remains distinctly non-liberal, both in the dominance of nationalism as the primary ideological foundation for the state and in the prevailing political-economic practices whose primary purpose is to enrich the small band of state-building elites.

The relationship between the region's peculiar political arrangements and specific patterns of economic accumulation is important and will be analysed in more detail in Chapters I and II. Suffice it to recall for now that exploitative economic practices exist in the West as they do in the Balkans. But in the case of the latter these practices are rooted in still largely coercive dispossession and looting, rather than standard capitalist property relations based on exchange and profit maximization. Or put more simply, and to use a common post-Yugoslav scenario, whereas the Western capitalist will exploit his factory workers through coercively low wages and union-busting, the Balkan elite will dismiss their entire workforce and bulldoze the factory in order to strip and sell it off in parts. Thus the dominant economic (and political) class in the former Yugoslavia is at best a kind of *lumpenbourgeoisie* but more accurately a bandit (or *baja*) class.[18] While they bear a resemblance to other post-communist oligarchs,[19] the rise of these post-Yugoslav elites has been shaped by the ubiquity and, indeed, necessity of the bandit during war, and cemented through international legitimation.

Finally, the reified status of ethnicity in the canon of Balkan statehood – both in ethnically fractured polities and those in which enforced homogeneity is the norm (e.g. Croatia, Serbia, and Albania) – all but denies the concept of citizenship and certainly the ideal of the demos or the plebes. And historically, this "ethnic card" has been kept up the sleeve of ruling elites in the region even when the nominal ruling order was non-ethnically constituted. This was done in order to prevent the emergence of a popular participatory conception of politics and the political as rooted in the power and consent of the governed, rather than the power and force of the governors. In other words, nationalism has been an instrumental and constitutive element of the Balkan elites' elastic authoritarianism. In these states the essential and exclusive ingredient of social cohesion is ethnicity and thus it is the only relevant category of identity. Despite the overt trappings of liberal democracy, there is no meaningful concept of a social contract that extends beyond or supplants banal invocations of blood and soil. As a result, contemporary Balkan states, despite their multiparty elections, negate the most fundamental aspects of democratic theory and practice alike: they reject the principle that genuine democratic regimes are the product of the participation, deliberation, consent, and agency of their citizens in both founding and administration.

In contrast to the primacy of the individual at the centre of traditional liberal democratic regimes, the preferred "ethnic majoritarian" interpretation of democracy (i.e. the pursuit of homogeneous ethnic enclaves under the guise of "democratic will") by the Balkan political elite – both today and at the moment of original state founding in the nineteenth century and again during the dissolution of Yugoslavia in the 1990s – is fundamentally anti-democratic and anti-participatory. Though writing in the context of BiH's peculiar constitutional order, the Bosnian political scientist Asim Mujkić's argument applies to the region as a whole precisely because the same essential processes are at work throughout. That is, post-Yugoslav elites are committed to "*presenting ethnos as demos*, where *ethnos* act like *demos* thus ... becoming an imaginary community of belongingness and connection", where it is the figment of the ethnic community and the nation that embodies the principles of "representation, decision-making and law".[20] Ultimately, what becomes definitive proof of one's appropriate ethnic identity is subservience to the ruling establishment.

That is how the authoritarian germ in the Balkans has persisted, through the adept incubation of nationalist tensions and resentments as engineered by local elites. After all, genuine democratic experiments are those that, on some level, attempt to challenge the state (or, at least, its existing incarnation) as the exclusive form of political association, and recognize that democracy is a practice, not a destination. In democratic societies the state is recognized as existing outside the citizens themselves and thereby existing only through their consent, a consent that is measured not merely through elections and referenda, but through continuous contestation and participation. Accordingly, the crisis of democracy which concerns this book is not merely the product of recent experiences of war and authoritarianism. It is a question of the prevailing political, economic, and social patterns that have shaped the emergence of these states and polities since the nineteenth century.[21]

Though it may at times read like a history of failure, especially in the context of the Balkans, the ideal and the aspirations of substantive democratic practice permeate this work. After all, no commentary on democracy could possibly foreclose the power of moments – "fugitive moments" as Wolin, again, frames them – in which the demos and the plebes are able not only to emerge but to truly affect change. Inasmuch as the democratic demands and aspirations of the Balkan peoples have been denied to them historically, it remains for the scholar and citizen alike to document these instances and to learn from them for future moments in which more may be demanded and won. It is clear that failing to steer a new course has as its result only further despotism.

Outline

With these theoretical claims now established, a brief note is presented here on how the remainder of the book shall proceed. Broadly speaking, the book is divided into two major thematic sections, spread over four chapters. The first two chapters lay out the complex and historically constituted origins or "causes" of the crisis of democracy in the Balkans, while the last two chapters anticipate two possible "effects" of the re-emergence of similar political patterns in the contemporary period. The factors which shaped the initial emergence, and evolution, of the state in the Balkans are established in the first two chapters, while the renewal of elastic authoritarianism as a defining feature of contemporary regional politics, and the nascent civil society response to it, are addressed in the last two chapters. Thus, while the respective sections each deal with distinct historical periods and scenarios, they are closely linked thematically. At the very least, the reader will note the distinct similarities in the manner in which Balkan elites navigated and negotiated the end of imperial hegemony in the nineteenth and early twentieth centuries and their response to the contemporary crisis of global liberalism.

Accordingly, the discussion opens with a chapter examining the twilight of the Ottoman Empire's hold on the Balkans at the end of nineteenth century in order to trace the origins of the local elites' unique ability to survive and thrive through repeated moments of otherwise total regime collapse; and, moreover, to posit this moment of regime entropy and accompanying elite elasticity as a defining feature of the socio-political experience in the Balkans. But contrary to still canonical treatments of the Ottoman period in the Balkans, this work argues that it was not that the region "fell behind" the rest of Europe in socio-political development per se, hopelessly delaying the area's democratic evolution in the mire of Oriental despotism. Instead, the region was arrested in its development by its own elites, who sought to preserve rather than reform key aspects of the previous imperial regime and especially their own role within it.

Recalling the ingenious manner in which a previous generation of Balkan elites navigated both the revolutionary upheavals of the nineteenth century and the collapse of the Ottoman Empire, the second chapter examines the reappearance of this strategy at the close of the Cold War during the last days of the Socialist Federal Republic of Yugoslavia (SFRJ). After reviewing the manufacture of ethnic tensions by regional elites that led to the dissolution of the Yugoslav state, as they similarly accompanied the weakening of the Ottoman Empire's hold on the region in the nineteenth century, this chapter will examine the post-war stability consensus that Western governments reached with local nationalist leaders. I will examine how, despite claims to the contrary, Western policymakers continually traded their commitments to genuine political and economic transformation in the region for security guarantees from local "big men", [22] especially following the events of 9/11.

In the third chapter, the focus shifts to the geopolitical dimensions of the collapse of existing, Western-built democratic institutions in the former Yugoslavia. Specifically, the discussion centres on the already apparent (and growing) dependency of local oligarchs on new foreign benefactors in the vacuum of coherent European and American regional policy, and what this will mean for the area's emerging civil society. Of particular concern in this chapter is the growing role of Russia, China, the Gulf states, and Turkey in the region's politics, especially in the light of similar (and more severe) processes of democratic rollback in each of these new partner countries. This chapter will conclude by arguing that European stability depends vitally on repelling these authoritarian incursions into the region, but that the best way to ensure this is not, as in previous years, for Washington and Brussels to attempt to make loyal clients of the region's big men themselves. Instead, the US and EU must find their new "stakeholders" among the region's emerging social movements and civil society – those who will truly infuse failing parliamentary institutions with the spirit of democracy. Failing to do so will merely prolong this haunting instability and the ferocity of its inescapable collapse.

To this end, the fourth and final chapter will examine popular local responses to the aforementioned stability consensus between local oligarchs and Western policymakers as well as the appearance of new authoritarian benefactors. While the resort to street politics amid failing government institutions is not without its accompanying dangers, the decisive collapse of civic trust in the existing political order also opens the terrain for an unprecedented popular democratic revolution in the Western Balkans. By focusing on the declared and demonstrated aims and strategies of the emerging mass movements in Slovenia, BiH, and Macedonia – three case studies with important lessons for broader regional dynamics – this chapter will portray these activists as the agents of a potentially profound political transformation in the Western Balkans. Specifically, these movements represent a transition from the politics of ethnicity and state-building (by both local and international actors) towards the politics of dignity and agency: substantive concerns with jobs, education, social services, and also popular self-rule. In other words, these movements are articulating organic demands for democracy in a way that mirrors similar eruptions of "people power" in other post-authoritarian states in the rest of the world.

And despite the focus on the "revolutionary" dimensions of these movements, the concern here is not with failed or otherwise marginal "utopian" projects (nor is it pained "Yugonostalgia") but rather with the concrete experiences of similar democratic insurrections in other post-authoritarian and post-conflict countries, especially those in ethnically divided societies (e.g. South Africa, Spain, Taiwan, and even Ukraine). This represents an original intervention into the literature on the contemporary Western Balkans. And at the very least, it reflects an earnest desire to shift the discourse on the region from tragedy to possibility.

Finally, as may already be clear from this introduction, this is a somewhat odd book. It is a text that sits (uncomfortably) at the intersections of political theory, international relations, comparative politics, and popular commentary. Scholars may find its claims sweeping, while the general-interest readers may be flummoxed by the complexities of Balkan politics. Nevertheless, the hope is that both sides will recognize the genuine urgency that motivates and permeates this work. This is not to suggest that the conviction with which these claims are stated merits praise per se. Rather, it is to say that this is a sincere attempt to articulate a sober analysis of the crisis of governance in the Balkans, the long-term origins of this crisis, and the bifurcating ways forward, and to do all of this, ultimately, with the Balkan peoples and their basic decency and irrepressible agency at the centre of the analysis.

In other words, this book holds absolutely, in the words of the American abolitionist Frederick Douglass, that those "who profess to favor freedom and yet depreciate agitation, are people who want crops without ploughing the ground; they want rain without thunder and lightning; they want the ocean without the roar of its many waters".[23] Those who desire in southeastern Europe the kind of stability provided by the functional democratic systems of the West cannot deny or ignore the long process of popular agitation that created these regimes in the first place. The Balkans' democratic revolutions, in short, are yet to come.

1

CLIENTS AND BRIGANDS
The Origins of the State in the Balkans

For all the horrors of the Yugoslav Wars and the bloodied political lines along which the SFRJ fractured, and along which the region remains divided today, the daily work of coexistence is the task of ordinary people who usually have neither the emotional nor financial means to begin their lives anew, together or apart, as the circumstances may warrant. And yet democracy as a social phenomenon has only ever existed when just these peoples, these plebes, this demos, this impoverished rabble, have won the right to govern themselves, wrested from the grip of their political and economic superiors through their collective agency. Over the course of the last century and a half, two imperial regimes have collapsed in the Western Balkans, two separate incarnations of Yugoslavia have met the same fate, and entire populations have been exterminated in the 1940s and again in the 1990s. Despite what appears to be the entropic quality of the state in this region, the defining feature of Balkan politics since the end of the nineteenth century has been the emergence of an elastic state form as the primary mode of social organization in the region. That is, while particular ideological regimes have come and gone, a peculiar *Staatsidee* (literally, idea of the state) has remained; one fundamentally and persistently patrimonial[1] and authoritarian. What is thus particular to the former Yugoslav space

17

(but true to some extent of much of the southeast of Europe) is that dramatic ideological mutations have been accompanied by stationary socio-political practices. A virtually identical cast of elites has survived revolutions, wars, and geopolitical realignment, while persistently suppressing the ability of ordinary peoples and citizens to participate meaningfully in the political process.

Why, then, though they have fought in the ranks of imperial and national armies and militias, and have been exposed to the machinations of virtually every major ideological movement of the nineteenth and twentieth centuries, have political conditions for the majority of people in the Western Balkans essentially remained static? The region is today, as it was at the end of the nineteenth century, overwhelmingly rural, economically backward, and politically dominated by a handful of socio-economic (and criminal) clans of supposedly mutually incompatible ethno-national persuasions. Though the twentieth century produced some of the worst horrors in the history of humanity, from the Holocaust to the Great Leap Forward to the Rwandan Genocide, it was also a century of tremendous positive change. From women winning the vote to decolonization, the world is in many places and in many ways far different from what it was at the end of the nineteenth century. And yet my descriptions of the Western Balkans' current social and political ills would be intimately familiar not only to my deceased grandparents, but to my great-grandparents and likely even my great-great-grandparents. As Refik Hodžić has observed concerning the struggles of genocide survivors in post-war BiH, "There's a connection between economic robbery and the trauma of the past ... Poisonous cynics are making money by undermining our attempts to bring peace. This is hatred as a smokescreen for robbery".[2] A similar argument, this book contends, could be made to describe much of modern Balkan political history: hatred as a smokescreen for robbery.

In other words, what has survived through all these generations is not some inherent Balkan idiocy that has made people in the region less capable of claiming for themselves "peace, order, and good government", in the words of the Canadian Constitution Act.[3] Though conditions appear to have remained static, in reality the nineteenth and twentieth centuries were a period of profound transformation for the entire region. During the four decades of communist rule, for instance,

Yugoslavia underwent a rapid process of economic modernization and industrialization that elevated living standards (in the cities, at least) to levels comparable to those in the West. But unlike the great social and class confrontations that defined the development of Europe's western half, in the Balkans neither representative democracy nor a capitalist mode of production followed from or accompanied, in any meaningful sense, this technological industrialization. The task in this book therefore is to explain how the state in the Western Balkans has remained perennially as an "organized protection racket", a term the sociologist Charles Tilly traditionally reserved for the initial stage of state formation. The task is to explain why the Balkan state endured, despite a series of apparently profound ideological transformations, as a largely patrimonial and authoritarian mode of social organization. In other words, why have the violence and coercion of the few over the many remained the overt and defining features of Balkan politics?

At the root of this peculiar and particular socio-historical pattern of development is the primitive nature of economic relations in the region – primitive in the sense that coercion is and has remained the primary mode of "production" in the Balkans, that is, the primary means of economic accumulation, an economic model severely limited in its genuine productive capacities. In this way, the Balkans differ significantly from the advanced capitalist economies of the West, where both production and accumulation occur through transactional circuits of capital (i.e. exchange and trade). Because such systemic forms of coercion are only possible in authoritarian regimes, local elites have consistently founded and re-founded such polities. And, indeed, the re-founding has been crucial and necessary because of the inherent instability of regimes based on violence and dispossession. Therefore, the elastic quality of Balkan authoritarianism features also an entropic dimension, wherein these regimes collapse and are restored, albeit within new nominal ideological parameters, in a virtually cyclical manner.

In framing the argument in this manner, this book deliberately deploys Marxist terminology, in particular from the work of the geographer David Harvey. Yet the point is precisely the opposite of what traditional Marxian accounts of the region have argued. In these analyses, the suggestion has been that while the Western Balkans are peripheral to the global capitalist economy they are nevertheless a site of neoliberal exploitation and that it is this external factor that should serve as the primary analytical tool for understanding local politics.[4] In contrast, this text argues that both historically and currently, the Balkans have taken a completely separate and distinct path of development. As a result, neither capitalist property relations nor bourgeois political formations (i.e. parliamentary, representative democracy) have emerged in this region in anything other than the most skeletal form.

It was through this persistent process of "accumulation through dispossession", that is, accumulation through violence, that the Balkan elite established themselves in the first place amid the collapse of the Ottoman Empire.[5] Of course, this is not to say that violence was absent in the economic histories of the West; indeed, periods of primitive, coercive accumulation accompanied the emergence of all of the world's major economies and are integral to the emergence of capitalist property relations in particular. But in the Balkans, economic practices remained permanently coercive, whereas in the West, accumulation and appropriation became increasingly formalized and essentially "voluntary", conducted through various forms of wage labour. While economic relations in the West became diffused and global from the nineteenth century onwards – marked by complex networks and circuits of supply and demand – they remained stubbornly territorial and terrestrial in the Balkans. The Western Balkans, in particular, remained (or re-emerged continually) as an economic regime founded on blood and soil and thus remained broadly feudal in a socio-economic sense.

The political structures these Balkan elites created (and preserved) in turn were ones that cemented not only their gains in various episodes of accumulation but their methods too; in short, the economic practices of brigands begot the political structures of warlords. Indeed, it was these static and retrograde economic practices that ultimately stunted the further development of a genuine polis – a substantive participatory democratic culture – in the Balkans, instead tilting the region continuously towards an emptying of the popular aspects of modern state formation that characterized the collapse of feudalism in western Europe. In place of liberal social contracts, the atom of social cohesion and association in the Balkans became the germ of the "nation-state" complex: a fiction of homogeneity in an inherently heterogeneous area possible only through successive episodes of war, genocide, and dispossession. The fantasy of the ethnically pure nation-state, ostensibly inspired by the French Revolution and later European revolutions, served in reality the interests of Balkan elites who wished to keep the region from undergoing precisely the profound social transformations that came to envelop western Europe at the end of the eighteenth century and continued throughout the course of the nineteenth and twentieth centuries. As a result, while western (and, increasingly, many eastern and southern) European states have spent the century following the World War I negotiating various forms of global governance – usually with words, sometimes with arms – Balkan elites have essentially spent the same century mired in provincial disputes over the fate of a smattering of villages along the Drina and Ibar rivers.

While nationalism is not a phenomenon unique to the Balkans, its persistency and persistently anti-democratic bent have significantly altered the course of social developments in the region as compared to the western half of the continent. While nationalism may have returned to European politics in the second decade of the twenty-first century, it has remained a factor in Balkan politics since the end of the nineteenth century. Here, however, it is important to distinguish this claim from essentialist myths concerning the "ancient ethnic hatreds" of the Balkan peoples. In short, nationalism in the Balkans is not a "natural" phenomenon: it is a particular, elite-manufactured political programme. Specifically, the embrace of nationalism ably obscured the primitive economic and political regimes of the Balkan elites, who traditionally relied heavily on the use of violence and dispossession against overwhelmingly rural (and uneducated) populations.

As a result, war and the outward appearance of regime change often roiled southeastern Europe but rarely did dramatic social changes follow in their wake. The emergence of the state form in the Balkans after and amid the collapse of the Ottoman Empire must thus be understood through these defining local characteristics. So must the experiences of the generations of ordinary Balkan plebes, who in the process of Balkan state-building became members of nations without ever becoming citizens, who were forced into the state, while being ejected from the agora and thus the polis as a whole. The remainder of this chapter examines in greater detail both the origins of the state in the Balkans and its characteristic elastic authoritarianism.

The Ottoman Dissolution as Model

How can we characterize the political and social patterns and structures that led to the formation of the early Balkan states and, linked to this, the kinds of governing systems they precipitated? In sum, the early Balkan state-founders gained their authority as formerly pliant clients of the Ottoman state or as bandits who were in turn "rehabilitated" by the Ottoman authorities. By the nineteenth century, the weakened Porte – the seat of Sultanic power in Istanbul – increasingly came to rely on various local "big men", as David Kanin refers to them, to maintain some semblance of law and order. The most effective big men proved to be individuals who had previously been the very bandits whom the empire wished to eliminate.[6] In other words, rather than eliminate them, the Ottomans legitimized the Balkan bandits, making them enforcers rather than opponents of imperial rule in the region.

In the non-capitalist political economy of the late Ottoman Empire, as in many collapsing regimes, wealth and privilege could only be secured through a complex system of patronage and favours that emanated from the centre of imperial power. When this centre began to lose its hold on the periphery of its empire, the economy fractured into parts, but its essential dynamic did not change. Accumulation still occurred through patronage and favours, only now the contest became one of deciding who would emerge as the new centre. Because the Ottoman system had been a military regime since its inception, at war for virtually the entirety of its six century existence, civilian political and economic institutions not geared towards explicit war-making capabilities were comparatively underdeveloped. This was especially the case in the Balkans, the contested borderland between the Ottomans and Austro-Hungarians for nearly three centuries.[7] Accordingly, when the Ottoman grip on the region waned, the only truly established patterns of governance and accumulation among the local elite were essentially martial. Because power and wealth were thus the result of non-economic activities (i.e. not trade and commerce but plunder and imperial patrimony), the post-Ottoman economy remained characterized by continuous processes of accumulation through dispossession.

The point here is not to suggest that the Ottoman Empire itself was responsible for the later political backwardness of the Balkans. Indeed, the legacies of the empire are complex, contradictory, and multifaceted, as evidenced by the significant political divergences among former Ottoman territories, stretching from the gates of Vienna to Basra, in the century since the empire's collapse. But in the Western Balkans, at least, the Porte's western-most military frontier, the empire's imperial regime combined with local patrimonial patterns of rule to produce a uniquely regressive mix; a mix whose potency was expressed especially in the manner in which it allowed local elites to navigate the empire's collapse rather than its actual existence. In short, this elite mode of navigating regime collapse meant that violence became the definitive feature of the post-Ottoman Balkan state: violence employed by state-forming elites against an overwhelmingly peasant population and against other competing sects of local elites. Rather than the emergence of representative parliamentary bodies through elite accommodation or popular rebellion and agitation as in the West, the hallmarks of this particular state-building project were the crushing of the peasant-led Timok Rebellion in 1883 and the bloody, generational Obrenović–Karađorđević rivalry, to use but two examples from Serbia. Violence alone, however, could not have ensured that such a system of brutally exploitative accumulation and governance would persist. What was required was a facsimile or, again, a model of popular participation that would nevertheless preserve the privileged position of the elite, an ideological project to create the illusion of popular representation without actual accountability. Nationalism became this model.

As P.M. Kitromilides argues, rather than nationalist movements giving birth to states in the Balkans, what happened was precisely the opposite.[8] Statist elites constructed and promoted ethno-national identities to entrench their own positions of power.[9] In the Yugoslav lands, the national question was used to undermine every other kind of political mobilization (i.e. those based on class or even more fluid conceptions of ethnic identity) against the new elites. What few reforms did eventually take place during the nineteenth and early twentieth centuries were almost in every case purposely constructed in ethno-national

terms – to mitigate their emancipatory political and economic potential. Accordingly, nationalism in the Balkans was from the outset a
fundamentally anti-democratic project and operated explicitly on the
idea of excluding or minimizing popular participation in the new
states. Thus, rather than nationalist sentiments underpinning all politics
in the region – as mainstream journalistic accounts still often claim – it
was a process of elites deliberately manipulating communal differences
so as to obscure the largely class-based antagonisms that defined the
genesis of the Balkan state. The relative success of these initial forays
instructed successive generations of elites in the region that they could
continue advancing the same essential programme of primitive accumulation through nationalist subterfuge, more or less unabated.

Accordingly, the result of the weakening hold of the Ottomans on
the Balkans after centuries of essentially military administration was
that "the most distinctive feature of rural relations in the South-East [of
Europe]", Perry Anderson notes, "was the break-down of any firm civic
order imposed from above: banditry became rampant, encouraged by
the mountainous relief of the region, which made it the Mediterranean
equivalent of flight on the Baltic plains, for the peasantry. Landlords,
conversely, maintained bands of armed thugs … on their estates, to
protect themselves from revolt and repress their tenantry".[10] And those
who were most comfortable and experienced in such a chaotic environment (bandits, landlords, and warlords of various sorts) would
thereafter remain the dominant members of the post-Ottoman Balkan
elite. Of course, in nationalist mythologies, these bandit-warlords have
been remembered as romantic freedom fighters, as *hajduks*, the local
incarnation of Hobsbawm's "social bandits".[11] The reality was entirely
more sordid. Though the sixteenth century was a stable period of
growth, by the late eighteenth and early nineteenth century, as the
Ottoman Empire's grip on the Balkans slipped and as widespread brigandry emerged as a major concern, the weakened Porte was forced to
turn many of these bandits into actual governors. The trend of turning
bandits into rulers, like the famed Ali Pasha (1740–1822), David Kanin
argues, is one that became a staple of imperial and later international
administration in the Balkans. Most of the formative political and social
elites in the region emerged from this paramilitary and criminal milieu.
Indeed, intellectuals and revolutionaries who espoused more progres-

sive views, of which there were some, remained marginalized and persecuted by this bandit class of elites.[12] In this respect, the process of Ottoman dissolution in the Balkans anticipated the dissolution of the SFRJ, which too was marked by a process of state capture by entrenched criminal and provincial conglomerates under the cover of national liberation.[13]

Contrary to the romantic image of the *hajduks*, Karen Barkey describes these bandits as a parasitic class, in collusion rather than in conflict with landlords and central authorities: "bandits [were] the malefactors of rural society. They hurt the rural community in several ways: they inhibited its potential for collective action; they plundered its resources and actively participated in its coercion by local power holders. These agents of the local strongman could not have been benevolent. Bandits were neither necessarily nor often enemies of the state."[14] Accordingly, she stresses the need to distinguish between "class-based movements that threaten the structural arrangement in society and a banditry that attempts to benefit from existing structural arrangements in society. These bandits, in the end, have no reason for the destruction of those structures of inequality from which they benefit."[15] Inasmuch as they eventually did participate in the destruction of imperial authority, the Balkan elite did so in a manner that would ultimately preserve their own local power structures.

Still, the Ottoman legitimization and institutionalization of these bandits in the governing order, argues Barkey, constituted the central element of the state consolidation process of the Ottoman Empire and was at odds with the norm in western Europe, where the practice was one of confrontation rather than negotiation with elements that challenged the state's authority. While the system functioned, the authorities "managed and played off different groups, responding to and curtailing their orbit of influence while keeping all groups dependent on the state. A state-centred culture was embedded in the structure of society by state action, with everyone from elites to bandits dependent on state-servicing patronage."[16] The banditry that prevailed in the Ottoman Empire, she argues, was thus the result of demobilized soldiers, local strongmen, and bandits seeking legitimation from the centre. These were not Hobsbawm's "social avengers", but were "status-seeking rebels".[17] Moreover, their ability to extract privileges from the centre while the centre still held, and then to shift allegiances to new benefactors when the previous hegemon lost its position, became the defining feature of the phenomenon of elastic authoritarianism in the Balkans.

Thus, the elites who emerged in the collapse of the Ottoman Empire were educated in generational patterns of clientelistic and parasitic behaviour. As wealth could only be obtained through plunder, through accumulation by dispossession, force was always required, and the state's monopoly of violence was the premier way to accomplish this. Individual opponents, when they emerged, were negotiated with accordingly. But the real threat to this order was the threat of collective, popular action. The Ottomans dealt with this danger through the non-hereditary *timar* system – a land tenure regime by which the Sultan essentially leased territories to local notables, called *sipahi* – which, aside from preventing the emergence of a western European-style feudal nobility, also largely precluded the possibility of peasant rebellions. Precisely because the *sipahi* were a military class, expected to go and furnish frequent military campaigns, and because their estates were temporary, patrimonial privileges, they were essentially "absentee landlords".[18] Moreover, the administrative lines of the *timar* estates were such that a single village might often be divided among several *sipahi*. Thus, peasants "who knew each other on the basis of living in the same or in contiguous villages did not necessarily deal with the same landholder. And, since peasants from the same village were bound to different landholders, they had no direct common enemy to ally against. Therefore, in most cases of peasant–landholder conflict, individual peasants were pitted against individual landholders".[19]

The system was virtually designed to prevent the kinds of class and social conflicts that had necessitated the emergence of complex representative and democratic bodies in the West. In contrast, the Ottoman Empire was "basically bureaucratic rather than feudal".[20] This was not a western European feudal mode of production, one that despite its similarly patrimonial structure nevertheless involved also a complex balance between the crown and the aristocracy. Unlike English lords, the "*sipahi* had no claim to the land itself; it remained part of the 87 percent of Ottoman territory in the 1528 census that was state land. His sons could inherit no more than a fraction of his income, not necessarily from the same *timar* and only if they too served the Sultan".[21] Instead, this was a "system of military occupation, staffed and controlled by the central government".[22] And if this was primarily a governance scheme designed for an overwhelmingly agricultural society, the situation was little better in the towns as the "urban guild system was likewise tightly controlled, explicitly designed to prevent the emergence of an independent, for-profit economy". Here, too, the guiding economic impulses were extractive: "As *timar* agriculture supplied food, the urban economy provided the army with weapons, uniforms and other equipment for pressing forward on the frontier. Both the urban and rural regimes were also designed to maintain civil order in the interior with a minimum of military force".[23]

Still, at the height of Ottoman power and prosperity, the life of the average serf in the Porte's dominions was better than that of his western European peer; they enjoyed free movement and, while taxed at discriminatory rates, non-Muslims were generally excused from military service. Class resentments nevertheless arose. Yet widespread peasant revolts in the Ottoman Empire came not during the *timar* period but rather once the so-called *chiflik* estates emerged, an eighteenth-century attempt to reform the *timar* system that instead begot an exploitative form of tax-farming.[24] The rise of these estates led to abuses of the predominantly Christian peasants by a newly empowered landlord caste with their own private armies on which the empire increasingly depended for its defence. In fact, the emergence of the *chiflik* system corresponded directly with the slow but discernible collapse in the authority of the central Ottoman state from the time of the death of Suleiman the Magnificent in 1566.[25] Indeed, only after the death of Suleiman does an economic order develop that is "eminently feudal [in] origins" and characteristics in the region.[26] Accordingly, the "agents of anti-Sultanic disobedience", Clemens Hoffmann argues, "were not an incipient commercial or even national class. Rather, they were a newly constituted seigniorial class, keen on retaining and enlarging its surpluses". Yet this "realisation of gains was … made possible much more by the politically constituted, unimpeded, higher level of surplus-extraction from the peasants based on the central state's inability to secure regional political control, rather than by exploiting the inequalities of markets". In other words, rather than creating wealth through commercial trade or circuits of exchange, Balkan elites physically dispossessed the local peasant class of what few agricultural and extractive (i.e. mining, lumber) resources they were able to produce. This eminently primitive economic practice meant also that the "collective interest" of local elites "did not consist in political and technological 'progress', but much more in stagnation and preserving the status quo".[27]

The *chiflik* system depended on the use of violence against peasants by newly empowered landlords and their bandit militias, amid the collapse of central authority, to extract economic goods. But more so, this system depended on the broader social and political climate which allowed for such a regime to emerge in the first place; one in which the centre came to rely on peripheral elites for its stability but was no longer able to extract from them, in turn, the kind of obedience once afforded to it at the zenith of the Porte's power. The parallels with the current plight of Euro-American diplomacy in the region should be obvious. More to the point, it was a period in which local elites began more earnestly parcelling off chunks of territory for their own control. And because the Ottoman regime, even at its apex, had prevented the emergence of a politically relevant merchant class, the transition from Ottoman to local control was accompanied by little social reform. Perry Anderson writes that the "characteristic Turkish town eventually came to be dominated by a stagnant and backward *menu peuple* that prevented any entrepreneurial innovation or accumulation. Given the nature of the Ottoman State, there was no protective space in which a Turkish mercantile bourgeoisie could develop, and from the seventeenth century onwards commercial functions devolved increasingly onto infidel minority communities".[28]

In contrast to triumphalist nationalist claims in the century and a half since, the transition from central to local control was not heralded as a grand emancipatory triumph at the time. The majority of the population in the Balkans recognized correctly that the diminishing role of the Porte in the region meant that local elites were now steering the ship; gone was the office behind the truncheon and all that remained was the blunt instrument. The local elite also understood the lack of legitimacy behind their rule, and it was the more clever and cogent among them that began to lean on confessional differences as a strategy of control. While the peasants urged the Porte to reassert strong, central authority and dismiss the corrupt *ayans*,[29] *pashas*,[30] and their various associates, thus directing their ire towards their local leaders, a segment of these local elites adeptly displaced this resentment outwards. By insisting that the primary conflict was Christian–Muslim, rather than between peasants and landowners, these elites discovered the contours of a nationalist ideological programme.

This account differs from traditional claims that the Ottoman *millet*[31] system provided the original basis for the separation of (what would later become) ethno-national communities in the region.[32] I reject this reading because it removes agency, both elite and popular, from the equation. If we recognize that nationalism and ethnicity are socially constructed, then there is little reason to believe that the *millet* system would have "birthed nations" if national identities were not intentionally prescribed and inscribed by elites. Like all political projects, the advent of nationalism in the Balkans required deliberate ignition and perpetuation. It is no doubt the case that a segment of these elites (and some progressive intellectuals) genuinely believed in the idealness of nations, while actively debating their "naturalness". However, their consistent educational and propagandist efforts suggest that they nevertheless understood that the masses had to be convinced both of their belonging to these nations and that this belonging was in their interest. Yet this nationalist ideal was unlikely to have become much more than another ideological fantasy had it not been recognized as an effective means of securing power for statist elites. It was only when nationalism became a state-sponsored programme that it began to speak to concrete material and economic grievances of the general population, precisely because it began to be used by these new elites to subvert class resentments and to channel these grievances into reactionary ethno-nationalism as a means of legitimating their rule.

So defining was the influence of these early nationalist elites on the region that the political economy of the Yugoslav lands continues to be dominated by the clientelistic and patrimonial patterns they established in the nineteenth century. Their programme has remained salient despite the modernizing efforts of the Ottomans, the Austro-Hungarians, the monarchist authorities in the first Yugoslavia, the communist regime, and the liberal democratic international community, each of which has variously vacillated between attempting to curb and to embrace the region's different nationalist causes. While the socialist period saw the emergence of large-scale industrial projects, a staple of state socialist regimes seeking to mimic Western development models, control over these enterprises remained patrimonial with only a bureaucratic veneer. This process continues today, coupled with repeated rounds of dispossession during both the war years of the 1990s and the post-war rush towards the panacea of privatization.[33] Thus, "criminals and other inhabitants of the [Balkans] ... continue to manipulate local and international officials by constructing rhetorical discourses of loyalty to the international regime, while at the same time pursuing illegal business activities in the tradition of [kleptocracy]".[34]

In short, the manner in which Balkan elites navigated the dissolution of the Ottoman Empire should be understood as a model for how they later dealt with the Austro-Hungarians, the Yugoslav crown, the fascists, and the Yugoslav communists, and how they deal today with the EU and US. Of course, each of these regimes was and is distinct, and its administration of the region is likewise specific. Moreover, segments of the local elite in each period genuinely invested themselves in the preservation of each regime. But these were the exceptions rather than the norm. To understand the structural dynamics of Balkan statehood and politics since the nineteenth century, it is more important to examine the moments of collapse and the periods of entropy. It is these that reveal what has remained lasting and durable in the region: an elastic politics of authoritarianism and an enduring economy of dispossession, masked by the dull sheen of provincial nationalism. We now turn to a more detailed account of how these patterns first emerged, beyond their initial germination during the late Ottoman period.

Creating the State, Inventing the Nation

Nearly a century before the Ottomans lost Albania in 1912, the last of their Balkan territories, the events of the First Serbian Uprising (1804–1813) established the essential contours of contemporary Balkan governance. Beginning a decades-long process of extraction from the fold of the Porte, a constellation of local big men, brigands, and firebrands from the Belgrade *pašaluk* (i.e. the province of Belgrade) adeptly cobbled together a programme of banal economic populism, religious fanaticism, and concocted sectarian grievances essentially to author the concept of Balkan nationalism. Cleverly recognizing an imperial regime in decline, opportunistic local elites began to transform themselves into and solicit the services of nominally "nationally conscious" bandits in an effort to win populations and regions to their respective causes, typically through "what was essentially state-sponsored terrorism".[35] Thus, while the uprising had been chiefly organized by little more than "hayduks, robbers and riff-raff",

> [the] genius of the first rebels against the Ottomans was to link these [bandit] traditions to a more general political struggle against a foreign overlord and eventually to constructions of national identity. This also meant that a certain kind of political roughness and violence became a central rather than peripheral part of post-Ottoman Balkan political life from the beginning of the nineteenth century. The first uprising against the Ottomans was led by Karadjordje ('Black George' whom *The Times* referred to by his Serb name of 'Czerni George' [*sic*]) who had been a one-time hajduk as well as an Austrian army auxiliary ... [The] existence [of these bandits] became a definitive part of national identity.[36]

The century of strife and contestation that followed the First Serbian Uprising, however, produced little in the way of political philosophy or theory on the nature of just governance. Precisely because the independence projects of the Balkan elites were based on little more than their own narrow self-preservation, what followed Ottoman imperial rule was not republicanism or democracy but monarchism, autocracy, and autarky. Nevertheless, local elites recognized that they required a programme to blunt their ejection of the expansive network of imperial institutions, norms, and privileges that characterized life under the Ottoman Empire, however limited these were in comparison to the situation in the west of Europe by the nineteenth century. They could hardly offer comparable "social services" or even basic security to their populations but they countered by offering a freshly minted sense of political belonging and the illusion of agency in constructing these new nation-states. Conveniently, elites created the conditions whereby targeted populations were cajoled or terrorized into declaring themselves as "ethnic" and "national" subjects of these new states. In short, the nation-state in the Balkans created the problems its architects purported to remedy.

The creation of "ethnically homogeneous territories on a mass scale … had no comparable precedent on the Balkan peninsula. The years that followed the collapse of the Habsburg, the Romanov, and the Ottoman empires after World War I witnessed a radical 'un-mixing' of populations in the former imperial realms. International treaties and national policies made diverse local communities into separate Greek, Turkish, Bulgarian, and Albanian nationals who were forced to relocate to new 'homelands'".[37] In Serbia, for instance, the 1860s and 1870s saw the expulsion of nearly the entire Muslim population and "the destruction of most mosques and other sites associated with Islam or the Ottomans".[38] Areas like BiH and Macedonia, which were the target of competing claims, witnessed an upsurge not only in nationally inclined schools, newspapers, and fraternal societies but also in militias and militant secret societies of every sort. The entry of these violent bands into villages and hamlets would quickly dissolve traditional societies, while the lives of the new "majorities" and fleeing "minorities" depended on declaring their allegiances according to the new rubric. The Balkan Wars (1912–1913) were marked by mass displacement and ethnic cleansing as the primary strategic objective of each of the combatants and in particular as an exercise by the new "Christian" powers in the Balkans in appropriately nationalizing the various territories and populations they coveted.

Importantly, the violence engineered by domestic elites was not strictly reserved for ethnic and cultural minorities, that is, the populations which became minorities (or majorities) as a result of their nationalizing projects. In the Serbian heartland the authorities were hardly above using violence to forcibly incorporate their "own" recalcitrant peasants into the new nation-state fold. In 1883, for instance, a rural rebellion in eastern Serbia erupted when villagers "refused to hand in their weapons to the military unless they received modern replacements".[39] Whereas the insurrectionary character of the peasantry had once been celebrated when it was necessary to foment anti-Ottoman sentiment, it now became an opportunity for King Milan (1854–1901) to test out the effectiveness and loyalty of his new army. While the so-called Timok Rebellion was short-lived, at one point "nearly a quarter of the country was under rebel control and the unco-ordinated peasant volunteers almost succeeded in dividing the country along an east-west axis". "Despite its short duration," Misha Glenny argues, "this was probably the single most important event in Serbian history between independence in 1878 and the outbreak of the Balkan Wars in 1912. The confrontation between an autocratic modernizer and a militant peasantry also established a pattern of militarization which was later repeated in other Balkan states".[40] This "modernization and militarization" approach, or simply autocratic coercion, was the process of state-building itself in the region, and it would remain as such throughout much of the next century. The overall result was that the Balkan polities never quite made the transition from protection racket and monopoly of violence to republic.

The policy and cultural literature produced in Serbia and Montenegro during this period is also instructive. Ilija Garašanin's famed 1844 *Načertanije* programme for the territorial expansion of the Serbian state, for instance, was a mixture of propaganda and jingoism.[41] BiH, as a primary target of Garašanin's program, was the place where the then Serbian Minister of the Interior expounded on the necessity for the national education of all the religious communities, in order that there might be established a "unity of Serbs and Bosniaks".[42] Yet the entire programme was premised on either a division or a shattering of the Ottoman Empire, inevitably by an assortment of established and emerging Christian states. It was a plan for conquest first and fore-most, and while it dabbled in politics, it was virtually on the level of phrenology. For its part, the Montenegrin Prince-Bishop Petar II Petrović-Njegoš's 1847 epic ballad, *The Mountain Wreath*, a cornerstone of Serb and Montenegrin national literature, revolves primarily around the extermination of the mountain principality's Slavic Muslim popula-tion by the defiant Christian nobility. While an epic poem should not be compared to a political programme as such, both the *Načertanije* and *The Mountain Wreath* were aspects of a single, emerging nationalist imaginary in nineteenth-century Serbia and Montenegro, which explic-itly linked the "liberation" of the Serb–Montenegrin nations with the expulsion and extermination of both the Ottomans and local Slavic Muslims. As Michael Sells argues, the poem later became the basis for Serb nationalism's anti-Muslim bent in the late nineteenth and twentieth centuries.[43] The poem popularizes, for instance, the concept of the *poturčeni Srbi* (Turkified Serbs), an idea that has since become a perennial feature of Serb nationalist discourse. This is, in short, the belief that Slavic Muslims – especially those in BiH, Serbia, and Montenegro – betrayed their "original" Christian faith (and, by extension, Serb ethnicity)[44] by converting to Islam. Their liquidation is thus an act of divine retribution. As Sells notes, such mythologized nationalist narratives were explicitly reanimated in Serb nationalist propaganda in the 1990s but appear in various forms throughout the twentieth century.

In this manner, both texts represent pillars of the broader "Greater Serbia" programme, a plan for a grand Serbian state stretching across the Balkans, repeatedly rejuvenated throughout the nineteenth and twentieth centuries. Of course, this programme was not always explicitly chauvinist, as proponents occasionally found themselves receptive to the idea of a South Slavic (i.e. Yugoslav) or a Balkan federation that would necessarily include non-Serbs as part of its population. Nor was irredentism of this sort exclusive to Serbia: Bulgarian, Romanian, Greek, and Croatian elites all dabbled in similar fantasies. Yet what is, arguably, unique about the Serbian incarnation of this nationalist project is its historical consistency and popularity among the successive generations of state-building elites in the country. The idea was openly advocated by leading government figures in Belgrade during the royal Yugoslav period, by Draža Mihailović's quisling Četnik movement during the 1940s, and the likes of Slobodan Milošević, Radovan Karadžić, and Vojislav Šešelj during the 1990s. Each of these were moments that not only corresponded to episodes of extreme violence against non-Serb populations in the region but occurred within periods of regime collapse.

Indeed, in order for the Balkan elite to survive the collapse of existing regimes, they depended on the use of violence to subvert popular demands for structural reform. Accordingly, during these periods of dissolution, elites scrambled to consolidate peoples and territories, both externally and internally. Thus Serbian domestic politics were dominated from 1804 to 1903 primarily by a blood feud between the Obrenović and Karađorđević clans, the two leading "royal" families in the country. The feud ended finally with the murder of the last Obrenović ruler, Alexander I of Serbia (1876–1903), by members of the secret military society the Black Hand (of later Franz Ferdinand-related fame). The bankrupt and cynical nature of post-Ottoman politics in the country, dominated by intra-oligarchic disputes, led the anarchist Mikhail Bakunin to remark sarcastically that in "Serbia, the overthrow of one prince and the installation of another one is called a 'revolution'".[45]

The post-Ottoman period produced little except for provincial intrigue in Serbia. Precisely because the Serbian "nobility" had not been imported from elsewhere in Europe but traced their ancestry to local brigands and peasant communes, the Obrenović and Karađorđević clans and their followers had to embellish their own humble origins. This process meant that any wealth the newly independent polity could create or lay claim to was quickly siphoned off by the elites for the purposes of self-aggrandisement. Moreover, the desire by the elite to immediately begin expanding their freshly minted kingdom (as their primitive, feudal conception of economics necessitated greater land and manpower, above all) meant that militarization and irredentism became the dominant political project of nineteenth- and early twentieth-century Serbia. This fact would also invariably influence its neighbours and Serbia's relations with them. While limited democratic reforms waxed and waned in the new state – amid vicious factional strife in the weak parliament – the jingoistic outlook of even the nominally liberal movement within Serbia severely constrained the possible shape of any actual participatory political project. Virtually all popular energy was channelled into an immobilizing nationalist rhetoric. As Dubravka Stojanović argues, the elites' rapacious thirst for expansion and war meant that, as a polity, Serbia became perennially "unfinished", both because its borders were never clearly established and because permanent military mobilization stunted the ability of any sort of autonomous civil society to emerge.[46]

The experience of the People's Radical Party (NRS), a mainstay of Serbian and Yugoslav politics between 1881 and 1945, is exemplary in this regard. While at times a leading advocate for liberal political reforms in Serbia, including the adoption of significant constitutional reforms in 1888, the party reserved its most fervent support for the various Serbian nationalist causes. These were primarily assisting the crown's assorted wars of expansion prior to 1918, and ensuring ethnic Serb political hegemony within the new joint South Slavic state after 1918.[47] The party's political radicalism was thus perennially undermined by their parochial nationalism, which they never ceased privileging over the former. As Nicos P. Mouzelis notes in a comparative study of Latin American and Balkan paths towards modernization, which likewise privileges early state-formation processes in the nineteenth century as key to understanding late-twentieth-century dynamics: "both the post-oligarchic broadening of political participation and the subsequent acceleration of the industrialisation process contributed, in different ways, to a polity with a highly unequal distribution of political power between rulers and ruled". He goes on to add that, as a consequence, there remained in both regions an "inadequate basis for dealing democratically with the staggering problems that post-war semi-peripheral societies had to face once their economies were becoming more industrialised and their politics more fully marked by high levels of mass participation".[48] In the case of the Balkans, though, this disconnect has continued into the present and, as I note throughout this book, it has been adeptly reinforced through repeated episodes of nationalist indoctrination, the ideological veneer for the preservation of elastic authoritarian governing patterns, which have elsewhere, including Latin America, significantly abated.

While nationalist narratives promised unity and emancipation, in practice they exclusively promoted the interests of the local elites' politics of dispossession and depoliticization. The Serbian socialist Dimitrije Tucović's (ornately titled) 1914 treatise *Serbia and Albania: A Contribution to the Critique of the Conqueror Policy of the Serbian Bourgeoisie* described this policy in the context of the Balkan Wars.[49] Drafted into the Serbian army during both the Balkan Wars and World War I, Tucović, along with an entire generation of young Balkan radicals, died in the trenches of the European war. If World War I dealt a significant blow to the international socialist movement, in the Balkans it virtually exterminated many of the youth most interested in democratic and anti-nationalist organizing.[50] Nevertheless, before his death, Tucović thoroughly indicted the nationalist leaders of his time, recognizing that the sequence of post-Ottoman wars in the Balkans were merely an effort on the part of local elites to consolidate their respective claims to the Serbian, Montenegrin, Bulgarian, Romanian, and Greek states.[51] Rather than liberation for the peasant and (what existed of) the working classes, as these upstart monarchs promised, this process was largely one of elite parcelization, conflict, and intra-elite accommodation and negotiation.

As national borders proliferated and ethnic minority and majority status took on mortal consequences, large segments of the Balkan population found themselves suddenly targeted for displacement or extermination. The entirety of the region's Muslim population, for instance, suddenly became branded by opportunistic ideologues in Serbia, Montenegro, Greece, Bulgaria, and Romania as Ottoman fellow travellers, co-conspirators, and beneficiaries of Sultanic oppression. The images of the despotic, exploitative Ottoman and Muslim *ayans*, *pashas*, and janissaries, a trope of (Orthodox) Christian nationalist narratives in the region even today, have their origins in this transitional period.[52] Meanwhile, Muslim elites in BiH, Albania, and Kosovo, in particular, continued to hold out hope in the ability of the Porte to reassert its rule in the region and thus to preserve their relatively privileged positions in the imperial architecture. Yet, as Ottoman rule in the Balkans clearly waned, local Muslim elites struggled to adapt as deftly as their Christian peers, who used their confessional differences as the foundation for their emerging nationalist projects. When the Muslim elite (and what existed of a Muslim intelligentsia) finally came round to initiating a national project of their own, it was largely in response to the violence of their competitors.

Thus in BiH, for instance, the Muslim national project struggled merely to assert a distinct presence from the larger and more well-developed Serb Orthodox and Croat Catholic movements. As one influential Muslim leader, Sakib Korkut,[53] argued in 1919: "There are no class differences. Muslim peasant and Muslim landlord feel the same way because neither has become dead to the demands of justice and will not covet other people's property".[54] As a result of their late nationalization campaign, identification by BiH's "ethnic Muslims" as Croats or Serbs (for professional or political reasons primarily) was the norm well into the twentieth century. This also became fodder to Serb and Croat nationalists, who used it as "proof" that Bosnian Muslims, in particular, but also Muslims in the Balkans more generally, were merely "lapsed" Serbs or Croats who had "forgotten" or "abandoned" their actual ethnic identities. Such crypto-racist[55] debates aside, the observation by Korkut concerned the experience of a community suddenly marginalized and persecuted, but his essential logic was one shared, indeed embraced, by all nationalist leaders. That is, peasant and land-lord alike ought to feel the same way because despite their transpar-ently different social and economic positions, their ethno-national or confessional identity inherently bound them in a newly salient manner. In a sense then, both those elites advocating genocide and those attempting to survive genocide began to stress the importance of belonging to an ethno-national whole.[56]

Yet the reasons for accepting this logic were dramatically different for the vast majority of the population and for the elites who claimed to represent them. Terrorized both psychologically and physically, local populations sought out the safety of any and all saviours, allowing elites to consolidate an immensely lucrative (and static) political system. By carving out antagonistic Serb, Muslim, and Croat ethne, that is, self-identifying ethnic communities, elites ensured the emergence of a permanently immobilized population, ripe for exploitation, from which any grumble of discontent could be stifled by insisting on the imminent danger of extermination by the "other". What was most dan-gerous to this system was not actually the wholesale extermination of one side or the other – notwithstanding large-scale killing campaigns – but the emergence of a different conceptual framework: a competing ideological programme that might recognize that peasant and landlord did not have similar interests and that, indeed, the Serb and Muslim peasant had more in common than the Muslim peasant and Muslim landlord or the Serb peasant and Serb landlord.

It is thus no surprise that in the late nineteenth century, as today in the early twenty-first century, within the nationalist discourse the most dangerous enemy was not "the national other" but rather those from within propagating any form of socio-economic or class analysis or even merely a more robust conception of identity politics. As such, it is important to stress how late and how contested this process of national coalescence was among the various communities in the region, especially among those (admittedly few) educated enough to recognize that it was a self-serving, elite-engineered contest of social constructs. As the central territory for national contestation, the case of BiH is once again instructive.

CLIENTS AND BRIGANDS

Branka Magaš, for instance, describes how the Bosnian Franciscans consistently rebuffed attempts by the Catholic Church and other political authorities in Croatia to "rechristen" them as "Croats".[57] Among these Franciscans, Ivan Franjo Jukić (1818–1857) remains perhaps the best known. An early proponent of religious pluralism, the friar often wrote under the pseudonym Slavoljub Bošnjak ("Slavophile Bosniak").[58] Jukić pleaded with the inhabitants of BiH to "grab a hold of books and journals,[59] to see what others have done, to gather the same resources and to lead our people out of the darkness and into the light of truth".[60] The light of truth he had in mind was clearly the emerging national identities of the Serbs and Croats that were aiding these communities along the path to political sovereignty of the sort Jukić desired for BiH. Jukić and his Franciscan cohorts mimicked the quasi-historical mythologies of their peers in Croatia and Serbia, claiming that their order "retained a memory" of the medieval Bosnian kingdom that had ended with the beheading of the last Bosnian king in 1463. In the midst of nineteenth-century political romanticism, the Franciscans hoped to revive the sovereign Bosnian Kingdom, complete with a corresponding Bosnian/Bosniak national identity that would embrace all of BiH's religious communities.[61] Ivo Banac, meanwhile, notes that as late as 1891, Safvet-beg Bašagić, a prominent Bosnian Muslim poet and activist, was able to pen an ode in which he bemoaned, "From Trebinje ... to the gate of Brod, there were never any Serbs or Croats".[62] Bašagić meant Trebinje and Brod to symbolize the southern and northern tips of BiH, and the lack of Serbs and Croats was a reference to the recent "conversions" of Orthodox and Catholic Christians to their respective ethno-national movements. Tellingly, by 1894 Bašagić had moved to Zagreb and declared himself a Croat.

This transformation of class antagonisms into ethno-national fratricide became a staple tactic of elites in the Yugoslav lands during the nineteenth century and a critical element of why democratic organization and analysis remain stunted to this day, especially in the context of nationalist revival in the late twentieth century. With a large, uneducated peasant population, often in fear of extermination or at least robbery, promises of security became a popular means of obtaining support. Because the socio-economic character of the region has remained largely agrarian, underdeveloped, and primitive, this strategy has remained effective. In order to advance my critique of the Euro-Atlantic project in the Western Balkans in the next chapter, it is necessary to examine earlier attempts at reform, especially those initiated by outside powers. It is also for this reason that the discussion continues to focus disproportionately in the next section on BiH, the Balkan state arguably most affected by the external influences of both neighbouring states and great powers alike.

Ottoman and Austro-Hungarian Reform Efforts

Struggling to cope with the lawlessness within their own borders (as noted), by the early nineteenth century Ottoman leaders began to realize that the survival of their empire depended on major reforms. Sultan Mahmud II first abolished the janissary corps – the Porte's elite military order that grew to rival the power of the Sultan himself – in the 1820s and then turned towards restructuring the tax and land system of the empire in the 1830s. Both moves were aimed at modernizing the Ottoman state and would prove especially controversial in the empire's periphery. In BiH, for instance:

> the landowners ... resisted every attempt at westernization made by successive Sultans. Mahmud II's formal abolition of feudalism finally destroyed the *Kapetanate* [sic], the privileged forty-eight beys[63] who, when the Empire was at its zenith, had been entrusted with administering the subdivisions of Bosnia in return for raising *sipahi* regiments for the Sultan's cavalry. But the *Kapetanate* [sic] went down fighting, literally. Open revolt against Mahmud in 1837 was followed by an even wider rebellion when reports ... held out the promise of legal equality and social upliftment for Christians and Jews. Not until March 1850 did a powerful Ottoman army ... finally suppress the Bosnian beys.[64]

However, by 1910 there were still some 444,920 peasant families in BiH that were classified as *kmets*, or customary tenants or sharecroppers, usually understood to be the closest approximation to serfs in the region.[65] BiH was at this point in the third decade of Austro-Hungarian administration after the Habsburgs acquired the country at the 1878 Congress of Berlin from the Ottoman Empire, initially as a protectorate under the continued suzerainty of the Porte and then as a province after it was completely annexed in 1908. The Austro-Hungarian arrival, however, "did little to change ... [the] system of backward, exploitative sharecropping left behind as the principal Ottoman legacy to the province".[66] In short, "maximizing tax revenue to defray the costs of military occupation was always the major Hapsburg motive in [BiH], along with maintaining military security", much as it had been for the Ottomans.[67]

According to the 1910 figures, 91 per cent of landlords with *kmets* were registered as Muslims, while 73 per cent and 21 per cent of *kmets* were registered as Orthodox and Catholic respectively.[68] The evident confessional imbalance in the country's economic relations was a definite social cleavage, but as an article of nationalist mobilization it still lacked substance. Ivo Banac stresses that it "must be remembered ... that most Bosnian landlords (61.38 percent) owned less than 123.55 acres of land ... The point is that the Bosnian Muslim upper crust was not made up of Oriental nabobs living in ostentatious luxury".[69] This "Oriental nabob" reference is nevertheless provocative, as it invites comparison with the relative wealth of BiH elites and colonial scions elsewhere. The term "nabob" originates from the British colonization of the Indian subcontinent, and refers specifically to "British subjects who had gone either to India or to the West Indies and returned to England with spectacular wealth".[70] In contrast, Bosnian Muslim *ayans* and *beys* were not nabobs anymore than the emerging Serbian and Montenegrin kings and princes of the same period were actual royals; nor was the Ottoman and Austro-Hungarian administration of the Balkans "colonial" in the British sense of the term. After all, British nabobs were members of a transcontinental, imperial-capitalist bourgeoisie. The Bosnian Muslim elites' wealth, status, and privilege, in contrast, largely came from the titles they could extract from the collapsing central Ottoman authorities and what they could appropriate from an impoverished peasantry. This remained true during the Habsburg period and was also true of the nascent Serbian and Montenegrin royalty, who in a single lifetime shifted from loyal Ottoman subjects to "national liberators". In fact, as noted earlier, they shifted from having been the enforcers of the Ottoman order, the very oppressors of the peasant classes, to posturing as their emancipators.

The reference to nabobs is illuminating because it alerts us to the complete non-existence of a bourgeoisie in BiH at the end of the nineteenth century. What existed in BiH, as in Serbia and Montenegro and the rest of the Ottoman Balkans, was elites whose conception of wealth and power fundamentally rested on patrimonialism, which in moments of regime crisis or transition relied on extreme forms of violence, intended to preserve the structural status quo of these societies with only minor ideological mutations. As a result, for all the claims of Ottoman economic and political backwardness, the Austro-Hungarian expansion into the region – Austria and Hungary had directly controlled Slovenia and Croatia for at least two centuries prior to the Ottoman conquest of Bosnia in the late fifteenth century – was little better. It was during this period that the agrarian question (i.e. the end of serfdom) ought to have been resolved with the grand entry of the Balkans into the Concert of Europe. Yet even a brief survey of Habsburg economic policy demonstrates how much the Austro-Hungarians themselves contributed to the peripheral status of their newly acquired territories. This was a reflection of Austro-Hungary's own quasi-capitalist development and dominant authoritarian political structure, which was likewise beset by parochial antagonisms. As Robert Donia explains about the Habsburg arrival in BiH:

> Economically, the Monarchy's officials mainly treated its colony much like other European powers treated their overseas colonial holdings: They imported raw materials from it and exported manufactured goods to it. But two factors made economic relations between the metropole and colony unique: the intense rivalry between Hungary and Cisleithanian Austria for domination of the Bosnian market, and the proximity of colonizer and colony ... the rivalry seriously impeded economic progress in BiH. The rivalry retarded infrastructure development (particularly railroad building), led to politically-motivated investments and capital allocation, impeded the development of free markets, and entailed policies that inhibited domestic industry while subsidizing manufacturing in both halves of the Monarchy.[71]

The development of BiH was thus limited again by an imperial administration already itself in the process of coming undone and beset by patrimonial and provincial disputes. As a result, the emergence of a local merchant class, a bourgeoisie of any real influence, remained unrealized. The situation in the territories long dominated by the Habsburgs was only marginally better. Serfdom in Croatia, for instance, was fully abolished in 1848 and then only as part of an empire-wide change following the 1848 Revolutions. It had little to do with pressures from the local Croatian nobility. Moreover, the Croatian territories were the least developed of the already comparatively underdeveloped Habsburg lands. The illiteracy rate in Croatia-Slavonia, for instance, in 1869 was 80.6 per cent.[72] And although the literacy rate in Croatia was nearly halved by 1910, in 1914 barely 10 per cent of the population in the whole of the Yugoslav lands lived in urban centres; the vast majority of the population was still uneducated, illiterate, and lived in the country.[73] Capitalism was not on the radar.

The Austro-Hungarian regime's fundamental inability to resolve its own contradictory policy approach towards the Slav lands (i.e. incorporation but not at the expense of diluting existing economic and political interests) meant that a series of stopgap measures were all that they adopted after the departure of the Ottomans. By 1918, the closest BiH, and, by extension, the whole of the region had come towards mimicking a capitalist mode of production (and political administration) was still but a facsimile, notwithstanding the presence of some minor industrial production facilities in Zagreb, Ljubljana, Subotica, Sombor, and Novi Sad.[74] The Austro-Hungarian Empire did little to develop its Balkan possessions beyond leaving behind colourful facades in the cities and a skeletal extractive infrastructure in the countryside. The quasi-feudal relations of the Ottoman period remained in place in BiH, while Croatia, Slovenia, and Vojvodina, though comparatively more developed, remained provinces all the same. Serbia, the lone sovereign polity in the region, masked its economic backwardness behind the veneer of patriotic pomp. Its illiteracy rate in 1901 was above 75 per cent, while the figure in Britain and France was around 14 per cent in the same decade.[75]

The final end of serfdom in the least developed parts of the Balkans came only after World War I, with the formation of the Kingdom of Serbs, Croats and Slovenes (from 1929, the Kingdom of Yugoslavia). Still, this did not mean a transition towards a genuine market economy in the region. Such was the case in BiH, following a set of agrarian reforms between 1918 and 1919, where the genuinely socially emancipatory dimensions of this shift were mitigated by elite insistence on patrimonial self-enrichment. Accordingly, rather than a process of redistribution, the early Yugoslav agrarian reforms were a process of elite-driven dispossession, albeit with a distinct sectarian tinge.[76] In BiH,

[by] July, 1919, more than four hundred thousand hectares of land had been taken from 4,281 Muslim landowners. Sometimes land was taken without any refund. In other cases, the compensation offered by the state – some of which was paid immediately and the rest in instalments – was well below the land's fair market value. All of this had a catastrophic economic and social effect on the Muslim community as many landowning Muslim families were reduced to poverty. One result was a new exodus of Bosnian Muslims to Turkey. The Muslims were also generally uneducated. In the 1930s, the level of illiteracy for Yugoslavia as a whole was 88 percent, while the figures for Muslims were even more dismal: 95 percent (99.68 percent for women).[77]

These nominal reforms also took place in the context of yet another campaign of violence against the Muslims of Yugoslavia (and especially in BiH), which in its most recent incarnation began during the course of World War I. The pogroms, led by ethnic Serb militias, were given a tacit seal of approval by the new government in Belgrade and resulted in the deaths of thousands of Muslims, peasants and landowners alike. The agrarian restructuring and extra-judicial killings amounted to a "systematic destruction of Muslims", as one observer noted at the time.[78] The resulting political, economic, and demographic shifts had lasting consequences as much for BiH as for Yugoslavia's overall development. The country's economic paradigm changed but within the context of a destructive, reactionary political environment, rooted in sectarian revanchism that would not easily dissipate.[79] Above all, it was yet another moment of ideological transition marked by violence and minimal social transformation.[80]

Accordingly, it was not until after World War II that the Yugoslav communists made a serious effort towards the "modernization" of agricultural relations, however crudely understood, in Yugoslavia as a whole. Beginning in 1947 and ending in 1953, the new communist authorities undertook the most centralized and directed redistribution scheme in the region's history. Ultimately, this scheme too failed, largely due to militant peasant resistance, combined with the need for the new Yugoslav authorities to maintain support among this population in the wake of the Tito–Stalin split of 1948.[81] By 1953, the communists attempted yet another socio-economic transformation. While this particular plan, which would eventually become the workers' self-management system of the late Yugoslav period, had significant political consequences, it was also another in a long line of revolutionary half-measures. Accordingly, G. E. Curtis notes:

> In March 1953, the government began dissolving collective and state farms [which it had begun forming in 1945]. Two-thirds of the peasants abandoned the collectives within nine months, and the socialist share of land ownership sank from 25 percent to 9 percent within three years. In an attempt to mitigate the problem of peasant landlessness, the government reduced the legal limit on individual holdings from 25 to 35 hectares of cultivable land to 10 hectares; this restriction would remain on the books for over three decades and would prevent the development of economically efficient family farms.[82]

Thus from the late eighteenth to the middle of the twentieth century the Yugoslav lands were in almost constant political flux but endured a form of relatively static economic organization. This meant that it was not until the 1960s that the local economies developed and stabilized enough for "the emergence in the Balkans of urban populations at a level close to the European norm, with its characteristic pattern of small families, high consumption, industry and services".[83] And even then, urbanization in the Western Balkans mostly meant the concentration of populations with otherwise largely untransformed socio-economic practices. To this day, for instance, the immediate downtown core of Sarajevo is surrounded by village-like hamlets and neighbourhoods complete with livestock. This odd arrangement – a capital nestled in a valley, surrounded by peasant colonies – is not (only) the result of the devastation of the recent Bosnian War (1992–1995) but has still more to do with older socio-economic norms. As a result, in the wake of the dissolution of the second Yugoslav state, the region is once again transparently dominated by economic brigandry and demographic collapse. In other words, the post-Yugoslav transition was only the most recent episode of elastic authoritarian consolidation in the Balkans, in which the previous ideological order collapsed without any fundamental change in the nature of political administration and economic accumulation.

Conclusions

Because Ottoman and post-Ottoman socio-economic dynamics in the Balkans were different from those in western Europe, the state form also necessarily took on a different shape in the continent's southeastern corner. Owing to the clientelistic and patrimonial economic and political practices which predominated in the region during the century of transitional Ottoman and Austro-Hungarian administration, the key experience of Balkan political development became the process of regime entropy and elite consolidation. To local elites, the state and sovereignty meant the preservation of predatory land tenure, tax-farming, and brigand practices. The Balkan state began, as all states do, as a protection racket, but it remained so and therein lies its specificity. In order to navigate the process of regime collapse, Balkan elites orchestrated calculated campaigns of "nationalization" through violence and terror. Nationalism subverted class hostilities between the new elites and their overwhelmingly peasant populations into ethno-national conflicts between Christians, Muslims, Serbs, Croats, Bosniaks, Bulgarians, Greeks, and so on. The basic economic model of the late Ottoman period, accumulation through dispossession, patrimonialism and clientelism, thus persisted for generations as a kind of elastic authoritarianism, changing in ideological veneer but not in fundamental political character.

The preceding account is necessarily skeletal and skims over all manner of significant minutiae, not least the short-lived experiment in democratic parliamentarianism in the first Yugoslav state between 1918 and 1929.[84] But its aim is not to provide a comprehensive history of the turn-of-the-century Balkans, but rather to advance a theoretical survey of this history, and show how it should inform our analysis of contemporary democratization and reform efforts in the region. In a wider sense, the point of this chapter is to illustrate the local histories which inform the efforts of local elites today to roll back nearly three decades of Western political and economic intervention. Like their predecessors in the nineteenth century, contemporary Balkan elites believe they are seeing the early signs of imperial collapse, and they are preparing accordingly. It remains to be seen whether they are right, whether policymakers in Washington and Brussels can reassert their role in the region, and what role both the region's nascent social movements and the West's geopolitical competitors will have in the years to come.

2

THE WARLORDS' PEACE
Yugoslavia's End and Aftermath

The post-war political order of the former Yugoslavia is a complicated patchwork of peace agreements, special bilateral accords, and international supervision. But the unifying principle of the international community's peace architecture in the region for the past two decades has been simple: in exchange for a cessation of hostilities, Brussels and Washington have sponsored the region's reconstruction along with its political and economic modernization. And following the example of (most of) the former Eastern Bloc states, the primary incentive for Western Balkan elites to allow for the region's stabilization and democratization is the prospect of their integration into the continent's dominant political and economic structures: the EU and NATO. That was the theory behind the international community's approach to the region. It is referred to in the policy and political science literature as "conditionality": EU and US political and economic aid is conditional on the meeting of certain predetermined objectives by local leaders (e.g. free and fair elections, privatization of formerly socially owned enterprises, peace). In return, elites benefit from increased economic prosperity and political legitimacy, as do their citizens.

This approach has played out rather differently in reality. In practice, the EU and US have spent the last twenty years paying hush money

47

to a constellation of largely unreformed and unrepentant war profi-teers and warlords. When pushed to implement (rather than merely adopt) reform policies, local leaders have routinely opted to fabricate political crises in order to extract renewed commitments from the internationals. In this manner, local elites have kept both local popula-tions and the international community in perpetual fear of renewed conflict, while simultaneously presenting their respective regimes as essential for peace. Thus, rather than conditionality, a "protection racket"[1] is at the root of the relationship between Western powers and local elites: the exchange of nominal stability for condition-free finan-cial and political benefits, in a situation where the local elite rather than the international community is the dominant party. As a result, while Slovenia and Croatia have successfully joined both the EU and NATO, and Albania and Montenegro have entered the fold of the latter, the dominant factors in the politics of each of these countries remain decidedly local, namely, the legacies of generations of authoritarian, patrimonial, and clientelistic regimes, and the wars of plunder that have traditionally accompanied moments of regime collapse and recon-figuration in the Balkans. That Zagreb's political establishment, for instance, appears primarily concerned with events in Belgrade and Mostar (i.e. Serbia and BiH) is no aberration but a historical pattern.

The aim of this chapter is twofold. The objective is to discuss both EU and US policy in the post-Yugoslav Western Balkans. By trading security guarantees for deferred commitments to genuine political and economic reform, Brussels and Washington have created perverse, inverted incentive structures for the region's elites. Rather than pro-moting reforms, this approach actually encourages local elites to perch deliberately in the grey space between "partners in peace" and "threats to peace". By alternating between the two, Balkan leaders are able both to continue receiving Western financial and political support and to maintain power through existing patrimonial structures and networks. Importantly, this approach suggests a fundamental misunderstanding of democracy and democratic governance on the part of the EU and the US. Instead of being grounded in popular participation and delibera-tion, or even a degree of organic tension between the "aristocratic" and "plebeian" instincts of established parliamentary regimes,[2] the democ-ratization process spearheaded by the international community in the

Balkans has become merely an exercise in "installing the right elites".[3] This not only evacuates ordinary citizens from the task of governance in the Balkans, it also obscures the vital popular and populist dimensions of Western democracy without which that democracy could never have emerged or survived in the first place. In the final analysis, this chapter asks what such a "pro-ransom" policy on the part of Western policymakers means for claims concerning the "transformative power" of the Euro-Atlantic institutional and political framework. More importantly, where does this policy regime leave the vast majority of citizens in the former Yugoslavia, who now feel both disenfranchised by local leaders and betrayed by the EU's and US's post-war promises? And above all, were there any viable alternatives to this approach in the first place and do they still exist today?

In order to discuss the failures of Western policy after Yugoslavia, it is necessary to account for the local factors that precipitated the Yugoslav crisis in the late 1980s. As noted in the previous chapter, the complex socio-political regime which characterized the second Yugoslav state – and the patterns of accumulation and governance out of which it emerged – remain fundamental to the contemporary politics of the Western Balkans. More precisely, the concern is with the underdeveloped but nevertheless important democratic tendencies and energies which existed in the SFRJ, especially in the form of the workers' self-management system. The dismantling of this political-economic regime by local elites, with the assistance of the international community, represents the dissolution of a policy framework that could have significantly strengthened the effort of post-war democratization. And yet even the mere echoes of this regime can and should still inform future discussions of political economy (and its reform) in the former Yugoslavia. After all, despite past international policy failures and continuing generations of local authoritarianism, there is no alternative but to finally begin the long winding journey towards a participatory democratic regime in the Western Balkans. But we need not, nor can we, proceed as though the region were a blank slate, bereft of any and all positive examples on which to base such a programme.

The Essential Contours of the Yugoslav Crisis

"We've got no dog in this fight," were the words of US Secretary of State James Baker in 1991 on the eve of the Bosnian War.[4] Baker advised President George H. W. Bush to steer the US clear of the mayhem accompanying the dissolution of the SFRJ. Bush concurred, as would his successor, Bill Clinton, for all but the very last portion of the conflict. But across the Atlantic, the mood was decidedly more optimistic. Despite heavy fighting in Slovenia and Croatia, Jacques Poos, chair of the Foreign Affairs Council of the European Economic Community (EEC), declared that "this is the hour of Europe".[5] With the ink on the German reunification treaty of August 1990 not yet dry, western Europe's diplomatic establishment was eager to ensure that "some damned foolish thing in the Balkans",[6] in the fateful account of Otto von Bismarck, would not compromise the emergence of the post-Cold War order that President Bush had envisioned two years earlier: "Europe … whole and free".[7]

Yet when the Yugoslav crisis tested the resolve of the West's combined commitments to this vision of Europe whole and free, and to the arrival of the continent's defining political hour, it proved wanting. The situation was certainly grim when viewed from the rubble of Vukovar and Sarajevo. But it was also a sign of the deep-seated crisis of Western leadership itself, at the very moment of its purported triumph over the Soviet Union. In a sense, the unwillingness of the US and the inability of the EEC in the 1990s to act decisively in the face of clear and present evidence of both massive human rights violations and a long-term threat to Europe's security heralded the much more evident cracks in the Atlantic relationship visible today. The political cleavages between Washington and Brussels initially revealed during the Yugoslav crisis remained and are today leading factors in the arguably still more muddled Western response to the conflict in Ukraine and the horror in Syria. And while the commitments at the core of the North Atlantic security apparatus appear strained, Russia, renewed as a world power, asserts its will from the Baltics to the Balkans and beyond, shaping geopolitics to its own ends.

The magnitude of the failure of Western leadership in Yugoslavia is difficult to overstate. A decade of warfare, sprawling from Slovenia to

Macedonia, marked the South Slavic federation's dissolution. Approximately a hundred and forty thousand people were killed in the fighting, most of them civilians, and another four million displaced.[8] In the Bosnian War alone, a hundred thousand died, many in the organized campaigns of "ethnic cleansing", which were later recognized as the first acts of genocide in Europe since World War II by the International Tribunal for the Former Yugoslavia (ICTY), and which were orchestrated by the Serb nationalist forces backed and directed by the Milošević government in Belgrade.[9] With the sole exception of the relatively minor ethnic Albanian insurgency in Macedonia in 2001, the essential contours of the Yugoslav Wars were the same from their onset during the Ten Day War in Slovenia in the summer of 1991 to their last major chapter in the Kosovo War (1998–1999). At the root of each of these conflicts was a multi-pronged effort by an alliance of authoritarian and extremist nationalist elements within the Serbian political establishment seeking to navigate, albeit for different and sometimes contradictory reasons, the crisis of one-party rule in the SFRJ in the twilight of the 1980s.[10] While the conservative wing of the communist establishment in Belgrade sought to roll back the SFRJ's progressive political liberalization, the nationalist camp took issue with one particular dimension of this liberalization process: the diminishing centrality of Serbia in Yugoslav affairs and the supposed marginalization of ethnic Serbs throughout the country as a result. In time, these two sides would merge their efforts through the leadership of Slobodan Milošević, who adeptly portrayed himself as a champion both of the conservative communist establishment and of beleaguered Serb nationalists. In attempting to realize their aims, they unleashed a cycle of violence from which the region has yet to recover, three decades after Milošević's initial rise to power.

Milošević attempted to reverse the democratic transformation of Yugoslavia which seemed imminent as a result of both a decade of dramatic economic decline (widely blamed on the country's sclerotic leadership) and the wave of anti-regime discontent roiling the whole of the communist world. When his initial effort failed, he exploited nationalist grievances with the aid of an assortment of hitherto marginal Serb extremists to forcibly carve out of Yugoslavia a "Greater Serbia" whose twin ideological pillars were to be authoritarianism and ethno-nationalism. That is, Yugoslavia would remain an authoritarian regime but in the name of the Serb nation rather than the working class. Yugoslavia's crisis was thus political, as were the objectives of the primary architect of its dissolution. The ethnic dimension of the subsequent Yugoslav Wars was a result but not the cause of the country's implosion. This key insight, however, was never truly grasped by leading policymakers in Europe or the US. Instead, the internationals preferred various versions of the argument that Yugoslavia imploded as a result of the eruption of "ancient ethnic hatreds" in the wake of Tito's death in 1980. To them, Yugoslavia was a tribal backwater, held together by a military strongman whose death inevitably signalled the end of the state as a whole. This tautological account was not only ignorant but it directly compromised the West's efforts to prevent the outbreak of war and later to ensure peace and promote democratization and reconciliation. After all, by insisting on an essentially apolitical, millennial explanation of Yugoslavia's implosion, Western leaders failed to address the concrete political motivations and objectives of the conflict's chief architects. And when the US and EU, in turn, secured peace by largely acquiescing in the preferences of local elites (i.e. the preservation of patrimonial and clientelistic socio-economic norms within an ethnically fragmented political framework), they virtually guaranteed the futility of all subsequent reform efforts. Accordingly, a more detailed analysis of Yugoslavia's post-World War II development not only illustrates the error of the international approach, but it also helps identify the alternatives that were available both before and after the war and that remain available today still, albeit in significantly diminished capacity.

War and Revolution

Like its monarchist predecessor, the Yugoslav state created by Tito's communists was a historical curiosity. At the time of the country's occupation by fascist forces in 1941, the Kingdom of Yugoslavia was already a state unravelling at the seams as a result of the crown's unwillingness to allow for the development of a genuine constitutional monarchy.[11] Like the Ottomans and Austro-Hungarians before them, the Serbian royals who claimed the executive of the first South Slavic state in 1918 remained variously incapable or uninterested in substantive reform efforts, notwithstanding a short-lived and acrimonious experiment in parliamentarianism between 1918 and 1929. Unsurprisingly, strongman-engineered sectarianism, with the occasional veneer of parliamentary procedure, continued throughout the first decade of the Kingdom's existence. On 6 January 1929, King Alexander I did away with even this pretence of participatory governance and declared a royal dictatorship. This reign, in turn, ended with Alexander's assassination by a Bulgarian gunman, sponsored by Croatian fascists, in 1934; he was the second Serbian-Yugoslav royal assassinated in three decades. As it turned out, the power vacuum created by the disappearance of the Ottoman and Austro-Hungarian empires could not be filled by the provincial strongmen who styled themselves as kings and governors in the region in their wake. And so the violence on which these local elites depended to perpetuate their political survival begot more violence.

By the time of the Axis invasion in 1941, Yugoslavia had still not recovered from Alexander's murder and, arguably, teetered on the brink of civil war. The ensuing guerrilla wars in the region, within the broader context of World War II, were as much an intra-Yugoslav war between the assorted nationalist-authoritarian sects as they were a war for popular "national liberation". The latter option, the one represented by (although not synonymous with) the communist partisans, was initially a peripheral phenomenon within the broader chaos. Yet it was precisely the moral and political bankruptcy of the various nationalist cliques – from the quisling Ustašas in Croatia who sought the extermination of ethnic Serbs, to the Serbian quisling Četnik movement which primarily pursued the extermination of Muslims[12] – that left the communists with their programme for an all-Yugoslav resistance as the only plausible alternative for the majority of the population.

From the start of the Yugoslav period, the Communist Party of Yugoslavia (CPY) enjoyed significant urban support at least, coming in fourth in the first democratic elections in 1918. By 1921, however, the party was outlawed and driven underground by the monarchist authorities. The communists spent the next two decades in intrigue, conspiracy, and fantasies of proletarian revolution in an overwhelmingly agrarian and rural polity. But when their opportunity to lead an uprising of the people finally came, it was not as a result of the mass embrace of Marxist ideology but because of the obvious brutality of fascist occupation and the likewise murderous provincialism of their assorted local collaborators. Nevertheless, the communists navigated their surging popularity with acumen. They would portray themselves as the vanguard of a national liberation movement, winning first the war and then later the peace.

The winning strategy of the communist-led partisan forces during the war and in the immediate period thereafter was most clearly demonstrated by the massive influx of peasants into what had hitherto been a largely urban working-class party.[13] Though the party numbered nearly eighteen thousand youth members in 1940, a year before the Axis invasion of Yugoslavia, the influx of peasants during and after the war permanently skewed the class basis of the movement from urban working class to peasant and what Marija Obradović, citing William G. Lockwood, calls "worker-peasants": "villagers incorporated into industry while still maintaining a partial economic base in private agriculture and still enmeshed in a system of social relationships largely located in their villages of residence".[14] In 1945, there were 141,066 peasants in the new CPY and by 1945 the number of "worker-peasants" had grown to nearly five hundred thousand.[15] Combined with the fact that three-fourths of the pre-war membership died during the war, the CPY that emerged in 1945 was necessarily dramatically reoriented,[16] even if its own leaders did not immediately recognize this.[17]

What subsequently became known as the Yugoslav Revolution or the National Liberation Movement (or Struggle) (NOP/NOB) of 1941–1945 was therefore marked by a delicate relationship between the leadership of the "vanguard party" and popular, mass mobilization. Like the October Revolution in Russia, the Yugoslav Revolution took on a socialist-communist character within the context of a wider conflict and in a country far from the level of capitalist development that Marx and his followers believed would precipitate a working class revolution. This meant that the popularity of the Yugoslav communists was tentative; not all partisans were communists, and officially the liberation war effort employed a popular front strategy, bringing together communists, liberals, patriots, and all manner of others to oust the fascist invaders.

With the fascists ejected, the Federal People's Republic of Yugoslavia (FPRJ) was established at the end of the war, which according to the Treaty of Vis (1944) was to be ruled in tandem by the royal government in exile and the victorious "National Front" until the first post-war elections could be held. This poll was held in November 1945 and, though it was boycotted by the opposition parties and held in an environment in which the CPY had already moved quickly to stamp out dissent, it nevertheless appears to have cemented the genuine popularity of the war-time National Front forces, that is, the communists.[18] Despite their overwhelming mandate and already pronounced authoritarian tendencies, the regime that emerged in Yugoslavia post-1945 both practically and ideologically remained invested in a kind of "managed democracy" in which a truncated mass politics always appeared on the dangerous verge of becoming genuinely autonomous. Ironically, then, in the first Yugoslav state the country shifted from a constitutional monarchy to a royal autocracy, where the royalist regime openly professed distaste for and eventually completely eliminated democratic institutions. In the second Yugoslav state, however, for much of its tenure the regime maintained an ideological commitment to radical, participatory democracy while significant elements within the ruling establishment worked to limit and reverse the effects of what would later become known as workers' self-management. The ideological veneer shifted radically, in other words, but the basic authoritarian character of the state remained profoundly elastic and durable.

At its core, workers' self-management was a complex political-economic regime, modelled on the idea of the Russian "soviet" system. Industrial policy was to be set by workers' councils while the political administration of the state would likewise occur through a network of neighbourhood councils (*mjesne zajednice*) and flow upwards towards the republican and state legislatures. In theory, it was a kind of federalist direct democracy writ large. In practice, of course, the whole exercise was deeply coloured by the regime's authoritarian control over the entire state and society. Nevertheless, the ideological and normative commitment to the idea of self-management was significant, especially among ordinary Yugoslavs, and this fact eventually began to create serious, unintended political consequences for the regime.

Federalism without Democracy: Yugoslavia, 1945–1991

With their political supremacy assured after the November 1945 elections, the CPY leadership turned to the task of rebuilding a country utterly devastated by war. In the process, they discovered that their seemingly unassailable political dominance of the new Yugoslav state was considerably more precarious than first thought. After 1948, as a result of geopolitical and local realpolitik as well as a diversity of views within the radically transformed party, the regime's chief architects realized that Yugoslav socialism, if it was to survive, required an ideological renaissance. Darko Suvin argues that the period between 1945 and 1952 was one of "postwar reconstruction and consolidation, [and the] centralist fusion of Party and State".[19] This was not unlike what took place in the rest of eastern Europe. After the break with Stalin in 1948, however, the leadership of the CPY realized that "Yugoslavia 'could not build socialism' in the way she had started building it, that is, on the Soviet model".[20] This meant in practice that the hard-line Stalinist stance the party had taken in the immediate post-war period, in the name of state consolidation, would have to be altered. What was required now was a way both to purge the party of "Stalinist elements" and to win back the popular support that had marked the war years.

The collectivization schemes that the party used to modernize agricultural production in the country after the war, modelled on similar Soviet attempts, led to serious rifts among the bulk of the peasantry and the party,[21] and in 1950 resulted in actual armed conflict in the Cazin region[22] of the Bosnian Krajina.[23] While there was a brief attempt on the part of the CPY in the immediate aftermath of the Tito–Stalin split to out-orthodox the Soviets (by insisting on even more rapid collectivization and industrialization), the strategy was untenable, as Katherine Bokovoy argues, once it became clear that the largest segment of the population, the peasants, were prepared to resist this process violently. The masses had won the war and brought the party to power and now, squeezed on all sides by hostile foreign powers, the CPY could simply not afford to lose their support. Owing to their official ideological commitments, even the most conservative elements within the CPY could not argue against what was clearly a shift in popular opinion of the party's policies. Nor could they deny what had

been the most critical element of their wartime success: the autonomous and participatory structure of liberated areas, such as the so-
called Republic of Užice (Serbia) and the Bihać Republic (BiH). As
Suvin notes, "the revolution was fought by a great majority of the
people as a war for national liberation and justice", and "[while] sparked
and firmly led by a hierarchic network", he continues,

> the struggle was by both design and chance conducted from below
> upwards, for freedom and against the totally corrupt and murderous
> authority of the old class systems – monarchist and fascist. The partisan
> army, the local Liberation Councils, the youth and women's organizations,
> even the rapidly expanding and still largely undercover Communist Party
> were parts and expressions of that plebeian singularity in occupied
> Europe: a people (or group of peoples practicing *fraternité*) freeing itself
> by its own forces, with postwar power not coming on the muzzle of
> foreign tanks.[24]

However fleeting, the experience of popular sovereignty within the
context of the war had radicalized the political expectations of the
masses.[25] Thus, despite themselves being steeped in a deeply authoritarian culture, in order to preserve their tentative grip on power the
CPY authorities had no choice but to shift towards a political model at
least resembling the war-time efforts in Yugoslavia rather than their
preferred Stalinist (or Titoist) orthodoxy. While the conservative, statist elements within the party momentarily accepted this decision, and
as the progressive wing of the CPY seized this opening to push through
what would eventually become the workers' self-management system,
the essential post-war cleavage of the Yugoslav state began to take
shape: how substantive was socialist democracy in the SFRJ actually
going to be?

On the one hand, "the lesson from the [Tito–Stalin split] was to
shun 'the deformation of any Communist Party which identified itself
with the State and with the police apparatus' so as to avoid its adverse
consequences, where 'the working masses had been isolated from government and separated from the execution of power'".[26] "The only way
out", Suvin argues, "was in reviving the people's power of the partisan
days – that is, self-management … [In so doing] the privileges of the
'bureaucratic caste' were in good part revoked. Between 1950 and
[the] end of 1952 professional Party functionaries were reduced from

11,900 to 4,600".[27] Yet Vladimir Unkovski-Korica notes, in a close study of the debates within the CPY amid the search for a new social model, that as early as 1949 a cynical conflation of so-called anarchism – that is, anti-regime sentiment – and the self-management system emerged within the conservative camp.[28] By 1968, the anarchist spectre had taken on an established role in the party's ideological imagination: "anarcho-liberalism". While the term was in one sense little more than communist newspeak, the attempt by the (newly renamed) League of Communists to conflate all democratic critique with a fictitious synonym for both naivety and bourgeois reaction aptly captured the regime's conundrum.

As part of their ideological liberation from the Kremlin, the Yugoslav communists needed a terminology both to critique Stalinist orthodoxy and to protect themselves from Soviet counter-criticism. Such criticism invariably painted the Yugoslavs as Western stooges or undisciplined rogues, a critique that mirrored earlier Soviet attacks on their assorted leftist critics across Europe.[29] By comparison, formulating a critique of Stalinism was easy; the true masterstroke by Tito and his chief ideologue, Edvard Kardelj, was coining a term to capture why the LCY's peculiar and curtailed brand of democracy was genuine "rule of the people", or self-management in other words, and why everything else, everything to its proverbial left, was propaganda (or worse). When one considers the broader question of democracy in the former Yugoslavia, the term's conceptual ambiguity is part of its informative potential. The argument by Kardelj and his cohort that anarchism and liberalism could be conflated points to the LCY's profound discomfort with genuine popular self-management. The sequestering of as massive an ideological terrain as suggested by the party's adoption of the term "anarcho-liberalism" tarred even the most sympathetic critics of the regime with the same traitorous brush. The practical result of this was a disastrous purging of the party's most democratically inclined cadres, a policy that led to the country's dissolution two decades later.

But, theoretically, the fact that such a policy even existed reaffirms one of the central claims of this book: even in periods when there was an official commitment to democracy, the actually existing state and its representatives in the Yugoslav lands operated primarily to deny political agency to the citizenry. In other words, even when democracy was invoked, in its assorted ideological incarnations, its most crucial element – popular participation – was marginalized and neglected. How this was accomplished (and maintained) in a period in which democratic self-management was ostensibly the primary ideological tenet of the state is key to understanding the centrality of this phenomenon in the broader social development of contemporary Balkan politics.

As Srđan Cvetković notes, in suppressing student protests in 1968 and the associated movements which first challenged the LCY's grip on power, the conservative wing of the party transformed "anarcho-liberalism" into its preferred term for the domestic democratic opposition.[30] From the outset then, the substantive democratizing of Yugoslav society was represented by the conservative political establishment as an attempt by shadowy bourgeois elements to initiate the "counter-revolution" that would "undermine, by weakening the state, the leading role of the socialist forces and thus prepare the way for anti-socialist forces".[31] In reality, the eventual counter-revolution would be led not by the "anarcho-liberals" but precisely by the conservative and reactionary factions within the LCY, whose desire to preserve their privileged positions within the state led them to dissolve the society as a whole.

Though he was in some respects the face of the progressive wing of the party, Kardelj played no small part in creating this anti-democratic climate. In the 1958 LCY programme, largely written by Kardelj and Veljko Vlahović, the authors expound not only on the intricacies of the self-management system as well as the process whereby the state would progressively "wither away" but also the acute dangers faced by this new socialist experiment in the interim. "The socialist state … is and must be a state of a special type, a state which is withering away", the programme declared.[32] "With the development of the socialist democratic system", the authors went on to explain, "the role of state administration begins to diminish in the direct management of the economy, in cultural and educational activities, health service, social security, and so on. The management of these activities is more and more transferred to various social self-managing bodies, independent or interlinked in respective democratic organizations". The "socialist democratic system" was the emerging self-management model that was meant to evolve progressively from a strictly economic programme to a general socio-political regime.[33] While the state would continue to "perform a number of functions ... in the performance of these functions [the organs of state] appear less and less as organs of political authority and more and more as social organs of the various working collectives in the enterprises and of territorial communities[34] of working people as producers and consumers".[35] Certain organs of the state would take longer to wither away (e.g. "security, justice, national defence") but the self-management model was clearly the beginning of the end of the monopoly of violence.

Yet the spectre of counter-revolution remained. Though now five years after the death of Stalin, and with Yugoslavia firmly on the receiving end of US financial aid[36] (as the face of a moderate communist regime with which the West could do business), counter-revolution was an internal rather than external threat. In moving forward, the authors of the party's programme warned, the LCY

> will in the further construction and development of the social system untiringly combat two tendencies in the social life of Yugoslavia, both equally dangerous and harmful in present times: first, the tendency of anarchist underestimation of the role of the state, pseudo-liberal attacks on its socialist character and any undermining of its political strength in the struggle against the bourgeois counter-revolution and social demoralization; second, the tendency of transforming the state into an all-embracing social force, a force above society which would in fact liquidate the direct social influence of the working masses on the policies of the state leadership – that is, the tendency of state idolatry.[37]

Obviously, Kardelj and his camp were attempting to walk a fine line in advancing their vision of a self-managed socialism between countering accusations of their acting as an anti-state element and, in turn, warning against the authoritarian tendencies of their conservative critics. In this respect, it is perhaps unfair to chastise Kardelj for authoring what was certainly a pan-party policy document, one meant to fuse the views of both camps into a coherent manifesto. Yet the ideas fleshed out in the 1958 programme were ones largely repeated throughout Kardelj's individual works. Moreover, in 1962, Kardelj himself nearly fell from power completely, as a conservative reaction in the LCY blamed a recession at the beginning of the decade on "excessive liberalization" within both the leadership and the state as a whole.[38] In expounding on the evils of "anarcho-liberalism", Kardelj had given his enemies the ideological weapon with which to bury him and the broader project of genuine democratic reform in Yugoslavia.

Nor was Kardelj the first or only prominent (former) reformer to suffer a fall from grace. A decade earlier, after rising to the post of president of the Federal Assembly in 1953, Milovan Đilas barely held the position for four months before he was removed. He would thereafter spend the next thirteen years or so in and out of prison. Đilas had committed the cardinal sin of alerting the reading public in Yugoslavia to the emergence of a "new class" of political oligarchs who used their positions within the state apparatus primarily to enrich themselves and their associates and who were quickly becoming a dominant faction within the ruling establishment.[39] Like Kardelj, Đilas appears to have been a "true believer" in the Yugoslav experiment and had expected the turn towards self-management to substantively deepen the democratic character of the socialist project in the country. Yet unlike the "court's ideologue", as Dennison Rusinow labels Kardelj, Đilas drew his conclusions about the Yugoslav self-management project's unravelling early and forcefully and, as a result, paid a tremendous personal toll for it. Unlike Đilas, Kardelj recovered from his brush with Tito's wrath, however, and in his last major work devoted considerable attention to revealing the supposedly secret reactionary tendencies of what he labelled the "ultra-leftist" current among the reformist intelligentsia.

Clearly directing himself at the participants of the academic Praxis group and their fellow travellers,[40] Kardelj sought to explain why the LCY had "already from 1941 ... objectively taken the most revolutionary positions" possible on all the relevant socio-political questions in Yugoslavia.[41] In other words, it was an argument that democratization in Yugoslavia was unnecessary; the country was already a socialist democracy whereas liberal democracy would strip the working class of its vanguardist primacy. Curiously, while Kardelj seemed to reserve tremendous animus towards these supposed traitorous anarchists – that is, democratic reformers – he paid little attention to the deeply entrenched and corrosive influence of Yugoslavia's conservative political establishment, the party's privileged *nomenklatura*, or what Đilas referred to as the new class. That reality was in equal parts epiphany and futility. Intellectually, Kardelj could not ignore that by the late 1970s the LCY was on an accelerating drift towards illegitimacy.

Unwilling to allow for substantive democratization, yet likewise unable to curb the party's growing irrelevance, the old guard was at an impasse. In a sense, the sheer vitriol of Kardelj's anti-reformist invectives only further exposed the utter bankruptcy of the regime's ideological and political programme. The regime was clearly dissolving even as the LCY purged what remained of its reformist elements. In the meantime, the authoritarian germ remained, quietly preparing itself for another round of elastic mutation.

New Class, Old Forms

By the end of the 1960s, the relative opening of the political climate in Yugoslavia post-1948 culminated in the 1968 student mobilizations. The official response to these protests made clear the boundaries of what was permissible political action in nominally self-managed Yugoslavia. In the intervening years, the likes of Đilas and Kardelj experienced individual consequences for their perceived liberal excesses, as did conservatives, like the head of the state security agency, Aleksandar Ranković, for daring to impinge on Tito's ultimate authority.[42] But the student protests in 1968 altered the political dynamic altogether. However half-hearted, the self-management project produced a generation of young people who, quite separately from the ruling establishment, were developing their own radical interpretations of what socialist democracy meant and, most importantly, who were now beginning to organize. To understand the origins of this new radical democratic awakening, it is first necessary to explain what it was about "actually existing" self-management that this generation of students and intellectuals found so disturbing.

The original impetus behind the self-management idea came from the lack of "[objective conditions] ... for the emergence of any kind of centralized administrative and government system and even less for centralized management of labour, economy, social and other fields", during the war and its immediate aftermath.[43] "What was needed then", Kardelj wrote in retrospect, "was the maximum degree of initiative, self-organization and independent assumption of responsibility on the part of all sections[44] of the national liberation movement, of everyone in every area and settlement on liberated territory".[45] In truth, the "lack of objective conditions" had not prevented the communists from attempting to impose a rigid Bolshevik-style regime during the first years of their rule. But after the Tito—Stalin split, a general revision of the entire social order was necessary, including historical revision of the sort previously noted, which Kardelj spent most of his post-war life authoring.

The pillars of the self-management system were put in place between 1948 and 1950 and were fully formalized under the 1953 constitution. The idea was that the socialist democratization of the factory would be replicated at the political level, through a delegate system that harkened back to the old Bolshevik slogan of "all power to the soviets". But Curtis notes that the relative democratic opening entailed by the 1953 constitutional changes was from the outset an "uneven, changeable phenomenon in Yugoslavia. A meeting of party leaders at the north Adriatic island of Brioni [sic] that year resolved to strengthen party discipline, amid growing concern that apathy had infected the rank and file ... Over the next several years, the party tightened democratic centralism; established basic party organizations in factories, universities, and other institutions; purged its rolls of inactive members; and took other measures to enhance discipline."[46] Yet in practice, self-management, on both the factory floor and at the political level, was more slogan than reality. As one observer noted at the time, as a result "non-participation" was the predominant attitude taken by most workers to this truncated self-management regime.[47] The distinctly "managerial" character of the system lent "substance to the charge that 'Statism' [reduced] worker influence".[48] Moreover, "the fact that when they [did] get involved ... [workers were] frequently unsuccessful in getting their interests satisfied [posed] ominous overtones for the system".[49]

The lack of substantive self-management was further exacerbated by the emergence of a rudimentary market-oriented socialism in Yugoslavia, in which the political managers took on the role of "capitalists" but without any of the substantive democratic institutions or norms to counter the resulting drift towards outright oligarchy. Kardelj and Kidrić had envisioned that in the transition away from centralized planning, the role of the LCY would be reduced to planning only the proportions of the economy, leaving enterprises to operate based on these proportions and "the law of supply and demand". Thus, as Kardelj envisioned in 1954, enterprises would, "through free competition with other enterprises on the market", become interested in achieving "the best results as regards quality and quantity of goods, lower costs of production and good marketing". Thus, the market, another form of decentralization, would replace state intervention in the economy ... By the 1960s, the Yugoslavs would abolish central planning, introduce commercial banking to allow for enterprise-driven investment, and open their economy to the world market.[50]

Even a cursory analysis of the realities of "market socialism" demonstrates, however, not the existence of a "free association of producers" but rather parasitic, oligarchic corruption, unleashed especially after the 1974 constitutional reforms. Three examples are instructive here. In 1978, Slobodan Milošević's first major political appointment was as the head of one of the new commercial banks, Beobanka, among the largest financial institutions in Yugoslavia. By the time he was in the process of orchestrating the dismantling of the Yugoslav federation in 1990, the then president of Serbia used his contacts at the Belgrade bank to move approximately US$1.5 billion to offshore accounts in the Republic of Cyprus.[51] Radovan Karadžić, Milošević's man in BiH, was, by contrast, a petty criminal. He and his close associate Momćilo Krajišnik, then an economist working for the Sarajevo energy giant, Energoinvest, were in and out of prison throughout 1984 and 1985 for real estate fraud and embezzlement.[52] For his part, Fikret Abdić, a war-time Bosniak collaborator with the Serb nationalist camp, made his fortune as the head of another industrial giant, Agrokomerc. In 1987 it was revealed that the management of Agrokomerc, with Abdić a key player, had been involved in an elaborate Ponzi scheme, borrowing in excess of a billion Yugoslav dinars from local banks, using the money for bribes and posh residences and gratuitously inflating the real performance of the firm. The scale of the corruption is difficult to overstate: "The profit of the entire Bosnian economy for two and a half years was roughly equal to the money Agrokomerc owed when the scandal was discovered."[53] While it has since been speculated, in Bosniak nationalist circles in particular, that the "Agrokomerc Affair" was an early attempt to weaken the position of prominent Bosniak

leaders by Serb nationalist sympathisers in the Yugoslav political establishment (e.g. Hamdija Pozderac, then vice-president of the SFRJ, who
lost his post in the process), Fikret Abdić became a willing accomplice
of the Karadžić regime once the fighting actually began. From his for-
tress in Velika Kladuša, with the aid of the Agrokomerc factories, Abdić
created a private fiefdom in opposition to the central authorities in
Sarajevo: the "Autonomous Province of Western Bosnia" (later referred
to as the Republic of Western Bosnia). Western Bosnia was no more
than a one-man criminal enterprise, though, and as a result Abdić was
later sentenced to twenty years in a Croatian prison for war crimes.

Yet Abdić's patrimonial grip on the Kladuša area was and remained
so strong that in 2016 he managed to return to politics and win the
post of mayor in the municipality. The result caused uproar across the
region but, in truth, Abdić's reappearance was merely the most recent
episode in a long string of such incidents. From Biljana Plavšić to
Dario Kordić, convicted war criminals have seamlessly reintegrated
into the nominally democratic regimes of the former Yugoslavia precisely because there has been so little substantive change in both the
tenor and make-up of the ruling elite, not only since the 1990s but
since the 1980s. In short, economic criminality in the 1980s, war
crimes in the 1990s, and contemporary corruption in the Western
Balkans should be understood as points along the same continuum.
The most recent instances were and remain only the most extreme
versions of processes begun in the 1980s and are in many cases perpe-
trated by exactly the same people. Earlier, when some semblance of a
principled democratic opposition still existed, these practices could
have been challenged, perhaps even reversed. But by the 1980s the
entire structure of the Yugoslav state was beset by the competing,
autarchic, and corrupt interests of the various republican cliques:
"More devastating for the specific ideology of *Yugoslav* socialism was
the fact that the economic crises of the 1980s provided fuel for
increased regionalism (often ethnically constituted) and a further
weakening of the federal centre as a decision-making force ... By 1986
federal policy-making had essentially ceased".[54]

But a decade earlier, Sharon Zukin observed the crucial role that
institutional fragmentation played in Yugoslavia's elite-dominated
regime. By fragmenting political and economic authority not only

across six republics but also across individual enterprises, the ruling establishment was able to keep socio-economic struggles local, not unlike the earlier Ottoman system designed to prevent peasant insurrections. Yet, as citizens were encouraged to identify not as Yugoslavs but as members of individual nations, the only category capable of consistently mobilizing mass movements proved to be nationalism. Originally, discouraging "Yugoslavism" was meant to reflect the consociational aspects of the new Yugoslav state as a free union among nations and working peoples. Unlike the royalist regime, post-war Yugoslavism would not become a byword for Serb hegemony, the communists insisted, and, in so far as it existed at all, Yugoslavism would be a synonym for federalism and socialism.[55] Therefore, the attempt to stifle the "natural" national and ethnic feelings of the various peoples of Yugoslavia, the communist logic went, was itself a combination of Stalinism and Serbian nationalism. Yet because the nation was preserved as an active category while at the same time the emergence of substantive democratic models of governance was prevented, workers' "grievances which should cut across national-ethnic and enterprise lines" remained suppressed until they were ultimately hijacked and reimagined as ethno-national hatreds by those seeking to preserve the oligarchic character of the regime.[56]

Moreover, as both Ellen Comisso and Ramnath Narayanswamy note, precisely because the Yugoslav regime insisted on a fiction of self-management, actual independent labour unions were absent in the SFRJ, even as the society was becoming increasingly exposed to market pressures. As Narayanswamy argued at the time, "a system of self-management of enterprises is certainly desirable [but] its consequences can often be perverse in the absence of an established democratic mechanism of coordinating economic activity, which is not the case in Yugoslavia, which is not only dominated by a one-party system, but like its centralized neighbours, is also a country where unions cannot exist independently of the power apparatus".[57] Instead, what prevailed was a system of political clientelism and dependence in the context of a peculiar brand of socialist-themed patrimonialism. Though strikes became a near-constant feature of life in Yugoslavia in the late 1980s, these were almost always isolated "wildcat" manifestations, with leaders and activists lacking the ability and experience to organize "general" actions. Everywhere there was talk of democracy yet nowhere was it applied.

The perverse consequences of this contradictory regime came to the surface especially after the 1974 constitutional reforms, which decentralized the country's administration among six republics and two autonomous provinces, envisioned by Tito and Kardelj as a substitute for substantive democratization. Instead, as Yugoslavia entered a prolonged period of economic crisis in the late 1980s, "high unemployment, over-investment, regional autarky, record inflation, poor export performance, dwindling foreign currency reserves and mounting indebtedness" combined to form the basic ingredients for a volatile mixture.[58] Worst of all, Yugoslavia was now "a country with not only wide inequalities in income, productivity and culture between north and south, but also with considerable divisions among the different nationalities. Serious conflicts of interest are bound to exist and if these are not allowed political expression, it is difficult to see how they can be meaningfully resolved".[59] After 1974, this "conflict of interests" would become one not only between managers and workers, elites and masses, but also one among the various and increasingly autarchic republican cliques, who then used these popular grievances for personal ends.

It is important to note that while the question of nationalism does obviously appear in analyses of Yugoslav politics and economics in the post-World War II period, it is almost in an inverse relationship to how familiar the authors were with the intricacies of the state's administration. Narayanswamy's short but lucid description of the country's economic woes is striking precisely for the fact that it introduces nationalism as a final, almost offhand "spark" in an already glowing tinderbox. The majority of his analysis is concerned with officials "worried about the prospect of [keeping] social peace if living standards ... continue to slide".[60] What Narayanswamy identified was not that nationalism itself would undo the Yugoslav federation but that nationalism would be used to subvert growing popular resentment against entrenched and corrupt political elites. To explain how this became a viable strategy on the part of the elite, a closer look at the events leading up to the 1974 constitutional changes and the political climate thereafter is necessary.

Protests and Purges

The 1974 constitutional reforms were the direct result of popular democratic agitation in Yugoslavia, both during the 1968 student protests and the so-called 1971 Croatian Spring. Yet while the country's administrative divisions were significantly altered and decentralized, the 1974 constitution failed to substantively democratize the Yugoslav state. Thereafter, the spectre of popular revolt became an inescapable political reality in the polity, a fact through which one can read the country's unravelling two decades later. In most authoritarian contexts, popular revolt is always a principal danger for the ruling regime, but rarely does this possibility actually take on an established ideological "shape". That is, protests are usually the work of almost generic terrorists, reactionaries, and counter-revolutionaries in such regimes. But the danger of the Yugoslav left, that is, the "anarcho-liberals", was precisely that they "took literally" the 1958 *Programme of the League of Communists of Yugoslavia*.[61] In other words, groups like the Praxis collective "demanded the total de-professionalization of politics, the spreading of self-management to all levels and spheres of society, the introduction of workers' councils at the regional, republican and federal levels, and even the introduction of participatory democracy through the abolition of the party itself".[62] The "anarcho-liberals" were dangerous precisely because they were ideologically committed communists and thereby exposed the sordid reality of LCY, that is, one-party rule in Yugoslavia.

One of the most thorough studies of the actual activities and positions of this Yugoslav "New Left", aside from the contents of the Praxis publications, is Fredy Perlman's account of the 1968 student strikes. Perlman's study is especially important because, unlike most critics of the regime, he actually was an anarchist – a leading figure in the movement in the US until his death in 1985. In the mid-sixties, Perlman obtained an MA and a PhD at the University of Belgrade and, upon returning briefly in 1969, set about composing the text of *Birth of a Revolutionary Movement in Yugoslavia*, the dissemination of which was, unsurprisingly, prevented by the local authorities. Perlman focused his analysis on the tensions between official LCY ideology and the actual nature of their rule: "In June 1968, the gap between theory and practice, between official proclamations and social relations, was exposed through practice, through social activity: students began to organize themselves in demonstrations and general assemblies, and the regime which proclaims self-management reacted to this rare example of popular self-organization by putting an end to it through police and press repression".[63] The primary target of the protests, Perlman argued, was the technocrats, Đilas's new class, who through their control of individual enterprises and political offices had established themselves as a new class of exploiters of the students and workers in the ostensibly post-revolutionary Yugoslav state. Subverting LCY orthodoxy, Perlman argued:

> According to official histories, Yugoslavia eliminated exploitation in 1945, when the Yugoslav League of Communists won state power. Yet workers whose surplus labor supports a state or commercial bureaucracy, whose unpaid labor turns against them as a force which does not seem to result from their own activity but from some higher power – such workers perform forced labor: they are exploited. According to official histories, Yugoslavia eliminated the bureaucracy as a social group over the working class in 1952, when the system of workers' self-management was introduced. But workers who alienate their living activity in exchange for the means of life do not control themselves; they are controlled by those to whom they alienate their labor and its products, even if these people eliminated themselves in legal documents and proclamations.[64]

In other words, the contradictions of the incomplete social revolution in Yugoslavia expressed themselves in 1968 in the form of a politically frustrated insurrection of youth and workers. As a nominally revolutionary communist regime, the LCY's ideological commitment to liquidating capitalist class relations in a non-capitalist society, or at least one lacking developed liberal democratic political institutions, meant that socialist Yugoslavia (re)produced merely differently constituted but nevertheless exploitative and alienating class relations. Students and workers in 1960s Yugoslavia were emboldened by claims of their ability to wield radical democratic political and economic power yet were simultaneously confronted by the existence of a deeply segmented and unequal society, one divided between the political class and virtually all the rest. In short, LCY apparatchiks at the local, republican, and federal level appeared to be a class unto themselves.

Moreover, reasonably well-versed in the basic elements of Marxist political analysis, many Yugoslav students could not but identify the existence of this class and the ensuing hypocrisy of such a regime as merely a different kind of exploitation.

With a robust legal-political structure already in place, democratically inclined youth and workers in Yugoslavia needed only to insist on the substantive implementation of the LCY programme to find a model for their movement and, accordingly, to find themselves at odds with the authorities. The 1968 protests were arguably the biggest crisis the regime in Yugoslavia had faced since the Tito–Stalin split and, in retrospect, it was perhaps the most crucial episode in the state's slow unravelling. This is not to say that the SFRJ's demise was inevitable, but it is to privilege the struggle for substantive democratization as the central conflict leading to the federation's eventual implosion. Of course, it is tempting to dismiss the relatively localized student protests at universities in Belgrade, Zagreb, Ljubljana, and Sarajevo as merely a quaint local manifestation of a global youth "awakening" in the famed year of 1968, and one which produced few real political consequences. Yet this is to ignore the lasting political changes and implications (as the authorities feared) that the '68 protests inspired in Yugoslavia and that culminated in the wholesale constitutional rearrangement of the state in 1974. But these truncated changes, rather than democratizing the regime, allowed for a final authoritarian mutation that would result in the extinction of the self-managed society as a whole.

When the protests drew to a close after several raucous weeks, the regime systematically began to crack down on what they identified as the sources of the students' inspiration. While dozens of trials of students and faculty followed the 1968 protests, the "anarcho-liberal" threat soon struck again. In 1971, concern among a segment of Croatia's intelligentsia about the republic's seemingly marginalized standing within the federation bubbled over into what has subsequently become known as the "Croatian Spring" but what was at the time primarily referred to as MASPOK (*masovni pokret* or mass movement). The name here is significant because it points, fundamentally, to a politics of process rather than of identity, with which it has subsequently become associated. In the Serb and Croat nationalist mythologies, the events of 1971–1972 are proof positive of either the inherently fascistic character of the Croatian people or their unbridled desire for sovereign statehood in the face of Serb or communist authoritarianism. Yet the mass protests, as well as the flurry of intellectual output at the time, "mixed anticentralist, reformist, democratic socialist, liberal and libertarian elements", a combination from which it is difficult to extract any one coherent priority.[65] But the response of the Yugoslav authorities demonstrates precisely what they feared MASPOK could become if left unchecked. In this respect, it is clear that the threat from MASPOK did not come from the right, that is, its nationalist dimensions, but rather from the left, its popular democratic aspects.[66]

While the idea of mass politics of any sort clearly terrified the Yugoslav regime, it was the democratic reformists in Croatia who suffered the brunt of the wrath of the conservative establishment. In fact, not only were the Croatian reformers purged but so was virtually the entirety of the left wing of the LCY. By the end of 1972, Savka Dabčević-Kučar, Miko Tripalo, and Latinka Perović were only some of the more prominent Croatian and Serbian liberals who found themselves expelled from the League after the events of 1968 and 1971.[67] The purges would extend throughout the universities as well. Most of the Praxis group were removed from public life through some combination of unemployment, imprisonment, or exile, and by 1974 the famed journal *Praxis* itself printed its final issue.

With the liberal opposition essentially extinguished, the old guard of the LCY, namely Tito and Kardelj, sought to roll out a hollow version of the original left critique of the regime. The 1974 constitution radically decentralized the state institutionally, but with few political reforms beyond this. The result was disastrous, creating precisely the kind of parochial and centrifugal incentives that the document had sought to undercut. Instead of taking up the cause of democratic self-management, the constitution effectively transformed the individual republics into autarchies in which the most logical means to assert power for republican elites became the cynical stoking of nationalist sentiments. Moreover, by purging the genuinely reform oriented cadres, "second or third rate leaders put in place by Tito himself were left to steer the country through the extraordinarily difficult period after his departure ... Although their dearth of political capital and skill was not immediately apparent as a result of the complicated mechanisms of collective leadership, which ensured their constant rotation and lack of accountability, it was only a matter of time before more charismatic and effective leaders came to the fore".[68]

Collective Failure

This was the vacuum of leadership and vision into which Slobodan Milošević stepped. As noted earlier, my intention here is not to provide a comprehensive retelling of a history which has been studiously and clinically laid out elsewhere. Instead, the point has been to stress the complex but important democratic struggles that preceded Yugoslavia's dissolution. These initiatives have been largely neglected as relevant aspects of what took place in Yugoslavia in the late 1980s and 1990s. And this neglect occurred even though the preferred Western narrative (i.e. the re-emergence of ancient ethnic hatreds as drivers of conflict) left little actual room for policymaking and conflict resolution. After all, if the fundamental problem in Yugoslavia was sectarian, as the international consensus held, the only possible international response was partition: separating and keeping apart the warring Balkan tribes and, when needed, allowing the messy (but necessary) process of ethnic cleansing to take its course. Then, when there were clean territorial segments to deal with, the international community could assist in imposing a new order. The approach was as cynical as it was catastrophically misinformed.

In BiH, where the approach was pioneered before being replicated across the region (and then later proposed in states like Ukraine, Iraq, and Syria), each of the peace plans laid out by the European and American negotiators "proposed [the] partition of Bosnia into ethnic-national cantons [which] meant that the first peace proposal for Bosnia embodied, prior to the outbreak of open and widespread conflict … the very nexus between identity and territory upon which the major protagonists in the later conflict relied".[69] Such proposals were only ever "charter[s] for ethnic cleansing", Josip Glaurdić later noted, adding that such plans were only inducements to "*create* new ethnic realities on the ground", meaning new Bantustans where once there had been mixed and pluralistic communities.[70] "Federalist" solutions that took as their basis historical, regional, or ecological boundaries, rather than exclusively ethno-nationalist ones, were rejected out of hand.[71] Ignored, above all, were the perspectives and proposals of non-extremist and non-elite elements, that is, the majority of the Yugoslav public. To this point, a standard policy wonk rebuttal would hold that international negotiators and policymakers are only able to work with the actors they actually encounter, not the ones they would prefer. And in Yugoslavia, by the time the international community became involved, the moment of hopeful, progressive, and democratically inclined mobilization was long over. This, again, is a convenient rather than accurate response.

As Glaurdić notes, Western involvement in Yugoslavia did not begin in 1991 or 1992, that is, at the onset of armed conflict. Western diplomats had been deeply involved in Yugoslavia's constitutional and political crisis since its earliest days. Slobodan Milošević rose to power in 1987 and methodically set about dismantling the existing Yugoslav regime. Warren Zimmerman, then US ambassador to Yugoslavia, described in detail every episode of Milošević's destructive pursuit of absolute power, reports which were largely ignored by both the outgoing Bush administration and its successor.[72] This policy of ignorance would constitute, in the words of Richard Holbrooke, the chief negotiator of the Dayton Peace Accords, "the greatest collective security failure of the West since the 1930s".[73] In the preferred American narrative since the end of war, however, US reluctance to intervene in the Yugoslav crisis stemmed from the strong European claim to leadership in its "backyard", and the aforementioned complex and intractable nature of the conflict. Holbrooke lays out these claims explicitly in his memoir, adding for good measure that after the first Gulf War and the intricate negotiations that accompanied the dissolution of the Soviet Union, Washington's foreign policy apparatus was exhausted.[74] Moreover, Europe's insistence on taking the lead in Yugoslavia only strengthened the urge inside both administrations to wash their hands of the whole fiasco.

Although indeed convenient, this narrative is at odds with the facts, and even the facts that were available to Western policymakers at the time. As noted, to ascribe the Yugoslav crisis to the period between 1990 and 1992, as Holbrooke largely does, is to ignore the events between 1987 and 1990. Specifically, such accounts ignore Slobodan

Milošević's so-called anti-bureaucratic revolution, the process by which the emerging strongman toppled LCY leaders in Serbia, Kosovo, Vojvodina, and Montenegro between 1987 and 1989, and replaced them, in turn, with his own handpicked loyalists. Unlike the majority of Western policymakers, Milošević understood that Serbs, and Yugoslavs more broadly, yearned for a democratic revolution. But because a real revolution would inevitably consume the grey apparatchik class from which he emerged – as it was already doing in much of eastern Europe – Milošević concluded that to survive and thrive in such an environment of growing anti-regime sentiment, a virtual revolution would be necessary. And like the original Balkan state-founders in the nineteenth century, he pinned his ideological transformation on the siren song of sectarianism and nationalism.

In less than two years, Milošević mutated from a stilted, Marxist lieutenant of Serbia's President Ivan Stambolić, to a raging, nationalist demagogue who exploited Serb–Albanian tensions in the country's poorest corner, Kosovo, to propel himself to power. After his infamous 1987 trip to Kosovo, in which a small team of his operatives and local Serb nationalists engineered an elaborate ruse to create the impression that the predominantly ethnic Albanian police were brutalizing the local Serb population, Milošević returned to Belgrade as a champion of the downtrodden Serb nation, driven from power in its holy land, and further fragmented across the six Yugoslav republics. "Within weeks", Glaurdić notes, "virtually all the media outlets (down to individual journalists) and the organizations of the political and economic system (down to low-level party functionaries or enterprise managers) were cleansed of the opponents of Milošević's line … Milošević demanded unquestionable loyalty, and by the end of 1987 he had it in Serbia proper".[75]

Over the next several months, Milošević would repeat this performance in the provinces and republics, so that by 1989 he held directly four of the five votes needed to seize control of the eight-member state presidency and, with them, Yugoslavia as a whole. In other words, the anti-bureaucratic revolution was no more than a slow-motion coup by means of which Milošević hoped to reverse the SFRJ's (perceived) post-1974 liberalization, and reassert authoritarian centralism through his leadership under the guise of thinly veiled Serb nationalism. And as the reality of his power grab dawned progressively on the rest of the country, especially the various republican elites in Yugoslavia's west, and as repeated attempts at domestic mediation fizzled, so fragmentation became increasingly inevitable. When his plan for a single, centralized Yugoslav state failed in 1990, Milošević adroitly reimagined his programme as the creation of a Greater Serbia – another nineteenth-century idea, according to which the rump Yugoslav National Army (JNA) and various militant proxies would be used by Belgrade to forcibly carve out of Croatia and BiH, in particular, "Serb lands" to be joined to Serbia proper. Ideologically, Milošević was resetting the clock by a century but, politically, conditions would remain static; thousands would be exterminated in the shift from "brotherhood and unity" to "only unity saves the Serbs", but the ruling elite would remain virtually unchanged.

While it is understandable that the Soviet dissolution (and the nuclear sword that hung over its head) consumed most of America's foreign policy energy and likewise the energies of the Europeans, it is unclear what alternative these leaders imagined for Yugoslavia. That is, without American and European mediation in Yugoslavia, what outcome did they expect from Milošević's attempt to transform the South Slavic federation into a Greater Serbia? In the most reactionary segments of the Western foreign policy establishment, men like Henry Kissinger and his associates in the Bush and Clinton administrations actively egged on or, at the very least, turned a blind eye to Milošević's war machine.[76] The idea apparently was that efficient genocide was preferable to protracted war. In this effort, they had compatriots in the John Major government in Westminster and the François Mitterrand cabinet in Paris.[77] Still others, like UN Secretary General Boutros Boutros-Ghali, simply denied that anything all that bad was taking place, even in BiH where the brutal intentions of the Serb nationalist campaign of expulsion and extermination were telegraphed ahead of time.[78] Taken as a whole, the Western reaction to Yugoslavia's implosion might be summed up as wilful, cynical ignorance. Because American and European policymakers did not want to deal with the crisis, they simply chose to avoid it.

Unsurprisingly, when the Western hand was finally forced at the end of 1995, with the NATO-led intervention in BiH, this too was ultimately a half-measure. Nearly five years of abandoned peace agreements, each of which had insisted on partition, that is, acquiescence to the ultra-nationalist cause as the "quickest" route to peace, culminated in NATO's Operation Deliberate Force. By the time the operation ended, less than thirty Serb military personnel had been killed in the month-long bombing campaign. This was in stark contrast to the approximately one hundred thousand individuals who had been killed in the fighting since April 1992, and it was another painful reminder of just how little Western force was necessary to bring the Bosnian and broader Yugoslav crisis to a close. Had leaders in the US and Europe exhibited even the smallest degree of proactive will to engage earlier, the whole bloody mess might have been avoided entirely. But because Western leaders refused to manage the Yugoslav crisis constructively throughout, each aspect of their involvement was short-sighted, short-lived, and geared towards fending off rather than resolving the issue.

In such a policy environment, it is not surprising that the broader experience of constitutional and democratic agitation in Yugoslavia between 1945 and 1992 evaporated. The ideals of the liberal wing of the LCY disappeared, as did the hundreds of thousands of citizens in Belgrade and Sarajevo who on the eve of war pleaded desperately with local leaders and the international community to intervene and negotiate to avert war. Time and again, events on the ground and the agency of ordinary citizens presented the international community with platforms for engagement. As late as 1992, by which time Belgrade-backed militias and the JNA had already initiated fire fights in Slovenia and Croatia, the citizens of Sarajevo began weeks of anti-war mobilizations, drawing crowds of fifty thousand or so that appealed for peace and the preservation of "brotherhood and unity" in BiH and Yugoslavia as a whole.[79] The protests, informally referred to as the "month of Valter", channelled the memory of Vladimir "Valter" Perić, a partisan guerrilla killed during the liberation of Sarajevo, as a kind of civic meme, and were a desperate interjection of radical political potential on the part of ordinary citizens into the cataclysmic confrontations of the ruling elites.

In other words, the protests were true "fugitive moments" as described by Wolin. According to Wolin, such moments "activate the demos and destroy boundaries that bar access to political experience.

Individuals from excluded social strata take on responsibilities, deliberate about goals and choices, and share in decisions that have broad consequences".[80] But these episodes are dangerous to elites because such genuine democratic experiments, although usually short-lived, are "born in transgressive acts, for the demos could not participate in power without shattering the class, status, and value systems by which it was excluded".[81]

In Sarajevo in 1992, this meant a popular turn against the entire edifice of nationalist rule, which though it had been established through multiparty elections in November 1990 clearly did not represent either the interests or the will of the majority of Bosnians. Accordingly, on 4 April 1992 a small, spontaneous protest by forty-odd students "demanding the resignation of all political parties" grew overnight to a protest of a hundred thousand people.[82] The crowds were encouraged by the production crew, staff, and reporters of Radio Televizija Sarajevo (RTS), who much to the irritation of the entire political establishment began airing a live, uninterrupted feed of the gatherings. At the centre of the decision to air this coverage was the production director of RTS, Nenad Pejić. Pejić decided that the moment for "objective journalism" had long passed; the only opportunity to avert bloodshed now rested with the people of BiH rising up against their political leaders.

"For [BiH's] political parties", Pejić writes in retrospect, "this was the greatest threat ever posed to them. An organic movement was spontaneously demanding their wholesale resignation".[83] Aggressive and threatening phone calls from both the leader of the Serb nationalists, Radovan Karadžić, and the Bosnian president, Alija Izetbegović, followed, with both accusing Pejić of attempting to orchestrate a coup d'état. Instead of terminating the broadcast as demanded, Pejić managed to have both men agree to a debate in the RTS studios, along with the presence of a European mediator, the (interim) leader of the likewise nationalist Croatian Democratic Union (HDZ), Miljenko Brkić, and General Milutin Kukanjac of the JNA. The subsequent negotiations were not broadcast; instead, another Yugoslav-era partisan film was aired. "Never in my life have I witnessed negotiations that were so important", Pejić recalls, "and were being conducted by individuals that were so irresponsible. Their bigotry, verbal traps, accusations, threats, and half-truths were appalling. They immediately dived into accusing and attacking each other while hundreds of thousands of citizens demanded peace on the streets of Sarajevo".[84] Pejić's desperation only increased as the evening progressed: "At one point [Karadžić] wanted to leave the studio … I held him by his suit as he stood up from the chair. Shortly afterward, [Izetbegović] … wanted to leave as well, so I grabbed him too. I held onto their suit jackets and implored them not to leave. By this point, their security details were on full alert and, like faithful dogs, they were ready to defend their masters. But both … sat down and my sweaty palms released their suit jackets, leaving a little wrinkle on each".[85]

This Party of Democratic Action (SDA) and Serb Democratic Party (SDS) leaders' debate took place while only a few blocks away crowds stormed and occupied the legislature and the first shots began to ring out through the city. In an RTS evening news broadcast of 4 April 1992, the sound of ambulance sirens mixes with the chanting of protesters. In an impromptu scene, the actor and writer Josip Pejaković is seen microphone in hand amid a large crowd, imploring viewers at home to come into the streets. "We have been left to ourselves," he declares, "… we must show them that we can come to an agreement … we must come to an agreement, as we always have. Come to the government buildings, do not be afraid. You miners … you hungry masses, come! We won't give up Bosnia! We won't!" The crowd picks up Pejaković's invocation and chants with him. A bystander leans into the microphone, shouting, "Long live the partisans!"[86] In a sense, the self-managed ideals of the dissolving communist regime only grew stronger once the horrific realities of the new, emerging nationalist elite became clear. Precisely because "actually existing" communism and nationalism had betrayed the democratic aspirations of ordinary Yugoslavs, it was now finally not only possible but indeed absolutely imperative for the citizens to intervene in the politics of the state with radical political aspirations. In more simple terms, this was an attempt at democratization from the bottom up – it was a revolution.

Admittedly, this movement probably began too late. Perhaps a year earlier, in March 1991, when similar protests gripped Belgrade and demanded the ouster of Milošević, a pan-Yugoslav citizen insurrection might have charted a different course for the now doomed polity. But Milošević had used tanks to put down the uprising and, confronted by such incredible violence, the people of Serbia retreated. By this point, in a climate of pervasive fear and paranoia, elites in the rest of the country easily engineered, explicitly and implicitly, electoral outcomes to cement themselves in power in turn. As such, Yugoslavia's crisis was not the result of the democratic legitimation of nationalist parties or politics by the masses. Instead, it was caused by the authoritarian tendencies of the Yugoslav elite who sought to navigate the crisis of one party rule, even at the cost of violently dissolving the state in its entirety. As V.P. Gagnon notes:

> the violence of the Yugoslav wars of the 1990s was part of a broad strategy in which images of threatening enemies and violence were used by conservative elites in Serbia and Croatia: not in order to mobilize people, but rather as a way to *demobilize* those who were pushing for changes in the structures of economic and political power that would negatively affect the values and interests of those elites. The goal of this strategy was to silence, marginalize, and demobilize challengers and their supporters in order to create political homogeneity at home. This in turn enabled conservatives to maintain control of the existing structures of power, as well as to reposition themselves by converting state-owned property into privately held wealth.[87]

This strategy likewise influenced how these elites managed the republican elections between 1990 and 1991. Of course, the very fact that Yugoslavia's republican elites managed to hold multiparty elections even as the federation was dissolving, and after four decades of one-party rule, is an indicator of how adeptly they manoeuvred and directed a crisis that appeared from the outside as a directionless storm. In Slovenia, for instance, the first democratic elections in April 1990 actually preserved in office the republican LCY wing, now redubbed the United List of Social Democrats. Milan Kućan, who was until then the chairman of the Slovenian LCY, was elected as the first democratic president of Slovenia. While the parliamentary results were somewhat more ambiguous, they nevertheless produced a strong mandate for Slovenia's left-liberal parties, including the Social Democrats. The results of Slovenia's vote were clearly an endorsement of Kućan's democratic reformist vision for Yugoslavia, especially as talk grew in the western republics (and Macedonia) of a "confederal" model for the new, ostensibly democratic Yugoslav state.

Indeed, as late as the spring of 1990, the leaders of Yugoslavia's western republics, including those elected on popular mandates, sought to negotiate with Belgrade even as Milošević's authoritarian ambitions grew. As Glaurdić notes, "pre-election polls in Slovenia showed 52 percent of Slovenes supported the transformation of Yugoslavia into a confederation, 28 percent supported Slovenia's independence, and only 8 percent supported Yugoslavia's remaining a federation".[88] Slovenia, Croatia, BiH, and Macedonia would only make decisive moves towards independence once Milošević made transparent his willingness to use extreme violence to preserve a version of the Yugoslav state that no one but the most hard-core of Serb nationalists supported. Even so, the "secessionists" largely left Yugoslavia with their own miniature oligarchies intact. Socialist Yugoslavia dissolved, like its imperial and monarchist predecessors, but the region's elastic authoritarian tendencies endured.

In Croatia, the parliamentary elections likewise failed to produce a landslide endorsement of nationalist politics, though unlike in Slovenia the majoritarian electoral rules produced just that. The newly formed HDZ, the mother party of the similarly named affiliate in BiH, won 41.9 per cent of the vote, while the successor list of the LCY in Croatia followed with 35 per cent of the vote. The Serb nationalist SDS, likewise the predecessor of the BiH wing of the party, managed only a meagre 1.6 per cent of the vote precisely because Serbs in Croatia voted en masse not for the Belgrade-backed SDS but the LCY successor bloc.[89] Despite winning only a plurality of the popular vote, the HDZ won 55 of the 80 seats in the new Croatian parliament, or nearly 70 per cent of the mandate. As in Slovenia, popular support was still clearly in favour of a single Yugoslav state, albeit with significant institutional changes: "51 percent of Croatia's citizens [supported] a confederation, 11 percent their republic's independence, and 27 percent a federation".[90] After Zagreb and Ljubljana's call for confederal reforms was strongly (indeed, violently) rebuked by Belgrade, however, the HDZ would use its super-majority in the republican parliament to turn Croatia sharply right, not unlike the way Milošević had already done in Serbia.[91]

Because institutional anti-nationalist and anti-war political options were summarily crippled by reactionary elements within the Yugoslav and republican state apparatuses, in particular those in Belgrade intent on achieving their goals through violence, the only remaining course for the vast majority of Yugoslavs was the politics of the street. In a sense, however, the desperation of such mobilizations likewise brought home the existential danger they posed to the emerging nationalist regimes. By circumventing institutional politics and relying instead on informal activist and solidarity networks like those that had toppled the one-party regimes of the Eastern Bloc, Yugoslav citizens were on the edge of their own revolution. Realizing this, the extremist nationalist wing of the broader authoritarian coalition which Milošević had stapled together decided to act. On 6 April 1992, as a massive procession marched down Sarajevo's main artery, Karadžić's snipers, holed up along with the rest of the SDS leadership in the Holiday Inn building across from the parliament, fired on the crowds. Panic ensued, the marchers scattered, as Karadžić and company fled the city for the last time. The same day, the EEC and the US both formally recognized the sovereignty of BiH.[92] The subsequent siege of the city, which began that night, was not fully lifted until the end of February 1996. In truth, the war had begun weeks earlier as entire villages were levelled and thousands expelled by the assorted SDS and Belgrade-backed militias across central and eastern BiH. But with the capital surrounded and months after similar scenes had played out in Slovenia and Croatia, the war had finally, fully, officially begun in Yugoslavia's central republic, where it would take its bloodiest and most brutal form.

The chief architects of Yugoslavia's unravelling (and BiH's cataclysm) met the last, desperate intervention of the demos with sniper fire. No other alternative was left to them when they were confronted by the organized agency and power of the country's citizens. The elite project to seize and thereafter completely dominate BiH and Yugoslavia politically and economically could only be accomplished through violence. While significant, this last-ditch popular attempt to sack the entirety of the BiH political establishment must also be understood in the context of the discussion in the preceding chapter – namely, the century-and-a-half-long history of nation-state construction in the Balkans. The political and democratic potential of Yugoslavia's citizens had for so long been suppressed that its re-emergence in the final moments of the country's existence was too weak and too late to dismantle the incredible apparatus of fear, violence, and plunder that had already begun to consume the polity. This movement and moment was "fleeting", in the very worst sense of the ideal Wolin imagines. Nevertheless, in different circumstances, 1992 might have been the beginning of a revolution and not the beginning of a war, a fact not to be lost sight of as it concerns the potential for democratic change in the post-Yugoslav space.

Moreover, the constellation of events that preceded the country's immediate dissolution must also be understood in the context of the decades of democratic agitation that preceded it. These experiences – widely publicized in the Western media and well-studied in Western universities and intelligence communities – should have informed Western policymakers that, as in the rest of eastern Europe, there existed in Yugoslavia a genuine constituency for change – one already familiarized with the theoretical principles of direct democracy through the workers' self-management system, now yearning for its substantive implementation. Accordingly, the refusal by these international actors to proactively dispatch peacekeepers (as large segments of the Yugoslav public and the leadership of BiH and Macedonia favoured) or to facilitate a peaceful and inclusive dialogue concerning the federation's future was not merely a lapse in strategy. The failure to act in a decisive and timely fashion in Yugoslavia amounted to wilful ignorance, which, in turn, precipitated the worst humanitarian catastrophe in Europe since World War II. And nearly three decades later, the unresolved legacies of this crisis could easily destabilize the continent once more. As a result, Yugoslavia's catastrophically mismanaged implosion was not only a historical error; it remains an active policy and security concern.

Lessons Not Learned, Paths Not Taken

The preceding summary of the broad contours of Yugoslavia's dissolution is critical to understanding post-war American and especially European policy in the Western Balkans. By and large, the lessons of the region's history have not been learned nor have the much more recent lessons of the Yugoslav crisis and the subsequent wars been adequately processed by leaders in Washington and Brussels. No serious assessment of the Euro-Atlantic project in the Western Balkans can thus be conducted unless it notes its origins in the wreckage of the "hour of Europe" and, by extension, the refusal of subsequent European and American administrations to critically reflect upon these events.

Indeed, it is also why in this book recent events (i.e. post-Yugoslav Western policy in the Balkans) appear almost like an afterthought to the comparatively detailed accounting of nineteenth- and twentieth-century Balkan history. It is not because the present does not concern me. Instead, it is a deliberate attempt to gesture firmly at the static nature of certain core dimensions and patterns of both local and international politics in the Balkans. In other words, if the structural dynamics of international engagement in the Western Balkans have remained unchanged for nearly three decades, and these are in turn segments of still older patterns, then to focus disproportionately on strictly contemporary affairs is to willingly discard not only context but, indeed, the primary engines and determinants of local politics.

That having been said, neither the US nor the EU is responsible for Yugoslavia's implosion as such. As noted, both the structural and immediate factors that led to the country's end were almost entirely the product of local factors and patterns of development. Nevertheless, the (mis)management of Yugoslavia's final years, much like the fate of its successor states, is inevitably in large part the responsibility of the international community. Not just because the West (falsely) pledged itself to "never again" allow the horrors of the Holocaust to repeat themselves. More practically, the end of Yugoslavia produced, and continues to produce, all manner of political and security externalities which should still deeply concern leaders in both the US and EU. Thus, while the Balkans appear as a marginal, peripheral zone in world politics, their stability is inseparable from the security of Europe proper – not least of all because, as the refugee crisis has illustrated over the course of the last three years, the Balkans are the thin membrane separating the core of the EU from the chaos of the post-Arab Spring Middle East. The only truly effective way to strengthen that membrane is not only to ensure the absence of active conflict but to invest in the sustained democratic consolidation of the various Western Balkan states.

As it concerns not only the refugee question, but also continental security more broadly, the matter cannot be resolved (as appears to be

the preference of many European capitals) by exporting and buttress-
ing illiberal tendencies in these peripheral states in the hope that their
strongmen will insulate western Europe from the realities of a rapidly
shifting world order. Quite simply, any international approach that
does not have as its primary objective the genuine democratic transformation of the region will end in crisis, sooner or later. Both the dissolution of Yugoslavia and the initial formation of the Balkan state system
after the end of the Ottoman Empire demonstrate that authoritarianism in this region cannot ensure long-term stability. Contemporary
attempts by the US and EU to invest in elite-dominated, managed, or
illiberal democratic regimes as a means to shore up or guarantee
regional stability merely replicate these past errors.

What then has informed the American and European approach to
the region after Yugoslavia? Of course, distinctions and disagreements
exist and, indeed, these have widened since the EU replaced the US as
the primary guarantor of Western Balkan stability following 9/11 and
the US-led invasion of Iraq. Nevertheless, on the core questions –
namely, that EU and NATO integration will provide lasting stability
and security in the region – Washington and Brussels have traditionally
been in concert. Yet this grand bargain obscures more than it reveals.
The European approach, in particular, has been an institutional and
elite-centred one. Brussels insists on the creation of effective institutional frameworks, staffed by responsible and accountable technocrats,
in order to ensure compliance with the EU's morass of membership
requirements. By adhering rigorously to these demands, previously
authoritarian regimes will eventually become democratic; in other
words, good laws will produce good outcomes – "installing the right
elites" will produce a rightly ordered society.[93] The local public, recognizing the inherent sensibility of this approach, are expected to do their
part by electing responsible technocrats, and giving them the mandate
to reform local regimes accordingly. In exchange, the EU provides
(along with NATO, the World Bank, the IMF, and all other relevant
international institutions) candidate and recipient countries with an
assortment of political and financial benefits for playing by the rules of
global liberalism.

This entire narrative rests on two absolutely nonsensical axioms,
namely, that a constitutional regime exists independently of its repre-

sentatives, that is, that institutions are legitimate and functional by virtue of their mere *de jure* existence. And secondly, that the post-Yugoslav elite have a shared sense of interests, not only with the international community but with their own citizens. Both assessments indicate not only a shocking misreading of the historical record but a fundamental misunderstanding of the very idea of democratic governance, even as it is conducted in the West. Consider the latter point first: as noted, the core mechanism for ending the various conflicts in the former Yugoslavia was a combination of Western military intervention and post-war state-building and democratization. In between those two events, however, was the bargain struck, not so much between the respective warring factions, but between the international community and the assortment of local warlords who now styled themselves as statesmen. The essential political premise of the Dayton Peace Agreement in BiH, the Kumanovo Agreement and later Ahtisaari Plan for Kosovo, and the Ohrid Agreement in Macedonia was an exhortation to local warlords and militia leaders to become democratic leaders. In return, the international community would guarantee the region's security, while simultaneously financing the former Yugoslavia's economic and political reconstruction.

To sweeten the deal, these agreements, especially the Dayton Accords, ethnically segmented these states so as to ensure that virtually every two-bit gunman could become a councillor or mayor in this hamlet or that village. Or more precisely, they froze the various conflicts so that gains won through force would, for the most part, not need to be abandoned through negotiation. Not only did this decision fundamentally concede the narrative of Yugoslavia's dissolution to the most reactionary elements in the region (i.e. that ethnically and religiously heterogeneous populations could no longer peacefully coexist) but it cemented the post-Yugoslav state system on precisely the kinds of primitive political and economic practices which the post-war development agenda was meant to curb. This approach reduced the role of the international community in the Balkans to that of handmaiden to authoritarianism. After all, any meaningful pretence of democratic accountability or transparency, even within the context of international supervision, could only be anathema to regimes presided over by war criminals and profiteers.

Built into the international supervisory regime in the Balkans, therefore, was an irresolvable contradiction between aspirational democratization and actually existing authoritarianism. Having been rewarded for their criminal wars of conquest, why would Serb nationalist leaders in BiH, for instance, bargain away their prizes during peacetime – not only in the sense of territory, as traditional accounts have focused on, but more importantly in terms of political practice? Having won concessions as warlords, where was the incentive for these elites to become genuinely democratic leaders, vulnerable to the wishes of a traumatized and embittered electorate? Such incentives never did and still do not exist, especially given the fact that the international community has traditionally placed its highest premium not on the region's democratization but rather its pacification.

In reality, if and when local elites require financial or political aid they have only to feign commitment to "Euro-Atlantic values" or to threaten to destabilize the region radically. Often, as in the case of Milorad Dodik in BiH's Republika Srpska (RS) entity, Aleksandar Vučić's government in Belgrade, or Nikola Gruevski's former regime in Skopje, they use both approaches simultaneously. In this way, local elites blackmail the international community – their actual power is minute, but the EU's and US's inability or lack of interest in engaging in meaningful democratization in the region has greatly multiplied their effect. Indeed, it is irrational for European and American policymakers to expect local elites to kill their proverbial golden goose, without the threat of consequence. After all, to replace the expansive clientelistic and patrimonial networks that have cemented them in power for decades for the sake of normative ideals of democratic legitimacy would be an unheard of act of political self-sabotage.

In their insistence on as much, the Euro-American approach clearly remains informed by the collapse of communism in the rest of eastern Europe. As their preferred narratives suggest, in eastern Europe the disgruntled masses voluntarily and autonomously overthrew the Soviet satellite regimes while a new class of elites likewise voluntarily affiliated themselves to and embraced Euro-Atlantic values: free and fair elections, parliamentary and representative governance, the rule of law, free markets, and EU and NATO integration. To the extent that large segments of the eastern European public and post-Soviet elite viewed it as a political priority to distance their regimes from Moscow, the preceding account is accurate, notwithstanding the tremendous socio-economic devastation that accompanied Western-sponsored economic "shock therapy" in these countries. Yet the turn against Soviet hegemony and the widespread embrace of democratic norms and values are two quite separate events. Separate also are the initial mass social movement mobilizations that toppled the one-party regimes of the Eastern Bloc and the fashion in which these were subsequently "constitutionalized", as Wolin would say, that is, the manner in which the diffuse and disparate demands of these mass movements were articulated by subsequent elected governments.

In this regard, the illiberal turn in Hungary, Poland, the Czech Republic, and Slovakia over the past five years should seriously undermine the pat technocratic narratives of the end of communism in eastern Europe.[94] Clearly, the anti-Soviet sentiments of east European elites were not necessarily an indication of their democratic convictions as such. Moreover, given the ongoing persistence of civil society and social movement organizing in the region since the end of the Cold War, it also does not appear that the essential "social question" in these societies has been resolved.[95] That is, social contracts rooted in transparent and consultative democratic norms have not yet been fully drafted, despite the integration of these countries into the formal fold of the EU and NATO.

In principle, similar concerns exist in the former Yugoslavia but they are further exacerbated by the legacies of conflict and systemic violence, with which the rest of eastern Europe, for the most part, has not had to contend. As noted earlier, the kinds of mass movement mobilizations which toppled the one-party regimes of the Soviet Union and Eastern Bloc were both less pronounced in Yugoslavia (partly because the Yugoslav regime was more "liberal" than its neighbours) and far more violently suppressed. In this respect, even the relatively limited degree of post-communist transition among elites in eastern Europe is years ahead of the glacial rate of transformation among the post-Yugoslav elites, whose regimes have done little to move beyond patrimonial and clientelistic as well as violent and coercive forms of governance. In other words, before we can use the end of communism in eastern Europe as an example of the kinds of transition paradigms which international and local actors should embrace, sober reflection on the extent of these changes is imperative, as well as on the structural and historical specificity of authoritarianism in the Western Balkans.

Accordingly, the eastern European example of democratic transition is clearly inappropriate in the context of the former Yugoslavia. Yet the international community's post-communist and post-war democratization policy in the Western Balkans remains wedded to this paradigm. There is a persistent and pernicious expectation that warlords will become democrats despite the lack of combined and consistent top-down and bottom-up pressure which marked at least the initial phase of anti-regime activities in the former Eastern Bloc. The West expects change in the Balkans without effective international sanctions for elites consistently acting in bad faith or without fully articulated grassroots, social movement, and civil society mobilization. Nor is the broader analytical merit of this approach helped at all, it must be said, by the accelerating deterioration of democratic norms in those formerly paradigmatic transitional regimes. Indeed, inasmuch as these states remain an example of successful democratic transition for the former Yugoslavia, it is as sites demonstrating the necessity for continuous civil society engagement and mobilization.

In contrast, in BiH, for example, where the process of ethnonational and administrative fragmentation was taken to extremes (in the form of an internationally brokered constitutional regime with fourteen separate governments for a population of less than four million people spread over an area smaller than the state of West Virginia), the utter lack of political and economic progress has been truly remarkable. This lack of progress is especially startling when compared with the nominally expansive architecture of the international community's presence in the country. The Office of the High Representative (OHR), for instance, an internationally appointed post with the power to sack elected officials and suspend laws when they contradict the writ of the Dayton constitutional order, has a mandate that is so extensive that critics once referred to the body as a "European Raj".[96] Of course, the comparison is inane; the brutality of the Bosnian War necessarily warranted mechanisms for ensuring that the assorted warlords could not continue their campaigns of extermination and expulsion through ostensibly "legal means" in peacetime. While the OHR was created through Dayton's Annex 10, the expansion of its mandate (the "Bonn Powers") came only in 1997 when the Americans and Europeans begrudgingly realized the lack of credible enforcement mechanisms in the original text. And, indeed, the persistence of just such politics has cemented the OHR's continued relevance since then.[97] Yet in the past decade, the OHR's actual exercise of its constitutional responsibilities has receded so dramatically (most worryingly, during a time of worsening political conditions in BiH) that the body is now a ceremonial post in all but name.[98]

The OHR's eclipse has been only a part of the international community's broader turn towards an abstract, rhetorical democratization policy in the region. The inherent elasticity of Balkan authoritarians has easily adapted to this shift, with catastrophic results for ordinary citizens. The insistence on "local ownership", a policy motif urging local elites to take responsibility for socio-economic reform efforts, for instance, has translated simply into a standstill in reforms. But this detachment from any meaningful promotion (and enforcement) of democracy is not new for the international presence in the Balkans, as I have stressed throughout. And in one sense, its most destructive episode – after the war itself – has already passed.

As regards any sustained effort at political and institutional reform, the underlying economic dynamics in the region are the bedrock for accomplishing such reforms. During the Yugoslav dissolution and the war years, historical tendencies towards kleptocracy and patrimonialism accelerated dramatically, taking the form of outright plunder. But when the internationals arrived in the region in 1996, after the signing of the Dayton Peace Accords, they not only refused to reverse these ill-gotten gains, but legitimized them through an assortment of convoluted and otherwise dubious privatization schemes.[99]

In the academic literature, much has been made of the neoliberal orthodoxies that guided the restructuring of previously planned economies across eastern Europe. In most of the formerly communist east, however, these economic transitions still had some semblance of an accompanying legal regime, even if often managed through political and criminal networks.[100] In the former Yugoslavia, the transition to "market economics", or rather the fragmentation of the workers' self-management system, occurred almost entirely through the process of accumulation by dispossession – that is, overt violence of a sort even more extreme than anything that had occurred in the region during the nineteenth and early twentieth centuries. In fact, the first batch of privatizations occurred in the midst of war, as early as 1994 in BiH and still earlier in Croatia, and involved not the legal transfer of socially or state-owned property into private hands but the seizure of commercial and industrial real estate and property by criminal cartels.[101] Opting in no meaningful way to reverse these developments, the arrival of the liberal democratic, free-market capitalist international community tacitly legitimized the (re)founding of the political and economic order in the Western Balkans through supremely primitive (and thus local) means.

To begin with, formerly socially owned properties – the central pillar of the workers' self-management system – were transformed virtually by (criminal) fiat into state-owned enterprises.[102] Although the self-management regime lacked substantive democratic qualities, as a legal category it represented the germ of potential, organic democratization. In principle, self-management in Yugoslavia was little more than aspirational co-operative economics, a feature of free-market economies from Spain to Canada. Instead of rehabilitating and modernizing existing economic (and political) structures in the region, Western advisers opted for a "one size fits all" approach that played directly to the interests of local elites. By insisting on the legal transformation of socially owned properties into state ownership, Western policymakers effectively transferred billions of dollars of public funds from the hands of citizens into the hands of elites.

Moreover, in the process, they dismantled a rudimentary but nevertheless important apparatus of accountability that could have immeasurably aided genuine democratic reform efforts. Consider, for instance, the example of participatory budgeting, most extensively implemented in certain low-income neighbourhoods in Porto Alegre, Brazil, and since expanded to dozens of locales around the world. While not a silver bullet for poverty reduction or economic reform, participatory budgeting significantly changes the power dynamics within communities by allowing ordinary citizens the opportunity to identify, study, and implement large-scale public works projects that are needed in their communities.[103] Similarly, the adoption of participatory budgeting or policymaking mechanisms, built on the experience of community and factory floor participation during the Yugoslav period, would not have entirely curbed post-war corruption and criminality in the Western Balkans. Yet such an approach would certainly have gone a long ways towards addressing the central missing element of existing local and international political practices in the region: the near total exclusion of ordinary citizens from the relevant decision-making processes. Importantly, the EU and the Council of Europe commissioned reports, studies, and research which showed the transformative effect that a turn towards participatory democracy could have on the region,[104] and, to this day, informed advocates continue to propose versions of this model.[105] Inexplicably, these suggestions continue to fall on deaf ears in both Brussels and Washington despite the obvious bankruptcy of existing approaches, which have divorced parliamentary institutions almost entirely from actual democratic accountability and participation.

As a result, the privatization process became an embrace not of free-market competition but of patrimonial redistribution by self-dealing militias turned political parties. In effect, the oligarchic concert that had characterized the late-Yugoslav period persisted into the post-war settlement, only now it was further legitimized by the presence of the international community. With little in the way of a "de-Nazification" process to accompany the international community's security guarantees, the authoritarians turned into warlords, then into nominally democratic leaders, all without ever losing power or abandoning any of their core values. Granted, key nationalist figures, like Karadžić and Ratko Mladić, were barred from office and eventually handed over to the ICTY. But, as Ed Vulliamy has observed, the "middle managers of genocide" largely went free and continue to serve in public offices, great and small, across the former Yugoslavia.[106] And this is to say nothing of the convicted war criminals, like Fikret Abdić and Momćilo Krajišnik, who have returned to politics after serving sentences for crimes against humanity.

Still administered as glorified protection rackets and political fiefdoms, the economies of the contemporary Western Balkans remain complete basket cases: a patchwork of collapsed and asset-stripped industries, over-priced and politically manipulated utilities, and a service sector that caters almost exclusively to (comparatively) wealthy foreigners and the itinerant diaspora. Unemployment, the most significant socio-economic indicator, among the region's non-EU member states continues to hover between 20 and 30 per cent, with those figures nearly double among youth.[107] In fact, economic prospects in the region are so dire that citizens are simply leaving, at rates not seen since the nineteenth century. Emigration is endemic, and birth rates are declining, meaning that the Western Balkans are facing both economic and demographic collapse.[108]

Amid such economic squalor, the post-Yugoslav political climate has remained, again unsurprisingly, thick and toxic with hate speech and chauvinist rhetoric. After all, violence and the mere threat of violence have been the historically preferred recipe of the Balkan elite for maintaining power, and it is a strategy that they have easily adapted to the era of managed democracy. The rhetoric of perpetual nationalist conflict, meanwhile, not only distracts the public from the socio-economic devastation around them, but obscures the manner in which local elites maintain control over the public administration apparatus (better understood as the bureaucratic remnants of overt authoritarianism) and the handful of cash-cow industries (e.g. utilities, telecoms, and energy companies for the most part) that keep their regimes afloat. The impoverished population, in turn, even when they are able to see through the veil of cynical, self-interested partisanship, are still so dependent on public administration jobs that they vote consistently for the same criminal clans who provide them with what little economic security they scrape by on. According to one set of figures in BiH, for instance, every third employed person in the country works in some sector of the public administration.[109] To be exact, the figure is upwards of a hundred and eighty thousand individuals in a country with an unofficial unemployment rate of approximately 40 per cent.[110] Since government jobs are the highest paid in the country, one can reasonably conclude that those employed in the public administration are in most cases the primary breadwinners, not only for their immediate but also their extended families. Those individuals have an active interest in preserving their patrons in power, even though these same political oligarchs have economically and socially devastated the society as a whole. In other words, despite failing to deliver much in the way of public goods, complex institutional incentives abound to maintain the current political status quo.

Clearly, then, the lack of legitimate democratic governance and the wider corruption and criminality that permeate post-Yugoslav political and social life are the product of both long-term local patterns of development and recently botched democratization and reform efforts by the international community. In this respect, while designed by the international community, the post-Yugoslav political architecture has fundamentally embraced the local elites' preferred political arrangements. From Dayton to Ohrid, the Americans and Europeans have largely presided over an armistice rather than a structural transformation of regional politics. Today, though the infrastructure for large-scale war has been dampened by the death of Franjo Tuđman in 1999 and the ousting of Slobodan Milošević in 2000, the chaotic division-of-spoils process largely persists. Thus, as Eric Gordy notes in addressing the political-economic dimensions of the Dayton regime, but in a context that can be broadened to the region as a whole: "[contemporary] politics … is characterized by political structures generated by outside actors, ostensibly with the goal of assuring peace and the development of democracy, but in practice maintaining ethnifying monopolies in politics and providing cover for impoverishing neoliberal monopolies in economics".[111] Even as the analytic stress of this account is on local, primitive patterns of dispossession and rejects the characterization of local socio-economic patterns as neoliberal, Gordy's observation here is spot on: political and socio-economic conditions in the Western Balkans have changed little since the dissolution of Yugoslavia, despite the international presence.

Conclusions

Alternatives to Yugoslavia's bloody disintegration existed as alternatives to the rise of the predatory and authoritarian nation-state in the Balkans existed all along. While the purge of the progressive elements of the LCY stunted the potential for democratically inclined leadership in the party, the broader self-management regime and relative liberalism of Yugoslav society still produced potential exits even in the dying days of the SFRJ. The crucial mistake the international community made in Yugoslavia and its successor states was not only in its failure to prevent mass killings and genocide – it was in the decision to accept as legitimate and unavoidable the consequences of these campaigns while simultaneously discounting and ignoring a far older and more pronounced history of aspirational but nevertheless important democratic agitation.

Now, it appears as though the post-Yugoslav states are trapped in a hopelessly reactionary, tribal, and primitive socio-political bind. The international community largely assists rather than challenges the most perverse dimensions of this "new-old" regime. Western leaders are blackmailed into propping up increasingly illegitimate and unpopular governments because they have continued to elevate shallow conceptions of stability over substantive notions of democracy and democratization. The aim of this chapter, although likely too ambitious for its own good, has been to gesture both at the alternatives that once existed and at the hopeless myopia of the present international approach in the Western Balkans. Yet the existing Western approach, much like the local regimes themselves, is unsustainable and in this there is both danger and opportunity. In the next two chapters, I examine in greater detail the internal and external sources of the region's instability and some potential paths forward.

3

GEOPOLITICS AND THE CRISIS OF DEMOCRACY IN THE WESTERN BALKANS

In the preceding two chapters the discussion focused on both the persistence of particular reactionary patterns of development in the Western Balkans and the failures of the US and EU to take stock of these in their attempts at state-building and democratization in the region after the dissolution of Yugoslavia. This analysis raises a simple, if loaded, question: what now? What do these past and existing local and international regimes suggest to us about the future of the Western Balkans and, in particular, the future of democratic governance in the region? In a sense, the final two chapters of this book are an exercise in fleshing out two possible versions of the former Yugoslavia's future. The first option, and the one examined in this chapter, concerns the marriage of local authoritarian tendencies with new, similarly authoritarian international patrons. Among these, Russia is the most noteworthy, but increasingly China, Turkey, and the Gulf states are also emerging as formative factors. How significant is their involvement in the region and how credible are the political and economic alternatives they offer Balkan elites and citizens? And what does the growing influence of powerful autocratic regimes in southeastern Europe mean for the continent as a whole?

To even entertain these questions, however, is to implicitly acknowledge that the Euro-Atlantic project, as a practical and normative ideal, is in considerable jeopardy. Aside from the exhaustion of international efforts and commitments, as a result of both local elite intransigence and Western ambivalence, it is the crisis of liberal democracy in the EU and US that now most imperils the former Yugoslavia. This crisis has already resulted in a tremendous inward turn among the former champions of globalization, leaving Russia in particular to create alarming new geopolitical realities across south and eastern Europe and the Caucasus. This historic realignment gives us occasion to reflect that for all the trappings of European soft power, the post-Yugoslav settlement in the Western Balkans was always primarily the result of the hard security guarantees provided to the region by three states: the US, the UK, and Germany. As of January 2017, two of those three guarantors have disappeared from the calculus of regional politics. Post-Brexit Britain and Trump-led America are no longer a factor in the politics of the Western Balkans. There has been and will be no official announcement, of course, and American and British aid of various sorts will most likely continue to flow to the region. But it will be directed towards marginalia, stopgap measures, and photo ops, not towards addressing and resolving the structural questions plaguing the region's development. After all, as these questions went largely unaddressed even at the height of liberal internationalism in the former Yugoslavia, they are unlikely to be resolved in the era of reactionary isolationism in the West.

The evacuation of British and American leadership and participation from the Balkans will leave Germany in a delicate position. Berlin is already under tremendous pressure as the apparently lone liberal democratic stalwart – notwithstanding the election of Emmanuel Macron in France – among a sea of reactionary populists. This solitary Germany holds together the European project in the face of still seething financial unrest in Greece, Italy, Spain, and Portugal, and against resurgent Russian revanchism across the continent. While Berlin will most likely continue to invest its energies into making the Union a functional and credible project, after Brexit it is clear that the EU is necessarily a German-led initiative. For the democratic project in the Western Balkans, Germany's success in holding together the EU is imperative, especially because local elites have already begun to hedge their bets on the dissolution of the Euro-Atlantic order. Recall, whether Ottoman,

Austro-Hungarian, Yugoslav, or Euro-Atlantic, the defining dimension of the elasticity of authoritarianism and patrimonialism in the Western Balkans has been the way local elites have navigated and survived the end of order. And from the perspective of local elites, we appear at present to be well within the midst of another such moment.

Accordingly, this chapter will outline what is essentially the worst-case scenario for the region in the years to come. Not the idea that international authoritarian and reactionary regimes can, substantively, replace the political and financial contributions of the West, but that even in trying to leverage one camp against another for their own political gain, local elites may precipitate real geopolitical crises, which could quickly spiral out of control. Or, worse still, that as the rift between Russia and the West deepens, and the Middle East sinks deeper into direct and proxy warfare, each of these regimes will attempt to weaponize their respective Balkan clients as a means of flanking their foes. While each of these scenarios is a projection of possible future events, the analysis is very much rooted in existing political dynamics. This chapter is therefore a warning to both local civil society and the international community – those historically and practically most committed to and dependent on democratic consoli-dation in the region. Building on the discussion in Chapter II, this chapter will continue the examination of the categorically "managed" nature of contemporary Balkan democracy and its accelerating drift towards outright authoritarianism. Tying these developments into the broader context of democratic retreat in Europe, the discussion turns to the international actors emerging as eager sponsors of neo-authori-tarianism in the Western Balkans. Finally, the chapter examines the broader geopolitical implications of the collapse of democratic gover-nance in the former Yugoslavia and what it will mean for the security and stability of the European continent and the West as a whole.

The Absence of Reform

The previous chapter spoke to the broad contours of the failure of the democratization project initiated by the US and EU in the Western Balkans since the end of the Yugoslav Wars and, in particular, their failure to make use of local proto-democratic experiences. Still, one specific question deserves particular attention and further elaboration: why have local elites resisted these reform efforts, especially in the light of the large financial benefits that they themselves would stand to reap by integrating within the broader political and economic framework of the Euro-Atlantic order? After all, this economic gospel is a core pillar of both the international and local discourse. Even the most stridently chauvinist elites in the Balkans argue that economic reforms, and eventual "prosperity", are a priority for their governments. European policymakers, for their part, are especially keen to distinguish between economics and politics, suggesting that politics (pejoratively understood as partisanship and sectarianism) are an impediment to sound economic policy and therefore a fundamental disservice to the citizens of the region. Some are even more specific in their claims, going so far as to suggest that particular infrastructure development projects ("connectivity") are the keys to economic vibrancy and thus, in the long term, peace and stability.[1]

This attempt to distinguish artificially between economics and politics, especially within the context of nominally democratic regimes, recalls the earlier discussion of "political" conceptions of democracy by Sheldon Wolin. Despite the worrying decline in democratic norms in the region, European policymakers appear keen to define politics in the Western Balkans in a manner that evacuates any substantive sense of contestation or deliberation from the process. They do this presumably because they have identified the nationalist-chauvinist narratives of local elites as the only relevant political framework in the region. This translates for local citizens and elites alike, however, as a policy in which the EU would rather have a "stable" Western Balkans dominated by warlords than an "unstable" Western Balkans rocked by democratic protests and grassroots mobilizations.[2] This is a dangerous preference. In continuing to concede to local elites their primary political project (i.e. ethno-nationalist fragmentation as ideological cover for the preservation of political authoritarianism and economic kleptocracy) decades after the end of the Yugoslav Wars, Western policymakers have consistently contributed to the marginalization of civil society in the once nascent, now unravelling democratic regimes of the region. Because of this commitment to bankrupt and short-sighted conceptions of stability, the EU and US have effectively sabotaged the possibility for genuine political reform in the Western Balkans. This fact is essential to understanding why Brussels' rhetoric, in particular, concerning the urgent need for reform in the region is fundamentally hollow and why even in the states that have joined the EU and NATO (e.g. Croatia and Slovenia) there is a cavernous gap between proposed and actually existing democratic consolidation.

From the perspective of the post-Yugoslav elite, reform is unnecessary and undesirable. These leaders are fully aware that the economic prosperity gospel preached by policymakers in Brussels and Washington necessarily entails political regimes founded on principles of constitutional government and the rule of law. Recalling perhaps aspects of their early Marxist education, they conclude correctly that capitalism is first and foremost a political rather than economic regime. For this reason alone, reform, whether economic or political, is a non-starter in the region. It is undesirable because it would almost certainly mean that the existing elite structures, especially their patronage networks, would have to be dismantled. And reform is unnecessary because of the patrimonial control these elites wield over the public apparatus and the still longer history of primitive accumulation and dispossession that has characterized the political economy of the region since the nineteenth century. After all, what rewards would these parties reap as a result of successfully implemented reforms? They already dominate the electoral process through a combination of fear and patrimonialism and, if anything, substantive changes to the legal order of the state would almost certainly result in their fall from power. Moreover, given the crass criminality that defines the existing political regimes in the region, such a fall would not be a gentle one; it would mean jail time. One observer notes this explicitly, citing as a precedent the case of Croatia. Noting that the leadership in BiH has obstructed all but the most cosmetic reform efforts in the country, Benjamin Pargan argues that "[this] stubborn blockade has been reinforced by a case in neighbouring Croatia, where the former prime minister Ivo Sanader was arrested and sentenced to ten years in prison for corruption. The image of a former government leader in handcuffs has left a lasting impression on his counterparts in Bosnia-Herzegovina, by showing them what could happen if the Bosnian judiciary began investigating corruption, with the EU's support".[3] A similar situation is currently developing in

Macedonia, where the government change in the summer of 2017 is showing signs of having as one of its primary outcomes the arrest and conviction of the former prime minister Nikola Gruevski and a number of his government's members.[4]

The same phenomenon can be readily observed in Serbia, Montenegro, and the region as whole. Indeed, it even accounts to a great degree for Croatia's own democratic backsliding since joining the EU. With membership came the end of the EU's ability to extract significant concessions from Zagreb and so, as in Hungary, the country's elites are reverting to form. Yet this absence of reform (or reversion to form) in the former Yugoslavia is not the result of some inherent backwardness on the part of the Balkan elite or citizens. Instead, as previously stressed, it should be understood as a deliberate policy on the part of local elites to stunt the socio-political progress of these societies. Rather than being the product of Ottoman, Austro-Hungarian, or, in this case, Euro-Atlantic influence, these patterns are the result of local elite agency and preference. In other words, this is a theory of power that is primitive and reactionary but nevertheless intentional, anticipatory, and elastic. Recognizing as much is central to explaining why Balkan elites are able to alternate fluidly between nationalist chauvinism and liberal democratic rhetoric (even the odd policy decision) and why they have historically so adeptly negotiated and navigated regime collapse. Because the actual networks and structures of power in the Balkans have remained informal, patrimonial, and clannish (and, most importantly, non-ideological in their fundamental conception of political and social order), they have persisted through otherwise seismic historical transformations.

This is perhaps best illustrated with respect to the nominal success stories of the post-Yugoslav transition: Croatia and Slovenia. Despite their having formally navigated and completed the complicated, bureaucratic EU and NATO accession processes, we would do well to ask what the genuine quality of Croatian and Slovenian democracy has been since joining these organizations. The facts are not encouraging. According to many analyses, both Croatia and Slovenia are the most corrupt states in the EU.[5] The Croatian elite likewise remain clearly authoritarian and provincial in their orientation; plagiarism among government ministers and members of parliament, for instance, is endemic.[6] According to Freedom House, the media in Croatia remain only "partly free",[7] while other monitoring organizations note that the state broadcaster, as in other former Yugoslav states, remains highly politicized and an arm of the embedded post-war elite, which in Croatia is centred on the right-wing HDZ.[8] The situation in Slovenia is marginally better, but the Freedom of the Media Representative of the Organization for Security and Co-operation in Europe (OSCE) has expressed grave concerns as recently as 2014 over the country's media climate.[9] And then there is also the problem of institutionalized chauvinism and nationalism, which in Croatia has not only been limited to events in the 1990s but has also entailed the wholesale rehabilitation of fascist and quisling movements from the 1940s.[10] Slovenia has not rehabilitated its fascist quislings but it did legally "erase" thousands of citizens and permanent residents after the country gained independence in 1991.[11] Two decades later, and thirteen years after Ljubljana joined the EU, the status of many of these individuals remains unresolved, making them effectively stateless,[12] despite repeated rulings against the country at the European Court of Human Rights (ECHR).[13]

When these observations are taken in conjunction with the waves of growing civil society mobilization that have gripped both Slovenia and Croatia in the last half-decade or so (which are the focus of the next chapter), it is difficult to escape the conclusion that integration with the EU and NATO has not been accompanied by a particularly rigorous or deep form of democratic reform in either country. Yes, formal one-party rule has dissolved and the extent and quality of civil rights and liberties enjoyed by citizens are doubtlessly much improved since the Yugoslav and war period. But neither state, in truth, is a consolidated democratic regime in any meaningful sense of the term. It is therefore no stretch to say that in both Slovenia and Croatia economic patrimonialism and a distinctly "managed" (if not outright authoritarian) form of political administration prevail. Granted, the situation is still worse in the region's non-EU and non-NATO states, the so-called Western Balkan Six (WB6). But that is precisely the point; despite their apparent post-war divergences, the essential socio-political character of the former Yugoslav republics remains more similar than not. Ultimately, what binds these states together is the political processes and events which have not taken place: the fundamental socio-political ruptures and confrontations between the elite and the plebes, the demos, the citizenry, that otherwise characterized the collapse of one-party rule (and have largely continued since then) in the rest of eastern Europe. In short, it is the absence of something like the 1989 revolutions which has continued to skew the political development of the Western Balkans, allowing the region's elite to survive regime collapse with only the most minor of ideological and technical readjustments.

To be clear, revolutionary episodes in and of themselves are insufficient for substantive democratic transformation. Indeed, the experience of the post-Soviet and former Eastern Bloc regimes clearly demonstrates as much. In this respect, the crisis of south and east European democracy as a whole is visible not merely at the margins but in the region's relatively prosperous core. In Poland and Hungary, for instance, one-time paragons of post-communist democratization, recent government decisions have targeted ethnic minorities, LGBT groups, civil society organizations, the free press, and even the independence of the judiciary.[14] In fact, a decade after the EU's 2004 "big bang" expansion, the Visegrád Group (Poland, the Czech Republic, Slovakia, and Hungary) has emerged as an influential illiberal bloc, markedly at odds with Brussels' traditional concert of democracies.

Of course, the complex democratization processes in the former Eastern Bloc have themselves been the subject of great scholarly scrutiny. Broadly, Marxist and critical approaches have focused primarily on the destructive neoliberal economic policies that accompanied the fall of communism in eastern Europe, presenting these as a foreign-imposed paradigm at the root of virtually all subsequent political and social crises in the region.[15] Yet such accounts have reduced regional events to mere ripples in the broader, global neoliberal turn while simultaneously diminishing the historic significance of the collapse of one-party rule in eastern Europe. By the same token, accounts of liberal institutionalists have tended to minimize the true toll of neoliberal restructuring in eastern Europe and the widespread socio-economic devastation such policies exacted on large segments of the population.[16] Yet while obscuring the realities of "shock therapy", these scholars also narrowed their embrace of democracy and democratization to shibboleth-like conceptions of multiparty elections and the rule of law. Absent from their accounts were the once vibrant social movements that had overthrown the former regimes in the first place. And with the erasure and implosion of participatory civil society came the demotion of democracy to mere parliamentarianism.

In contrast to both of these approaches, the contention here is that the current anti-democratic climate in eastern Europe must be understood as a local, political project and one that reflects the incomplete transformation of eastern European society following the collapse of communism. And while the focus of this work is clearly on the former Yugoslavia, it is an observation that speaks also to recent events in the former Eastern Bloc. In short, while eastern Europe's economies were restructured, the accompanying political transformations lagged behind and as a result a genuine transition in the values of the elite (and large segments of the populace) never occurred.[17] But with respect to eastern Europe proper and the previously cited example of the Croatian and Slovenian transitions, distinctions must nevertheless be drawn. While the revolutions prompting the collapse of one-party rule in eastern Europe have been insufficient for the broader task of democratic transformation, they have nevertheless been indispensable to beginning such a process all the same. In this respect, the fact that social movement agitation continues to define politics in these countries (especially in Romania, Bulgaria, and Poland) is a reflection of the vibrancy and maturity of civil society in these states. So, while these manifestations are the product of an incomplete post-communist transition, they are nevertheless evidence that this failure to progress is being contested by the grassroots, the citizens, those on whom any substantive democratic regime ultimately depends.

Thus it is not merely that the initial collapse of one-party rule in the former Yugoslavia did not occur through the efforts of civil society, but that in the decades since, civil society has remained largely stunted and marginalized. The absence of reform has therefore been intrinsically tied to the absence of certain revolutionary impulses in the civil society of the Western Balkans. The worst aspects of the Euro-Atlantic integration process, from the perspective of participatory democratic norms (i.e. the technocratic institutionalism which was also clearly present in the former Eastern Bloc states), have consequently been especially acute in the Western Balkans. In other words, when observing the entire artifice of post-Yugoslav state-building and democratization there is a cavernous and structural implementation gap, one that has become truly definitive of the Western Balkan polities and of civic and political life within them. The nominal legal foundations for democratic regimes are widespread and well developed in the region; *de jure*, the Western Balkan states have some of the most progressive legal regimes in the world.[18] In practice, however, these laws are not enforced and the nature of political authority in the region remains patrimonial and authoritarian.

Such a situation would be worrisome and unsustainable at the best of times, that is, were the broader project of democracy and democratization healthy and thriving at a continental and global scale. Obviously, this is not the case and at present we are confronted with an alarming confluence of factors: the decline of democratic norms in the principal states of the liberal democratic world order and the resurgence of outright authoritarianism at its peripheries. The latter, however, is only a complicating factor; the real crisis, the one with the most consequence for the Western Balkans, lies in the West. However flawed in practice, however deeply compromised by histories of colonialism, imperialism, racism, and sexism, the struggles to enact and expand the full promise of democratic government in the West have served as an important beacon for the rest of the world. In dimming, if not extinguishing that light outright, the US and EU leave regions like the Balkans in the dark of creeping authoritarian retrenchment.

The Crisis of International Liberalism

The 9/11 attacks radically transformed the American perception of foreign affairs, at least when compared to the optimism of the immediate post-Cold War period. Despite the deep neoconservative bent of the second Bush administration, the purpose of American foreign policy after 9/11 and the invasion of Iraq was no longer about promoting democracy but, in the words of the president himself, about pre-emptively confronting terrorist threats and their state sponsors.[19] Unsurprisingly, 9/11 and Iraq also prompted the initial, post-war drawing down of American involvement in the former Yugoslavia, as Washington's foreign policy focus shifted to the Middle East. The US remained present, of course, but politically it was the EU that now took the lead in the Western Balkans.[20] And this basic fact changed little during the Obama years, as the new administration was consumed by the process of disengaging from the Middle East, then managing the consequences of that disengagement, and attempting to pivot towards Asia in the interim.

In response, the Brussels establishment took the position that the integration of the Western Balkans into the EU and NATO could essentially be understood as a synonym for the completion of democratic transition in the region.[21] That is, the very process and act of joining the EU would turn the states of the former Yugoslavia into fully fledged democracies. Even if certain states proved especially recalcitrant or difficult to integrate into the Euro-Atlantic fold, like BiH and Kosovo for instance, then sufficiently expansive legal and economic linkages could be established between these states and the EU to stabilize the region as a whole. There was, in other words, a level of "stable instability" that the EU could and would tolerate in the region, provided there was no resumption of outright conflict.

The approach was conceptualized as the height of realpolitik, albeit with a generous dose of European liberal institutionalism. Much as the EU had emerged from the wreckage of two world wars, so too could the Western Balkans emerge from the former Yugoslavia through the EU. In reality, however, it was an expedient illusion, one that played to the latent indifference of leading European policymakers to events in the continent's southeast (and was, incidentally, the same approach that characterized their indifference to Yugoslavia's implosion in the first place). The EU's true interest in the Balkans was to manage the post-conflict environment, for which the promise of eventual Euro-Atlantic integration was necessary. Yet it was doubtful from the very outset whether Brussels actually wanted to absorb the region as such. After all, by refusing to commit to the substantive, generational task of democratic transformation in the Western Balkans (i.e. like the broader democratic transformations that took place in western Europe after World War II) Brussels merely slowed the process of democratic retreat in the region, painting over it with the veneer of technocratic accession jargon. Little, if any, thought was given to what would happen if the day came (as it soon did) when local elites concluded that this arrangement was not in their interest, or, worse still, the geopolitical climate changed so much that other external actors could begin to legitimately obstruct Euro-Atlantic expansion in the region.

This state of suspended animation was interrupted by a succession of global crises: the 2008 financial crisis, the Arab Spring and the subsequent post-revolutionary wars in Libya and Syria, the refugee and migrant crisis, and, above all, the Brexit referendum in the UK and the election of Donald Trump in the US. While the 2008 financial crisis significantly affected the already weak economies of the region,[22] it was the changing political climate surrounding the refugee crisis, the Brexit referendum, and the Trump election that left the biggest mark on the region. Indeed, the resurgence of far-right and otherwise xenophobic sentiments in the West has fundamentally changed how policymakers in Europe view the position of the Western Balkans, especially the non-EU states of the region.[23] The Euro-Atlantic integration of the former Yugoslavia is no longer a historical or moral responsibility of the West, nor is it even a geopolitical or security priority. Increasingly, it appears the Western Balkans are some combination of the embodiment of precisely the kind of "foreign" elements that the newly salient far-right in Europe wants to eject and erase from the continent and the compliant authoritarian regimes that will protect the borders of Europe from invading hordes of refugees.[24] Both perspectives represent a catastrophe for the genuine democratic aspirations of the Balkan peoples.

In other words, not only has the process of Euro-Atlantic integration ground to a halt in the Western Balkans, it seems as though the sun has also set on the broader project of nurturing liberal democracy in the region. Growing segments of the European political establishment believe not only that substantive democratic reform is unlikely in the region but that it is not in the interests of the EU to promote democracy per se in the Western Balkans. Or, more precisely, it is not in the EU's interest to promote disruptive, antagonistic, or populist forms of democracy in southeastern Europe at a time of democratic crisis at home. Accordingly, the calculus of some policymakers in Brussels – or, more properly, within many European capitals – now suggests that in order to preserve the stability of liberal regimes at home, the EU needs essentially to shore up authoritarianism in the former Yugoslavia. Strongmen who keep the peace are now partners, not because of instability in the Balkans but because of instability in Europe. As the journalist Norbert Mappes-Niediek has surmised: "Europe is the powder keg [and the] Balkans are the fuse".[25]

The political scientist Florian Bieber concurs with this sentiment but, importantly, reframes the issue in the context of consequences for local reformers: "if you are an activist … for liberal democracy, for a pluralist open system, then of course you are in trouble because your ally in the past has been the [EU], and now all of a sudden it looks like [the EU] may prefer alliances with more authoritarian leaders instead".[26] We may conclude then that the EU now depends more on Balkan elites than they depend on Brussels. It is a startling reversion to form as far as the phenomenon of elastic authoritarianism in the region is concerned. Rather than remaking Balkan elites, the Balkan elites have remade Europe in their own image. Why has the calculus shifted so radically? It is a matter of domestic politics above all. In the age of resurgent nationalism and far-right sentiment, if the Gruevski government in Macedonia, for instance, is able to stem the tide of Syrian refugees headed for Germany, Austria, and the Netherlands, then the insurgent far-right in those countries will weaken, thereby preserving the semblance of liberal democratic decency within the EU. To ensure this, these EU states will sponsor not only the hardening of southeast European border regimes, but will sponsor the stability and preservation of these regimes as a whole. And given that the discourse on refugees and migrants in the West has now become all but entirely reframed as a security rather than a humanitarian issue, such an approach can be deemed as (once again) prudent and sensible realpolitik. As a result, even though Europe's moral and political compass has veered sharply to the right, or rather towards accommodating authoritarianism and illiberalism, the official rhetoric from Brussels and the various member states remains as measured and optimistic as ever.

In one respect, of course, this approach is merely a continuation of the EU's well-worn policy of tolerating blackmail and protection rackets as legitimate local "stakeholder" activities, thereby playing the junior party in the relationship with Balkan elites. As noted earlier, this is an approach Brussels has taken more or less from the outset of its engagement in the region. Yet rarely has the EU so directly and explicitly endorsed the authoritarian tendencies of local regimes without even the slightest pretence of liberal sensibility. Witnessing Austria's then foreign minister, Sebastian Kurz, campaigning on behalf of the ruling regime in Macedonia in 2016, a government that had precipitated the biggest crisis in Macedonia since the signing of the Ohrid Accords, resulting in the largest anti-government protests in the country's history and necessitating the direct involvement of European and American mediators, was as astounding as it was telling.[27] So was the sight of far-right French MEPs parroting the talking points of extremist Serb nationalists in BiH, with whom they now openly associate, along with their joint benefactors in Moscow.[28] But Kurz and the French far-right are merely making explicit the spirit of Brussels' policy direction since (at least) the outset of the refugee crisis.

The 2016 migrant deal struck between the EU and Turkey was emblematic of this policy. Suddenly unfreezing Ankara's long paralysed accession process (or at least the promise of it), the deal was ostensibly meant to regulate and curb the influx of Syrian, Afghan, Iraqi, and various African refugees into the EU. In practice, the deal actually encouraged European and Turkish "policymakers ... to drastically cut legal corners, potentially violating EU law on issues such as detention and the right to appeal", that is, to violate their own core norms and principles to keep out of western Europe unwanted (i.e. black, brown, and Muslim) refugees.[29] This "potential" for human rights violations noted by observers at the time was already a reality, however, as the UN noted within days of the deal being struck. Turkish authorities simply continued to routinely brutalize asylum-seekers but now in the name of European civility.[30] For their part, European leaders could feign moral outrage while still reaping the political and electoral benefits of keeping the refugees at bay. More than a marriage of convenience, it was a betrayal of the supposed transformative power of the EU, as Brussels linked Turkey's renewed "European perspective" explicitly to Ankara's successful refugee clampdown.

Unsurprisingly, after the botched coup attempt in Turkey in July 2016, as the authoritarian tendencies of the Erdoğan government exploded into a frenzy of revanchism, the refugee deal became an explicit tool with which the regime now dictated policy to the EU.[31] Despite symbolic handwringing in the European Parliament concerning Erdoğan's draconian crackdown on journalists, academics, and the whole of Turkish civil society in the wake of the coup, the refugee deal remained (and remains) formally in place, meaning that the EU is directly sponsoring a candidate country's overt turn to authoritarianism. And all of this occurred while the entire refugee population that has entered the EU since the beginning of the refugee and migration crisis represents less than one per cent of the total EU population.[32] Indeed, the severity and speed with which EU states have back-pedalled on basic concerns with human rights and democratic legitimacy since the outset of the refugee crisis has been disturbing and suggests that the bloc will struggle to navigate the still rougher waters of the decade to come. Apparently the largest and most prosperous economic bloc in the history of the world is not only incapable of accommodating a minor spike in its overall population but its leaders are so squeamish about an almost entirely fictional transformation of "traditional" European demographics that it is in a headlong rush to abandon the most central pillar of the EU's existence in the first place – namely, in view of the centuries of internecine strife that have characterized the continent's complicated and bloody history, that genuine democratic governance is far and away the best guarantee for peace and stability, and that Europe can never again allow intolerance, nationalism, and, ultimately, warfare to grip the mainland.

This was both the logic behind the formation of the EU and the historical perspective which guided its attempts to incorporate the Western Balkan states in particular. Putting aside for a moment the manner in which the EU already abandoned those values in the 1990s in Yugoslavia, Brussels is betraying its principles again, and again it is southeastern Europe (along with Ukraine) that is ground zero for this dangerous hypocrisy. To be clear, the EU's toleration of authoritarian backsliding in the region was always problematic, as a question of both historical responsibility and practical policy, but since the refugee crisis it has become an undeniable threat to the EU as a viable political compact.

As the history of the Balkans readily illustrates, authoritarian regimes are inherently unstable. The appearance of their stability is temporary, rarely surviving one or two generations. Such regimes are certainly capable of mutating,[33] hence the deployment of the term "elastic authoritarianism" to summarize the modern political history of the Balkans. But even during moments of regime survival or reconstitution, violence, strife, and factionalism are the norm rather than the exception. Only constitutional regimes rooted in the rule of law, free and accessible democratic participation, and vibrant civil societies have shown themselves to possess true generational stability and longevity. And yet it is the nurturing of just such regimes that the EU and US appear to have now abandoned in the Western Balkans and perhaps in the world more broadly.[34] Ironically, they abandon the Balkans in order to preserve the edifice of liberal democracy within the European core, thereby embracing an inherently illiberal binary and zero-sum conception of the world. Democracy and liberalism are in the new calculus finite resources to be rationed and preserved for the Western heartland. It is a troubling replay of history. Where once European and American imperialists of the nineteenth century spoke explicitly of how only the white man was suited for civilization and free government, today these same regimes are in crisis because reactionary elements within their midst frame and reframe all manner of socio-economic challenges along explicitly racial, cultural, and demographic lines.

"Liberal technocracy"[35] – the supposedly post-ideological, managerial style of politics that the EU and US have patented since the end of the Cold War and have tried to export at the expense of participatory and civil society-focused forms of democratic governance – has proved incapable of mustering a coherent defence of its core values. Above all, liberal technocrats have struggled to defend multiculturalism and the universal promise of democracy as a right of all peoples in all lands. The retreat of substantive liberal democratic values, ideas, and principles in the era of Trump, Brexit, and the resurgent far-right means not only that liberal internationalism will not live to fight another day. It may very well mean its end as a relevant political project in the twenty-first century. After all, what kind of European liberalism can possibly prevail while democratic governance, however flawed its existing incarnation, unravels completely in the continent's southeast? What liberalism worthy of the name would allow the re-emergence in Europe of authoritarians and their razor wire less than three decades after the collapse of the Berlin Wall? Such liberalism is itself clearly in crisis, and the desperate illusion of security and stability to which it clings is its very undoing.

The rhetoric of values and ideals aside, why is the security of the entire EU compromised by Brussels' abandonment of substantive democracy promotion in the Western Balkans? How can events in the periphery endanger the core to such a dramatic extent? The matter is quite straightforward and the relevant realignments, those necessary for the re-emergence of significant security concerns emanating from the Balkans and protruding into the centre of the EU, have already begun. The political vacuum left by the EU and US in the former Yugoslavia is already being filled by a collection of new international actors whose foreign policy aims are not compatible, to say the least, with liberal democratic values. More to the point, at its extreme this new authoritarian axis has as its ultimate objective the dissolution of the entire liberal democratic world order. In this effort, the Western Balkans are not necessarily the most important geopolitical leverage point to realize such a realignment, but they are a useful one all the same.[36] Moreover, the mere attempt at leveraging or weaponizing this volatile region – as is clearly the policy of Moscow, at least – is itself dangerous. The manner in which the already failing democratic institutions in the former Yugoslavia may implode in the event of further authoritarian sabotage is unpredictable. Quite simply, in the age of precarious global stability, the chaos and chain reactions unleashed by actual democratic and state failure in the Balkans are a concern for the international community as a whole. An examination of the specific actors now active in the former Yugoslavia makes this point explicit.

Authoritarian Internationalism in the Balkans

1. Russia

Since the start of Russia's invasion and occupation of Ukraine, considerable energy has been expended by policy analysts and academics attempting to ascertain Moscow's next foreign policy gambits as well as the broader ideological turn informing Vladimir Putin's agenda.[37] Increasingly, the Western Balkans has emerged as a popularly identified "next" geopolitical skirmish zone between Russia and the West.[38] Despite this, most analysts have likewise soberly concluded that Russia's ambitions in the Balkans are relatively conservative: Moscow intends to play "spoiler" by complicating the region's EU accession and, if possible, halting NATO expansion altogether.[39] Ultimately, however, the received wisdom holds, Russia cannot seriously challenge the EU and US project in the Western Balkans because the region is already so completely dependent on Western funds and loans and already so significantly integrated within the network of Euro-Atlantic political and economic structures. Russian meddling, like Chinese or Gulf market penetration, cannot bump the Western Balkans off their road to Brussels.

Yet to assume that Russia is content to play spoiler in the Western Balkans is to ignore the determined revanchism of the Putin regime and the direct link it draws between its power and the weakness of its neighbours and other international actors. Moreover, this account dangerously overestimates the EU's ability (and the Trump administration's willingness) to defend, in hard security terms, its position and interests in the region. Recall Moscow's actions in Ukraine, Georgia, and Moldova, where the Kremlin has used direct and proxy assets to forcibly carve out chunks of territory to administer as breakaway satellite states; Russian interference in free elections across Europe; and the Kremlin's direct financial and political support for far-right and extremist movements across the continent. Vladimir Putin's Russia is no mere spoiler; it is an aggressive authoritarian regime with a reactionary but nevertheless sophisticated ideological and political programme to weaken and dismantle the EU and NATO. Moscow aims thereby to reclaim the territories it "lost" in eastern Europe and central Asia with the dissolution of the Soviet Union and, more generally, to cement itself once again as a genuine superpower.[40] True peace between such an autocratic and imperialist Russia and the liberal democratic US and EU is impossible, assuming both parties remain invested in and committed to their respective ideological positions. For European and American policymakers and analysts to claim otherwise is to implicitly give cover to both the Putin regime and its far-right proxies across the West. And to believe that Russia would not, if it saw fit, seriously destabilize the Balkans, as Ivan Krastev among others has observed, is once again to make policy according to preference rather than reality.[41]

That having been said, it is certainly the case that Moscow, with an economy smaller than that of South Korea, does not have the financial means to replace the EU or US role in the Western Balkans. But that is not Moscow's intent, no more than local Balkan elites have rushed to integrate themselves into actual free market or global capitalist circuits of production. Such banal monetarist analyses betray a profound ignorance of the deeper socio-historical patterns of power and accumulation that have defined these societies and, in particular, the views of their elite establishments. The Russians, for their part, are fully aware of their limited financial and strategic capabilities. For this reason, Russia has set about investing its resources not in spoiler effects but in wedge issues and the extremists who exploit them. The result, from Ukraine to Syria to the Trump administration, is inevitably chaos, both at the geopolitical and local level, as extremist movements of every sort have now been mainstreamed and set about attacking the foundations of liberal democracy and the liberal democratic world order. That Russia does not direct every aspect of these crises does not diminish the fact that it has engineered their appearance in the first place. Indeed, Russian engineering and sponsorship of the Western far-right, and penetration of the broader Euro-American political establishment, have been so effective and potent that micro-management of these assets has been unnecessary.

In the Western Balkans, this means that Russia invests in and encourages the already latent anti-democratic sentiments of particular elites. Chief among these are the Dodik government in BiH's RS entity,[42] the Vučić government in Belgrade,[43] and Nikola Gruevski and the VMRO-DPMNE in Macedonia.[44] This is in addition to the sponsorship Moscow provides for a host of smaller far-right movements, especially those in Serbia, which may not be electorally viable but nevertheless serve to pollute the broader public discourse.[45] In a sense, Russia merely provides the international muscle and recognition for these leaders' existing policies of blackmailing Brussels (and Washington) into particular political and financial concessions. The immediate objective is to deplete and undermine the credibility of the EU in the region among ordinary citizens, while simultaneously undermining support for enlargement within the EU, and maintaining a sense of permanent crisis that is seemingly intractable but requires constant micro-management by Brussels and Washington. And, again, Russia does little to provide a credible political alternative or financial substitute for the EU or NATO, aside from Serbia's growing military cooperation with Moscow.[46] But its stated objective of attempting to create "a strip of militarily neutral countries"[47] in the Balkans is one fundamentally incompatible with either EU or NATO integration in the region. Thus, while there may be no "positive" Russian project in the Western Balkans, the consequences of the Kremlin's anti-Euro-Atlantic campaign in the region are nevertheless significant.

Take only the purported Russian-backed coup in Montenegro in late 2016. The full extent of Moscow's involvement in the apparent attempt to assassinate Montenegro's long-time leader, Milo Đukanović, remains unclear months after the fact.[48] But the consequences for Montenegro, on the doorstep of NATO, have been clear: near fistfights in the parliament, resignations, violent demonstrations – in short, chaos. Thus the most minor investment on Russia's part (in this case, soliciting the services of a handful of armed goons) has as its effect political instability and scandalized and alarmist media headlines across the world. Montenegro, a state whose contribution to NATO is almost entirely symbolic (notwithstanding the alliance's now near full control over the entire Mediterranean coastline in Europe), is in the process recast as the latest geopolitical win for a newly resurgent Kremlin, whose reach appears to grow by the day. Yet the toll such operations take on public trust in legitimate, transparent, and democratic processes in the region is all too real. And this, ultimately, is the point of the Russian efforts: the piecemeal destabilization of vulnerable states and regions in order to deplete the resources and strategic capacities of the West. It is an exercise with far-reaching consequences and yet, contrary to the standard financial mantra, entirely unconcerned with Russian economic investment in Balkan industry.

But what of the local elites who cooperate with these Russian efforts to destabilize the Balkans, what do they receive? Simply, Balkan elites believe they can play the spectre of the Russian threat against the US and EU while receiving strategic tribute from both sides. To this end, in recent years, Dodik has dispatched his prime minister to plead for IMF loans,[49] while he travelled to Moscow to ask for the same from the Kremlin.[50] In Serbia, Aleksandar Vučić generally presents himself as the Western-oriented pragmatist, while Tomislav Nikolić took the role of the ardent Russophile.[51] After securing the Serbian presidency in 2017, Vučić will most likely continue to play both roles himself. Meanwhile, Belgrade also willingly participates in joint Russian war games,[52] and "humanitarian" exercises,[53] and eagerly solicits the purchase (or "donation") of Russian arms.[54] Skopje, too, once a leading contender for EU expansion, has since fallen far behind in the crawl to Brussels, and at present the VMRO-DPMNE party, the country's only recently ousted ruling group, is adopting an ever more explicitly anti-Western and anti-democratic tone.[55] Even in opposition, its ability to affect Macedonia's stability is significant, despite the apparently determined reform efforts of the new government. It is a path already successfully beaten for Gruevski and his party by Milorad Dodik, who was initially installed in power in BiH's eastern entity through direct US military intervention in 1998, only to reinvent himself as an ardent ultra-nationalist after 2006.[56] Even Montenegro, the former coup victim, plays the game. Milo Đukanović has led the tiny state, in one form or another, since 1991, during which time he has gone from being one of Slobodan Milošević's closest allies,[57] to a frontman for Russian organized crime and money-laundering,[58] to an ardent Western Atlanticist – and all of this without ever losing power.[59] Đukanović is elastic authoritarianism incarnate.

In a perverse way, everyone profits from these arrangements, though: the conservative establishment within the EU that is not entirely committed to EU enlargement in the region to begin with, the local elites who are likewise not truly committed to Euro-Atlantic integration, and, of course, the Russians, who are decidedly anti-EU and anti-NATO. Everyone benefits by keeping the region in a permanent state of fluid instability, that is, except for the ordinary citizens of the former Yugoslavia who are in desperate need of transparent and accountable governance, which remains impossible to establish under such conditions.

This delicate dance is also dangerous for the EU and even the local elite. As far as the locals are concerned, the broad contours of their objectives are obviously based on Tito's "non-aligned" strategy: the creation of a third, neutral bloc of states during the Cold War – spearheaded by Yugoslavia, India, and Egypt – to resist and balance the competing interests of the US and the Soviet Union. But the approach of contemporary Balkan elites fails to appreciate some important historical details. For one thing, Tito's Yugoslavia was a far more significant geopolitical player than any of the individual post-Yugoslav states or even the post-Yugoslav region as a whole. And even then, Yugoslavia was ultimately a marginal state. Indeed, for all of the marshal's bravado, Yugoslavia was for almost its entire existence a recipient of aid from both the US and the Soviet Union.[60] Yugoslav neutrality was on loan from both Washington and Moscow, to one extent or another, at a time of direct conflict between the US and Soviet Union and when both of the superpowers ultimately viewed it in their interests to keep southeastern Europe stable. While it was not the end of the Cold War per se that undid Yugoslavia, the end of the need for geopolitical balance did affect the country, especially in the form of the overwhelming indifference that characterized the West's response to the dissolution crisis.[61] The result was disastrous for the people of the Western Balkans then, and today the international climate is even more inhospitable to their welfare.

With American hard and soft power in rapid decline since the election of Donald Trump – more broadly since the expensive US adventurism in Iraq – and the entire European project straining as a result of the centrifugal forces unleashed by the Brexit referendum, Vladimir Putin's Kremlin can virtually taste a historic geopolitical and continental realignment. Importantly, from the Russian perspective, this realignment would be the result of direct Russian assertion of a sort unseen since the days of Yalta. It would signal, in other words, Russia's return to the world stage as a genuine superpower, a status it has lacked since the dissolution of the Soviet Union. Accordingly, Putin and his advisers (correctly) believe that the Euro-Atlantic project, the very existence of the EU and NATO, is one or two major crises away from collapsing entirely. Because Putin, in particular, blames the West for the Soviet Union's collapse and the string of "anti-Russian" colour revolutions across the post-Soviet region in the 2000s, he is eager to orchestrate similar scenarios in the EU and the US.[62] So far, the Kremlin has accomplished just that, through the proliferation of dozens of minor and major crises across the West, and in regions where the EU and US have strategic interests, the sum total of which has collectively eroded the foundations of the post-World War II international liberal order.

Both Brexit and the Trump election have advanced this agenda considerably and, accordingly, Russia views it as its interest to invest in and manufacture all manner of chaos that precipitates infighting and fragmentation between Washington and Brussels, and within Europe. While Moscow may indeed be a "regional power", as President Barack Obama opined,[63] it is a regional power that can easily shape world events when the West is riven by scandal and squabbles. Here again, the inaction and disagreement that characterized the West's botched response to the original Yugoslav crisis provides a good indicator of the kind of catastrophic consequences that further Russian assertiveness (compounded by Western strategic withdrawal) could have for the Western Balkans. Yet in the intervening three decades, the costs of similar mismanagement in the region have grown exponentially – as the internationalization of the Syrian conflict has likewise illustrated. Even though it may often be a slow burn, whether it is the Balkans or the Middle East and North Africa, as far as the stability and security of the West are concerned there is simply no longer such a thing as a "local crisis" or a "local conflict". At least, that is very much the view in Moscow: to never let a regional crisis fail to reach its global significance apex, or not deliver its full shock to the Western public's appetite for international governance, mediation, or involvement.

After all, in the 1990s the broader southeast European neighbourhood was relatively stable, notwithstanding the dramatic shifts that accompanied the end of the Cold War. The same is obviously not the case today. Much of the state system in the Middle East and North Africa has unravelled completely; Turkey is in a state of virtual civil war and on the precipice of outright dictatorship; Greece still teeters on the edge of financial ruin; the US has essentially abandoned its global leadership role; while the EU is internally fragmented. In short, the attention and perspectives of the Western powers are turned decidedly inwards, while a multiplicity of far more pressing crises than the fate of democracy in the Western Balkans dominate international headlines and policymaking. And yet the lasting instability of the former Yugoslavia, its craven and self-interested political elites, and their dependence on foreign sponsorship make the Balkans ideal for geopolitical manipulation. In a sense, given Russia's ideological and geopolitical aims, it would be foolish for it not to invest in further instability in the region, knowing full well that the Americans and Europeans neither want to nor can, at present, devote significant hard or soft power to stabilize the former Yugoslavia.

2. China

Russia is not alone in having designs on the Western Balkans. The Chinese, for instance, still largely a phantom on the horizon, are growing in influence. China's aims are in some respects less sinister than Moscow's, as Beijing is primarily concerned with completing its "New Silk Road" project, also known as the "One Belt, One Road" initiative.[64] Following its efforts in Africa to meet its growing demand for raw resources, China is interested in improving the basic infrastructure of (south)eastern Europe, which it views as a future entry point into Europe proper for its economic products.[65] The transparent corruption and cronyism that have otherwise undermined economic and industrial redevelopment in the region are not an impediment to China because, as in Africa, Chinese companies would simply import their own workforce.[66] And knowing full well how desperate local elites are for the hard cash needed to keep their failing regimes afloat, China trusts it will have willing and compliant partners in these efforts even if local citizens might balk at the outsourcing of desperately needed jobs to foreign workers. If anything, an overt turn to authoritarianism by local elites is better for China's way of doing business, even if Beijing has little interest in being seen to sponsor these transformations as such. Still, China does have some broader political ambitions in the region as well.

At present, China is building one of the largest "Chinese cultural centres" in the world in Belgrade, with a hundred-year plan for cultural exchange with and activities within Serbia and the region.[67] This grandiose (and somewhat comical) blueprint nevertheless belies China's serious interest in broadening its international reach. In practice, this means rehabilitating its image as a serious international player, one with a stable government and prosperous economic model, especially at a time of perceived turbulence in the West on both the political and economic front. In this respect, China is not interested in "imposing" its model on others in any overt sense but is instead keen to have its interests recognized and supported, especially by small, pliant states whose affections it can easily afford. The purchase of these affections occurs both through direct investment in high-visibility infrastructure like highways and railways, and the cultural and language centres, blossoming through the region, which serve politically to familiarize Balkan elites and citizens with China's interests and expectations.[68] The locals, in turn, are delighted at the attention and funds, especially as China's presence in the region still very much registers as a novelty and a lucrative economic opportunity for all involved. The first ceremonial marking of the Chinese Lunar New Year in Sarajevo in 2017, for instance, was attended by representatives of each of the country's competing political camps and was organized by the local Chinese embassy at the National Theatre.[69] This was a small but telling gesture in a country often racked by bitter factionalism and duelling boycotts: regardless of political or ethnic allegiances, the Chinese are a most desirable benefactor for all local elites.

As far as China's interests and expectations are concerned, as a permanent Security Council member Beijing is not shopping for UN votes. It is, however, eager to ensure (to cite but two prominent examples) that Taiwan remains internationally marginalized[70] and that its activities in the South China Sea are, at the very least, ignored. To this end, the recent South China Sea arbitration case at The Hague was a good indicator of China's interest in increasing its diplomatic pull in ostensibly marginal regions like the Balkans. Aside from receiving backing for its position during the dispute from the likes of Russia, Syria, Iraq, and Sudan, China's claims were implicitly and explicitly backed also by Serbia and Montenegro, respectively.[71] Slovenia and Croatia, meanwhile, helped to water down the EU's eventual statement on the verdict, albeit mostly because of their own maritime dispute.[72] Still, it was a helpful act from the perspective of Beijing, which, like Russia, benefits strategically from divisions among its competitors and their perceived proxies on both sides of the Atlantic.

While the support of these small states is not crucial for any of China's interests (although it does no harm to avoid embarrassing votes on the status of human rights, freedom of the press, or brutal occupation regimes at the UN General Assembly), these moves nevertheless further a kind of macro-objective – namely, to present more generally a competing, illiberal, and authoritarian incarnation of the international community: what Moscow succinctly refers to as the "Russian World" (*Russkiy Mir*) and which it has tried to formalize within the Eurasian Economic Union (EAEU).[73] For their part, the Chinese have tried to mimic the approach with their own claims to great power status and dominance in east Asia especially.[74] That such initiatives cannot possibly supplant the multitude of institutions and norms established in the West since the end of World War II is irrelevant, as this is not their point. Their objective is not to advance a competing set of "rules" for the international system but precisely the opposite: to reshape international politics, with the world divided into mutually exclusive spheres of influence, carved out accordingly by the respective great powers, in which they alone determine permissible conduct.[75] In other words, instead of twenty-first-century international community, both Russia and China ultimately prefer nineteenth-century great power politics.

3. The Gulf States, Turkey, and the Islamic State

If Russia's role in the region is actively malignant and China's is comparatively pragmatic, then the activities of the petrol monarchies of the Gulf are a third variation. Of course, the presence of the Gulf regimes in the region immediately raises the question whether there is a credible Islamic extremist threat in the Balkans. It is therefore pertinent from the outset to state what the Gulf states are not doing in the Balkans: they are not proselytizing Islam or financing extremist movements. Their presence is not entirely benign either, as these countries provide further illiberal and autocratic models for local elites to embrace and advance as counterpoints to the notion that economic prosperity is dependent on democratic governance. Troublingly, as the EU has already reframed its own presence in the Western Balkans in almost strictly financial terms, and amid persistent economic devastation, decisively severing the link between prosperity and democracy is both ideal for elites and acceptable to citizens. The elites are preserved in power, the citizens are promised jobs and pensions – an idyllic authoritarian arrangement.

The Gulf monarchies are investing in commercial and real estate opportunities in the region for somewhat particular but nevertheless transparent reasons. Like the Chinese, the Gulf countries are interested in expanding their economic linkages with Europe proper and view the Balkans and southeastern Europe more broadly as a useful launching pad to do so. The region's proximity to the core of the Eurozone is also helped by a degree of cultural affinity in the form of large autochtho-nous Muslim communities in BiH, Albania, Kosovo, and Macedonia, as well as Montenegro and Serbia to a degree.[76] This has especially spurred commercial and tourist investment in BiH, where Gulf Arab visitors represent an ever larger share of the country's growing tourist sector.[77] As of 2017, Sarajevo is home to a number of multimillion-dollar shopping and residential complexes built by Gulf investors (almost exclusively for Gulf tourists),[78] while Belgrade's largest (and most controversial) redevelopment initiative in decades, the "Belgrade Waterfront", is a $3.5 billion project led by an Abu Dhabi consor-tium.[79] The flag carrier of the United Arab Emirates (UAE), Etihad Airways, also owns a 49 per cent stake in Air Serbia,[80] while low-cost airline Flydubai offers nearly a dozen flights per week to Sarajevo. The Gulf Arab presence in the Western Balkans has become so economically significant that even BiH's and Serbia's famously acrimonious foreign ministries have taken to organizing joint junkets to the region.[81]

In this regard, Balkan states are especially interested in selling to one particular Middle East market: arms and munitions. Since the beginning of the Syrian war, millions of dollars' worth of arms and munitions from the former Yugoslavia have ended up on the killing fields of Syria, Iraq, Yemen, and Libya, with Saudi Arabia as the main buyer. In 2015, Croatia alone sold €101 million worth of arms and munitions to Riyadh.[82] Serbia[83] and Montenegro[84] have done the same, while Slovenian munitions have been discovered in Islamic State depots in Iraq, Syria, and Libya.[85] Arms traced back to the Balkans have also shown up in terrorist caches in Paris and Brussels,[86] and on both sides of the war in Ukraine.[87] Governments in the former Yugoslavia have feigned concern over such instances but the reality is that weapons sales to the Middle East, like tourism and property speculation from the region, are rare cash cows for Balkan elites. And as the conflicts in the Middle East (and elsewhere) continue to grow, so too will the flow of arms and munitions from the Balkans. Indeed, given the lack of oversight and transparency that Balkan governments afford to weapons purchasers, and the tremendous financial incentives to ensure that this remains the case, the region is likely to stay a premier destination for those in the market for mayhem.

Notwithstanding the fact that Middle Eastern states like Saudi Arabia and Iran financed a number of mosques and religious centres in BiH and Kosovo in the immediate aftermath of the Yugoslav Wars, recent commercial linkages (in terms of tourism and weapons) represent a far bigger degree of engagement and interest from the region in the Balkans. Thus, for instance, between 2005 and 2015 Saudi Arabia invested nearly US$300 million in BiH alone, while similar sums were invested by the UAE, Qatar, and Bahrain.[88] Moreover, the biggest recipient of Gulf money in recent years has not been Muslim-majority BiH or Kosovo but Serbia.[89] And while the total amount of Gulf Arab investment is still only a small fraction of what Austria, Germany, the Netherlands, and the EU as a whole have invested in the region, the social impact and visibility have, arguably, been significantly greater.[90] Consider only the Qatari-funded launch in 2011 of Al Jazeera Balkans, which, until the launch of CNN International's local affiliate N1 in 2014, was the first regional news television station with a mass market audience since the breakup of Yugoslavia. Today, Al Jazeera and N1 compete in a crowded media marketplace that also includes (in addition to popular European and American entertainment channels) Turkish- and Russian-funded news outlets.[91] Yet when combined with their mushrooming shopping malls and entertainment complexes, it is clear that the Arab states enjoy an outsized presence in the perceptions of the Balkan public.[92] And the political consequences of this public perception are only beginning to come into view.

Despite the overwhelmingly commercial nature of their presence in the region, concerns about Saudi (and Iranian) influence in the Balkans have remained since 9/11 and, more recently, since the emergence of the Islamic State group in Syria and Iraq. With respect to the question of Islamic extremism, it is a relatively well-known fact, for instance, that during the 1990s Iranian arms travelled to the Sarajevo government in the midst of the Bosnian War. These shipments came with the tacit approval of the US as an attempt to circumvent the UN arms embargo, which had demonstrably skewed the regional balance of power towards Milošević's regime and its proxies, who already controlled the brunt of the massive Yugoslav military apparatus.[93] The Clinton administration did not want to intervene directly in the conflict at that early juncture and so initially turned a blind eye to these shipments. Later, as US and NATO involvement became increasingly unavoidable, Washington shifted towards active encouragement of these transfers to ensure a degree of (post-war) military equilibrium.[94] The Saudis, for their part, are mostly associated with having looked the other way at the small stream of mujahideen volunteers who went to BiH, some of whom later became members of al-Qaeda.[95] And although the number of foreign and local self-identifying mujahideen in BiH's war-time forces never numbered more than a few hundred and at most four to six thousand individuals out of combined total of one hundred and twenty to two hundred thousand soldiers in the Army of the Republic of BiH (or less than one per cent of the total), it has remained a controversial and popular topic.[96] Popular, that is, primarily within revisionist accounts of the war, which falsely claim that the multi-ethnic Sarajevo government aspired to turn BiH into a strictly Muslim state.

Similarly, assessing the contemporary Islamist presence in the Western Balkans is best done in local rather than geopolitical terms. And in this respect we are once again forced to discuss the crisis of democracy and governance in the region rather than any of its symptoms, whether those are corruption, geopolitical meddling, or extremism. Thus the former Yugoslavia's weak governance regimes have resulted in weak and politicized security and police institutions which have impeded concrete counter-terrorism efforts. While Bosnian and Kosovar[97] authorities have arrested a number of returning (and local) jihadis in high-profile stings in recent years and foiled a handful of domestic terror plots in the same period (e.g. the attempted New Year's Eve bombing in Sarajevo in December 2015[98] or the plan to bomb an Albania–Israel football match in Tirana[99]), actual court cases have often fallen through. The recent release of Imad al-Husin (aka Abu Hamza) after seven years of detention without trial in BiH is only a prominent example of broader police and judicial incompetence.[100]

The result of this incompetence is a growing but misinformed perception in the Western press that the Western Balkans are a hotbed of Islamic radicalism.[101] In reality, Muslims in the Balkans have grievances, but these are difficult to divorce from both the specifics of regional politics and the structural socio-political dynamics affecting all communities in virtually equal measure in the former Yugoslavia.

Accordingly, in both BiH and Kosovo, the sources of the majority of Islamic State recruits from the Western Balkans,[102] the primary impediment to more efficient governance and policing are the secessionist elements within both countries, which are backed by Serbia (and Russia) in each case. The Milorad Dodik government in BiH's RS entity, in particular, has dangerously undermined the security structures of the Bosnian state, causing a near shooting incident between state and entity police forces in 2015.[103] The incident was only a dramatic example of a nearly decade-long policy of provocation by the government in Banja Luka, which has not only engendered a tremendous amount of resentment and ill will among BiH's Bosniak and Muslim communities but landed Dodik on a US Treasury Department blacklist in early 2017.[104] Despite this, the Dodik government still toys with the idea of holding an RS independence referendum in 2018.[105] Were this to occur, in 2018 or at any future point, it would inevitably elicit a response from the Bosniak and Muslim communities in the country, whose commitments to a territorially unified and sovereign BiH are viewed as an existential question of national survival – much as for the Jewish community in Israel – especially after the war and genocide in the 1990s.

If anything, then, the underlying issue fuelling resentment among Muslims in the Balkans is the progressive withdrawal of American (and European) security guarantees in the region, not their imposition. Washington's disengagement from the Western Balkans, in particular, has opened space for reactionary elements in Banja Luka, Belgrade, and Moscow to reframe the Muslim population of the Balkans as an extremist threat that has never been representative of the actually existing Islamic communities in the region, even at the height of the Yugoslav Wars.[106] Yet the sense of abandonment by the West on the part of Balkan Muslims is doubtlessly compounded and complicated by the broader Middle East crisis. In so far as a coherent conclusion about local Muslim perceptions of the wars in Syria and Iraq can be drawn, it may simply be "we stand alone". The desire for American assistance, combined with a sense that the US is nevertheless structurally to blame for the chaos in the Middle East following the invasion of Iraq, means that Muslims in the region are primarily suspicious of being drawn into broader geopolitical conflicts. Indeed, even members of the most conservative segments of the Islamic population, like the tiny Salafi community that has emerged since the 1990s, express a strong preference for local authorities to focus on socio-economic rather than geopolitical issues.[107]

Still, as events in Syria, Iraq, and the former Yugoslavia have all shown, ethnic and confessional identities can be rapidly radicalized in the right circumstances. The key to de-radicalization ultimately is to prevent the emergence of such circumstances in the first place, and, where they exist already, to create mechanisms for inclusive and participatory conflict resolution. In other words, democratic regimes which allow the full participation of all citizens are far and away the best security protocol. This prescription, however, is markedly at odds with the nature of elite control in the region, and therein lies the crux of the problem for the Western Balkans, not just as it concerns the question of potential Islamic radicalism but the potential for significant instability as a whole. The growing sense of frustration, anxiety, and desperation among ordinary citizens in the Western Balkans is not exclusive to local Muslim communities and is instead a latent feature of the political situation in the region as a whole. The lack of democratic and institutional accountability, the lack of socio-economic prospects, and the lack of mental health services (in a region with endemic rates of PTSD)[108] are exacerbated by widespread corruption, organized crime, the availability of arms, and drug and alcohol addiction. The result is a social time bomb with a short fuse and in search of a match.

This particular assessment should put the question of geopolitics in the Western Balkans into stark relief. What we are witnessing at present is the shrinking of US and EU influence in the Balkans and its replacement by an assortment of authoritarian and autocratic regimes. With the growing assertion of each of these new actors comes increased potential for significant instability in the region and all manner of security concerns for the rest of the continent. While each of these regimes brings with it particular concerns and agendas, the structural issue is that democracy promotion is most certainly not part of any of their programmes or plans for the region. Thus it is not merely a matter of one set of international actors replacing another in the Balkans; it is a profound ideological shift in values and norms. Or, still more simply, it is a dangerous combination of malevolent outside actors importing instability into a region already struggling to resolve its internal crises. If these circumstances persist, it is difficult to dismiss even the most pessimistic projections for the former Yugoslavia's future.

Here it is useful to cite a fourth regional actor, Turkey, to illustrate certain emerging trends. As the Erdoğan government began cracking down on real and mostly imagined coup plotters in Turkey in 2016, Ankara became particularly concerned with followers of the Gülen movement, the socio-religious movement founded by the one-time Erdoğan associate Fethullah Gülen. Once Erdoğan formally blamed Gülen for the coup attempt, Turkey began not only arresting followers of the movement in Turkey but seeking also the shutdown of all Gülen-affiliated schools and programmes across southeastern Europe. Within a matter of weeks, Ankara successfully secured the closure of multi-million-dollar Gülen campuses in BiH thanks to the close association between Erdoğan and the Bosnian president, Bakir Izetbegović, and called for the same in Macedonia, Albania, and Kosovo.[109] Prior to this particular situation, analysts had years earlier noted Turkey's growing influence in the region, especially in BiH, referring to Erdoğan and his then long-time lieutenant, Ahmet Davutoğlu, as having "neo-Ottoman" ambitions in the Balkans.[110] But Ankara's imperial romanticism, like Putin's interest in the region, was and remains mostly a matter of realpolitik. For Turkey this has meant leveraging various political and geopolitical concessions from Brussels and Washington by reason of its important geopolitical and strategic position between the Balkans and the Middle East proper. To this end, the Balkans have traditionally been a bargaining chip rather than a primary interest of Turkey. Yet since the start of the Syrian War and the 2016 coup attempt, Turkey's relations with both the EU and NATO have become considerably strained. Ankara's traditional support for the Euro-Atlantic integration of the Balkans appears to be waning, quite independently of whether or not Erdoğan's apparent rapprochement with Putin proves to be short-lived.[111] And therein is a neat summation of the danger of authoritarian regimes replacing democracies as the primary partners of the Western Balkans.

The internal and external policy positions of authoritarian regimes are inevitably synonymous with the preferences and whims of one person or clique and thus are lacking in procedural, institutional, and

participatory norms or durability. Such regimes are categorically incapable of advancing something akin to Germany's Ostpolitik and its
continuation in Berlin's post-Cold War commitments to the EU and
NATO – that is, a generational plan towards stimulating political
change and reform in neighbouring states through the development of
complex interdependence structures and regimes, ones widely
embraced by competing factions within the state who nevertheless
share a basic set of principles and commitments to stability (achieved
in Germany's view through the rule of law, constitutional government,
and democracy).

In contrast, one might say that authoritarian regimes practise great
power politics as opposed to foreign policy; they favour tactics over
strategy and short-term, zero-sum benefits for particular leaders rather
than long-term, positive-sum stability for complex polities. To the
extent that particular priorities can be transmitted through episodic
mutations of individual authoritarian regimes, the realization of such
aims is nevertheless compromised by and contingent on the extreme
patrimonialism of the ruling elite. And while the effects of these provincial forms of international relations have adverse effects for domestic populations, they primarily victimize the objects of their intrigue
– in this case, the peoples of the Western Balkans.

Conclusions

This, then, brings us to the matter of concrete outcomes for the
Western Balkans in the event that the region's primary international
partners become a constellation of autocracies rather than the existing
concert of democracies. In both the short and long term, the result of
such a transition would be not only the dissolution of all existing political and economic reforms, however conservative in scope, but also a
rapid reversion to profound instability. After all, no significant stability
can be guaranteed in a region that is politically fragmented and governed by weak and failing democratic institutions, and in which each
of those fragments is increasingly backed by rival geopolitical powers.
Add to that widening social and economic inequalities and cleavages
and widespread and easily manipulated ethno-sectarian grievances, and
we have a blueprint for chaos. Quite simply, the security, stability, and

political coherence of the Western Balkans depend on the maintenance of the Euro-Atlantic aegis in the region.

Imagine only the consequences of an (entirely plausible) scenario in the near future in which Turkey and Russia attempt to strike at each other's interests (as a result of competing interests in Syria or possibly the Caucasus) through their respective proxies in the Balkans. Or, even more simply, let us imagine overt Russian backing for further ethno-territorial fragmentation in the region, the basic framework for which is already Moscow's policy in backing the Dodik government in BiH's RS entity. Or, just as plausibly, imagine the effects of the accelerating Saudi–Iranian proxy conflict on the Balkans, if either of those regimes committed itself to "recruiting" the region's elites to its cause. The result of each of these gambits, as their architects know, could very easily be a rapid return to conflict in the region. While this conflict might not be on the scale of the Yugoslav Wars, with Europe already reeling from the blowback from multiple conflicts in the Middle East and Ukraine, and from growing security concerns in eastern Europe more broadly, does Brussels or Washington have the capacity to address yet another crisis in the Western Balkans? Ironically, given the broader geopolitical context, a failure to respond to such a renewed crisis in the region in a timely fashion would almost certainly have worse consequences for the West than the diplomatic and security failures of the 1990s. In short, the Balkans are a low-cost, high-profit target for any and all actors interested in sabotaging US and EU foreign interests. And it seems only a matter of time before some enterprising revanchist pulls that trigger or lights this fuse.

Yet it is also useful to think beyond these scenarios and entertain, however briefly, the idea of what comes after the Western presence in the former Yugoslavia. That is, can any single actor or even group of benefactors credibly replace the EU and NATO? From a strictly financial standpoint, the answer is obviously no. But it is from the standpoint of political and institutional arrangements that the authoritarian presence in the Western Balkans is most alarming. Like their regional counterparts, international authoritarian elites have an essentially primitive conception of politics and economics, structurally based around the idea of zero-sum interactions. Thus any alliances struck between such regimes are necessarily temporary, lasting only for as long as they meet the immediate needs of the more powerful of the respective actors involved. Accordingly, while authoritarian regimes often have networks of client or satellite states, they lack genuine alliances. In a sense, then, authoritarian foreign relations mimic the instability and antagonism of domestic Balkan politics – unsurprisingly, of course, as domestic politics have been historically defined by their persistent, elastic authoritarianism. Such politics is necessarily extractive, exclusionary, and conflict-prone, incapable of producing either mutually beneficial economic relationships or political alliances based on complex rules and norms. While the eventual causes of conflict in such domestic and international regimes are usually trivial, the results are devastating for entire populations.

Those in the Balkans who believe that the region would benefit from Russian, Chinese, Gulf, or Turkish hegemony would do well to review both the catastrophic state of human rights in each of these regimes and the discord in their various neighbourhoods. Such a review would also be useful for a great many policymakers in the US and Europe as well. The Western Balkans are relatively peripheral to contemporary world events but not irrelevant. And the weaker the Western position in the region becomes, economically but especially politically and strategically, the more central the Western Balkans will become to the security considerations of Washington and Brussels. For the US and EU, the costs of preventing a major escalation in the Western Balkans are still low, especially when compared to the bedlam of the Middle East. But that price point is quickly evaporating.

If events in the Western Balkans proceed on their current course, with the EU and US only nominally present but fundamentally unresponsive to emerging political developments in the region, then the exponential growth of authoritarian internationalism in the former Yugoslavia may be slowed but not halted. Basic democratic and constitutional norms will continue to deteriorate, a process that will be especially aggravated by the continued infusions of cash into the region's weak and failing economies from all manner of questionable sources from the wider authoritarian world. Given the double-digit unemployment figures across the region, the ability to keep patrimonial employment networks afloat is a virtual guarantee of power. Or, more to the point, it is a guarantee of power while there are funds to dole out and keep the populace relatively pacified.

Yet even with these infusions, the corrupt and clientelistic economies of the region are on their last legs. A shrinking tax base, the result of declining birth rates, growing emigration trends, and few viable economic sectors, is creating an unsustainable situation. The political apparatus, meanwhile, remains strangled by patrimonialism, preventing new leaders and movements from emerging through legitimate, electoral means. Of course, local elites are not ignorant of the self-evident crisis of legitimacy their governments face. It is why they have welcomed and actively solicited the arrival of new benefactors, whose assorted illiberal and authoritarian ideological programmes (even more so than their money) are the instrument on which local elites will lean to facilitate their next elastic transformation as they seek to survive the coming upheavals.

And upheavals, tumult, and revolt are coming to the Western Balkans. It is the only genuine certainty in the region in an era of great and many unknowns. Grassroots civil society and social movements have already emerged as a factor in regional politics over the past five years, as we shall see in the next chapter, through dramatic assertions of civic agency in Slovenia, BiH, and Macedonia in particular. Still, these movements remain small, fragmented, and sporadic in their abilities to organize sustained campaigns. And yet it is on them that the project of genuine democratic governance in the Western Balkans now depends. US and EU state-building and democratization efforts have created the basic institutional frameworks for constitutional government in the Western Balkans. While its practice remains impeded by local elites, its salvation and articulation are ultimately the responsibility of local citizens. Accordingly, whether these emerging social movements are able to overcome the obstruction of the elites is the essential political question that will determine the future of the Western Balkans. Doubtlessly, local elites will rely on a mixture of violence, nationalism, and assistance from their new foreign benefactors to survive these confrontations. It remains to be seen whether the US and EU will have the courage of their convictions and the strategic foresight to back and defend Balkan civil society in a similar manner.

4

THE COMING UPHEAVALS
IN THE WESTERN BALKANS

The most dangerous myth of contemporary Western Balkans politics, and the one most popular in Brussels and Washington, is that the present combination of democratic backsliding, anaemic economic growth, and geopolitical flux can persist indefinitely in some kind of stable form. So far, this book has focused primarily on illustrating the manner in which local elites benefit from such comfortable delusions and their still more reactionary designs emerging as the region veers towards the end of the Euro-Atlantic consensus. Largely absent in this analysis, especially as it concerns the fate of democratic government in the region, has been the role and agency of citizens – that is, the ability to affect the politics of the various polities of the region by those who actually constitute democracy as a system of social order: the demos, the plebes, the citizens, as discussed at length in the introduction. The omission is deliberate.

Civil society as a social phenomenon remains embryonic and underdeveloped in the Western Balkans. Its development, as this book has traced, has been purposely stunted by generations of authoritarian regimes in the region. In order to understand why the Balkans have historically lacked genuine democratic upheavals, it is insufficient to begin such an analysis in the late 1980s or after the end of the Yugoslav Wars. What is necessary is instead a detailed account of the complex origins and persistently authoritarian mutations of the state in the region, an analysis that recognizes the lack of democratic governance in the Balkans as the product of deliberate elite manipulation, preference, and policy. Compounding this domestic anti-democratic climate is also certainly the fact that in the last two decades support for the emergence of an autonomous and antagonistic civil society by American and European policymakers has been largely offset by their still deeper commitments to elite-managed "stability". In the process, the US and EU have played handmaiden to the bankrupting of genuine democratic reform and government in the Western Balkans, the one true guarantee of stability.

Yet democracy, while it is in its parliamentary form a complex set of norms, institutions, and processes, is also a series of ruptures and inversions, and a (relatively coherent) thread of moments of collective agency and revolt that over time transform how a society conceives of legitimate decision-making. It is a slow shift from the whims of the few to the deliberations of the many. In order to establish in the first place, and to preserve thereafter, parliamentary and institutional forms of democracy, a society must develop and maintain a culture of civic participation, engagement, and protest. When these are absent, democratic institutions either fail to develop or begin to fail. It is arguable to what extent democratic institutions and norms ever existed in the Western Balkans, notwithstanding two decades of multiparty elections in most of the region since the 1990s. What is unquestionable, though, is that we have yet to see the kinds of popular, sustained forms of social protest in the former Yugoslavia necessary for the development of a genuine participatory culture, one in which elites fear being ousted from power through both the ballot box or the street when they govern arbitrarily and without the explicit, sustained consent of those who are governed. After all, most democratic regimes were the direct product of revolutions or else revolutionary upheavals were necessary for the establishment and expansion of core democratic principles (i.e. the full franchise). Nor has the necessity of democratic revolutions and revolts abated in the twenty-first century, as the Arab Spring, the Taiwanese Sunflower Movement, and the Ukrainian Euromaidan have all illustrated in recent years.[1] Above all, substantive democratic regimes remain the result, as they have ever been, of the agitation and organization of the demos.

The central claims of this chapter then are twofold. Firstly, the substantive democratization of the Western Balkans requires that local civil society realize and make the shift towards antagonistic, popular opposition to the existing elite and that such opposition is, in turn, necessary to produce eventually new parliamentary representatives. That is, the process of civil society agitation must necessarily produce a multiplicity of outcomes that range from a shift in values and perceptions of the nature of government and governance among ordinary citizens, to the emergence of new social movements, political parties, and political actors. Secondly, there are reasons to be cautiously optimistic that we are in the very early stages of just such a paradigm shift. Indeed, the era of civil disobedience has already begun in the Western Balkans, and given the right conditions these existing and emerging developments may very well blossom into full democratic revolutions in time.

While such a claim may appear fantastically naive given this book's otherwise pessimistic tone (and the generally gloomy disposition of analysis and scholarship on the Balkans as a whole), it is a view rooted in a simple, fundamental truth about the nature of democracy: the rule of the many requires them to discipline and resist the authoritarian tendencies of the few. This process of popular disciplining is a generational one, requiring decades rather than years, and is susceptible to rollback and retreat throughout. The re-emergence of the far-right as a credible political force in the West should remind all of us that no democratic regime is so stable or so mature that it cannot be undone by determined reactionary elements. Nevertheless, the process of and insistence on popular accountability as both an institutional and extra-institutional phenomenon are essential if our aim is to change course in the Western Balkans from state failure to democratic renewal.

Political Vignettes

To begin with, what follows should not be taken as a definitive account of social movement mobilization in the region as either a contemporary or historical phenomenon.[2] Obviously, the history of democratic organizing and agitation in the Western Balkans is complicated by the fact that the dominant patterns of socio-political administration and accumulation have traditionally been decidedly authoritarian. Yet, as argued in Chapter II in particular, within this context important proto-democratic developments and episodes have nevertheless occurred. The refusal of the international community to harness the democratic potential and lived experiences of the workers' self-management regime in the process of post-war economic and political restructuring is a relevant precedent in this respect. Similarly, the still-nascent social movement manifestations emerging in the Western Balkans today represent a genuine possibility of democratic innovation in the region. But to succeed, these movements will require both popular local support and a fair hearing in the international community. The latter aspect of that combination is especially important as it concerns the significance and intent of this book. In fact, at its heart, this entire work is an attempt to provide a fair hearing for a different kind of analysis and conception of the Balkans – namely, one in which the defining cleavage of the region is not ethnicity but agency and the defining struggle of the present, as well as the past, is between those who have monopolized the exercise of and access to political agency and those who are attempting to redistribute it among the emerging Balkan demos.

Accordingly, we may think of the incidents of populist discontent that have gripped the region since 2012 as "political vignettes", akin to Wolin's "fugitive moments" of democratic articulation, in which the dormant capacities for popular self-administration explode into frenzied episodes of activity. In these instances, both those participating and observing such manifestations gain new social insights – receive vignettes – of new political possibilities and their own abilities to realize them in these societies. And in a sense, the more hopeless and reactionary the society, the more dramatic and important such insurrectionary moments become. As with the Euromaidan in Ukraine and its now oft-overlooked predecessor, the Orange Revolution of 2004–2005,[3] or even the Tunisian Revolution[4] (which begot the broader Arab revolts), the most dramatic manifestations of civic agency occur precisely in those places that are most deeply sunk in the muck of despotism, subservience, and apathy. After all, it is here that such revolts are most necessary and most deeply felt. Moreover, the assumption of apathy[5] (so common in the Balkans that even the term "politics" has a sour reputation and "democracy" is dismissed almost outright) masks in reality the teeming (albeit largely unseen) struggles and indignities that prepare the social terrain for almost certain ruptures. Of course, the success of any such explosions of anger and agency in producing lasting institutional changes depends on a number of complex and contradictory factors, which is only to say that revolution is no guarantee of democracy in and of itself. But sustained agitation and advocacy for a participatory redefinition of the phenomenon of democracy (and of politics as a whole) can produce revolutionary changes in time. And that is the juncture at which this work aims to intersect with the present situation in the Western Balkans.

Still, it is perhaps worth articulating from the outset an example of popular agitation and insurrection that appears not to have created sustained democratic changes: the October 2000 toppling of Slobodan Milošević in Serbia. Much has been made in both the academic and popular literature of Western financial and logistical support for the primary group behind Milošević's ouster, Otpor (Resistance).[6] Indeed, among the nominal "anti-imperialist" left in the West and conspiracy-minded apologists for authoritarian regimes in the "second" and "third" worlds more broadly, Otpor is synonymous with Western-engineered "regime change".[7] The trouble with such narratives, however, is that they are utterly historically ignorant. And yet their accounts must be addressed precisely because they have polluted so much of the discussion and discourse surrounding actual democratic organizing and its capacities for substantive regime democratization in the Balkans. At the very least, Serbia's experience with Otpor has been profoundly misunderstood by large segments of the international policy community and by still larger swathes of the local public.

To begin with, Otpor was an organic, local manifestation that grew directly out of the nearly decade-long student, anti-war, and civil society opposition movement in Serbia.[8] There had been previous attempts to oust Milošević through the mobilization of popular power, as in 1991 and 1996, but these revolts, as discussed in Chapter II, were violently suppressed by the regime. In other words, large segments of Serbian society were opposed to Milošević throughout his tenure, but it was not until 2000 that they were able to marshal enough popular and intra-elite support to eject him from power. His ouster was preceded by four disastrous wars, large-scale campaigns of genocide and ethnic cleansing directed from Belgrade, and the complete collapse of the Serbian economy. But, ultimately, Milošević's end came when he lost the faith of so many Serbian citizens that he became a liability to those segments of the elite, like Montenegro's Milo Đukanović, who sought to survive his regime.[9]

As such, Milošević's fall was both a moment of popular insurrection and elite elasticity — a familiar, albeit contradictory, feature of democratic organizing within authoritarian regimes, as previously illustrated in the discussion concerning nineteenth-century state formation processes in the region, as well as the New Left manifestations in the second Yugoslav state. And while Western support for the October 5th Revolution was logistically important (e.g. paying for cell phones, flyers, zines, banners, and T-shirts),[10] the crowds which the organizers convened for weeks leading up to Milošević's final exit were anything but manufactured.[11] Nor was there anything fabricated about the fact that virtually the entire Serbian political establishment implicitly or explicitly abandoned Milošević in his last days. And despite significant internal disputes among his democratic successors, it was Serbian police who took Milošević into custody and it was the Serbian government (then still nominally "Yugoslav") that extradited him to The Hague. These are not irrelevant details but integral aspects of what actually existing revolutions look like, complete with the emergence of messy, complicated, short-lived, and often self-serving alliances between disparate and (otherwise) opposing elements within society. Their success is not measured, however, by the romanticism of their declarations or aspirations but in the consequences of their organizing and mobilizations. By this account, the October 5th Revolution in Serbia was doubtlessly a major breakthrough for the democratic project in that country and the region as a whole.

Ironically, the authenticity of the popular opposition to Milošević's regime is best attested to by the fact that Otpor itself almost immediately and completely fizzled out after his fall.[12] Had Western financial backing been truly so decisive, and so strategically brilliant, then presumably the organization would have easily mutated into a successful political party. Instead, like many oppositional social movements, it was successful in mobilizing popular anger against a reviled autocrat and in opening up the political arena as a whole. But precisely because Otpor was, in the final analysis, merely a conduit for a heterogeneous constellation of anti-Milošević actors – including many Serbian nationalists, like Vojislav Koštunica who succeeded Milošević as the last president of the Federal Republic of Yugoslavia (FRJ) – it withered away once the strongman was gone. Since then, in particular since the assassination of the liberal reformer Zoran Đinđić in 2003[13] by a recalcitrant alliance of the security apparatus and organized crime figures, Serbian politics has remained seemingly in perennial flux, riven by political and economic instability.[14] Indeed, it is a central thesis of this work that politics in Serbia, as in most of the former Yugoslavia, have remained fundamentally authoritarian since Yugoslavia's dissolution and since the end of the Yugoslav Wars. Especially since Aleksandar Vučić's assumption of power in 2012, Serbia is definitely back on the path towards strongman rule.[15] So what significance, if any, did the October 5th Revolution have for Serbia's democratization and how should it inform a discussion that invokes the need for such spectacular uprisings?

While such questions are understandable, they belie a categorical misunderstanding of the nature of social transformation, one especially common in the region itself. As one might expect, living in impoverished, corrupt societies that are not yet one full generation removed from a devastating series of wars, preceded by nearly half a century of outright authoritarianism, many citizens in the Western Balkans are in essence psychologically immobilized by a potent mixture of trauma, frustration, fear, and resignation.[16] They appear to genuinely desire change, both great and small, but are unwilling or unable to invest themselves in realizing it. One dimension of this phenomenon is the persistently patrimonial Balkan economies, as previously discussed. After all, the livelihoods of citizens still largely depend on political acquiescence to the ruling regimes. A broader, sociological aspect of this perceived conservatism is the widespread, essentialist narratives popular in the region which hold that in the Balkans "nothing ever changes". These claims also fit neatly with similarly Orientalist accounts in the West that argue the region is one with too volatile a history and populace to be governed through institutional arrangements found in other complex polities.[17] That is, whereas legacies of conflict, persecution, and multi-ethnicity might be possible to navigate in the West, in the Balkans only partition or despotism are an appropriate form of control. These socially and politically immobilizing narratives are thus confirmed and enforced from within and without, the result being a kind of latent susceptibility to demagoguery of every sort.

In reality, the Balkans were historically incubated from the sectarian wars which rocked the rest of Europe for centuries, and it was not until the twentieth century and, arguably, not until the 1990s that there was a genuinely, thoroughly "local" conflict in the region, one whose origins and conduct were primarily the product of local politics, with no significant external drivers.[18] But such narratives persist in the region itself because they benefit the ruling elite and because they displace personal and communal responsibility for prevailing socio-political realities onto abstract notions of "history". In a sense then, they are a coping mechanism for a civil society which has not yet developed the tools to coherently articulate its opposition to the status quo. Moreover, lasting social change, especially democratization, cannot be distilled into one episode, into the toppling of one strongman. Democracy, in addition to its complex institutional and parliamentary components, is a continuous process of participation, deliberation, and (when necessary) protest and dissent that involves the society as a whole. As a result, it is a generational project, requiring decades (if not centuries) to take root and mature in a given polity. And even then, as recent events in the US and Europe have shown, retrogression is possible, even in the most developed, prosperous and stable democratic regimes. For the short-term prospects of the Balkans, though, Ukraine's decade-long interval between the Orange Revolution and the Euromaidan (and ongoing civil society agitation in the face of Russian invasion and intra-elite factionalism in Kiev since then)[19] is representative of the kind of sustained mobilization and activism necessary to bring about lasting change.

Because such sustained activism has been largely absent in Serbia and the region as a whole for the most part, it is odd to expect a greater degree of democratic "quality" than what is evident and available in the region. Unlike in Romania[20] and Ukraine, for instance, the Balkan demos have yet to truly demand self-made democracy and, as a result, we have available only illiberal parliamentary regimes backsliding into overt authoritarianism. Thus, the critique of the October 5th

Revolution, and similar smaller social revolts since then, as having precipitated few lasting changes is itself confused; as a critique of democratic agitation it implicitly reflects the need for greater and more frequent activism of just that sort, if the rule of the many is to truly take root. And, importantly, contemporary Serbian activists have recognized just this. Indeed, their analysis has continued to evolve and shape post-Milošević politics in Serbia, unlike the stilted (and deeply reactionary) apologia[21] of the former regime, which is at the heart of much of the anti-Otpor literature.

Accordingly, in the protests against the Vučić administration in the summer of 2017, the crowds explicitly likened the newly elected president to Milošević,[22] not so much because of their previous associations but because Vučić had begun to disturbingly emulate Milošević's form of governance[23] by clamping down on free media and on NGOs critical of the government, and by labelling large segments of the parliamentary opposition as anti-state elements. And although these protests were, in some respects, a continuation of the series of anti-Belgrade Waterfront re-development manifestations,[24] which have stirred the capital in recent years, they also represented a moment of maturation on the part of Serbian civil society (and youth, in particular)[25] in which the individual actions of the Vučić regime began to be recognized, and openly articulated, as part of one illiberal and authoritarian whole. Thus, regardless of their individual and particular views of Otpor as an organization, this latter-day generation of activists were clearly engaged in channelling the fundamental necessity and legitimacy of such mobilizations in confronting this would-be heir to the Milošević legacy. This kind of historical and political memory (or realization) is a heartening and positive sign for the future of Serbian civil society even if, in the short term certainly, the prospects for the country's democratic development under the Vučić regime appear grim. At the very least, the stakes and necessary responses to such a government are beginning to be popularized in Serbian society.

In short, democracy is inherently procedural and thus requires constant participation; it exists only as a process, not as an artifice. Indeed, its permanently unfinished form is precisely its greatest distinction, as "complete" polities are invariably the ones where contestation and deliberation have been artificially and arbitrarily extinguished.

Accordingly, it is now necessary to examine further the emerging forms of social mobilization in the region and offer some concrete suggestions as to how these movements might become more than merely disruptive. In other words, how can emerging social movements in the Western Balkans become genuinely transformative and revolutionary? While Serbia offers an important starting point for these reflections, the most striking examples of contemporary democratic organizing in the Western Balkans, both in terms of parliamentary and street-level activism and the fusion of the two, have been in Slovenia, BiH, and Macedonia. This is not to say that important struggles are not simultaneously taking place elsewhere, such as in Kosovo and Montenegro for instance,[26] but that for the purposes of this discussion these three polities are of special interest. As with the historical analysis in Chapter I and II, this examination of democratic activism in the region is not exhaustive or definitive. Nevertheless, the particular strands and patterns of organizing and contestation which the next section highlights are applicable to the region in its entirety and represent the foundations for an alternative conceptual framework for thinking about what is possible in the Western Balkans. Specifically, this discussion is an illustration of what is still required and is also achievable in terms of the region's democratization, as both a domestic and international policy objective, one that nevertheless remains a generational project that must be led by local, grassroots mobilizations.

A Region in Revolt

1. Slovenia

The current generation of Balkan revolts began in Slovenia in 2012. Notwithstanding some minor protests in the 2000s, which either targeted individual leaders or were confined to university campuses, the 2012–2013 Slovenian protests were the first since the anti-Milošević revolt in Serbia to demand genuinely systemic change. Ironically, or perhaps fittingly, the call for systemic changes in the region began, as in the 1980s, in its most prosperous and liberal corner. The cause of the protests in Slovenia was initially economic, a response to the government's mishandling of the lasting effects of the 2008 financial crisis and to Prime Minister Janez Janša's insistence (at the behest of the EU) on the continuing need for strident austerity measures to stabilize the economy.[27] But the protests mutated quickly into a rejection of both Janša's government and the broader post-Yugoslav political establishment, which had continued to dominate the country's electoral politics since 1991. As one observer noted at the time, "Janša is not the reason for the massive protests, he is merely the symptom ... of a much more fundamental dissolution of Slovenian political space, and the embodiment of alienation of politics from the people".[28] Instead, at the heart of the uprising was "the clear recognition that the state was hijacked by political elites ... The slogan that has accompanied the demonstrations since the very beginning addresses this fact very clearly: 'They are finished!'"[29]

This slogan, importantly, was taken directly from the October 5th Revolution, when Serbian activists rallied under the banner of "*Gotov je!*" ("He [i.e. Milošević] is finished!"), one that has reappeared throughout the region in the decade and a half since Milošević's fall. The slightly modified use of the slogan by the Slovenian activists signified a valuable recognition on their part – as activists in Serbia have realized recently as well – that the ousting of Milošević was not only successful and important but also that substantive political transformations required the ousting of entire regimes and establishments, not just mere individuals. Accordingly, the first street protests, initially numbering no more than a few hundred individuals, began in November 2012 in Ljubljana. By February 2013, there were twenty thousand in the streets of the capital,[30] a parliamentary expense report – which grew out of popular demands – caused the collapse of the government, and criminal proceedings against Janša began shortly thereafter. The true success of the protests was seen at the next general elections held in July 2014. These were marked by the emergence of entirely new political forces in Slovenia's parliament, hitherto a virtually unseen phenomenon in the region. A newly formed centre-left party swept to power, headed by a political novice, the law professor and former legal adviser to the parliament, Miro Cerar.[31] Cerar's government has not been scandal-free, as it was rocked by repeated plagiarism scandals among its ministers, an endemic problem among Balkan politicians (as noted in the previous chapter) keen to legitimize their administrations with the stamp of academic rigour.[32] On the whole, however, the new government proved competent and tolerable, notwithstanding trilateral disputes between Ljubljana, Zagreb, and Budapest as a result of the refugee and migrant crisis.[33] At worst, Cerar's administration has proved to be a functional technocratic regime, one which has kept Slovenia stable, even if its "post-ideological" or "centrist" veneer is more aspirational than actual.

But arguably the most significant shock of the 2014 polls was at the margins. To begin with, for the first time since the collapse of Yugoslav communism, Slovenes elected a self-identifying "anti-capitalist" party, the Združena levica or United Left (ZL).[34] Yet this ideological surprise obscured the real significance of the ZL: it was a constellation of civil society and social movement activists who decided to transfer their struggles from the street and into the parliament.[35] Similar efforts elsewhere in the former Yugoslavia had either consisted of attempts to resuscitate various incarnations of the different LCY blocs or were led by urban intellectual types, such as BiH's "Our Party" (Naša stranka).[36] In contrast, ZL was the first party initiative to attempt to shift from genuine street-level activism to governance and to do so while embracing an explicit (non-nationalist) ideological programme. While it remains to be seen how durable the ZL will be as a party, Alen Toplišek notes astutely that its handful of MPs have already had an outsized impact precisely because of their direct connection with Slovenia's civil society.[37] Accordingly, the ZL was instrumental in pushing forward Slovenia's recent same-sex marriage law, for instance, despite the fact that the option had been decisively defeated at a referendum in 2015 (albeit on a turnout of only 36 per cent).[38] Especially important in this respect has been the ZL's collective leadership model and the significant degree of internal democracy in the party, a reflection of the fact that ZL is in reality a coalition of several smaller left-wing initiatives and civil society groups. In the traditional party literature, rigid hierarchies and the cult of "strong leadership"[39] are prerequisites for electoral success. But in societies with long histories of popular disenfranchisement, it is transparency and accessibility that represent the path towards meaningful political alternatives.

Of course, by Western standards the ZL's success and internal dynamics are not particularly shocking. For instance, far-left parties have been a mainstay of politics in Scandinavia in particular, and western Europe as a whole for decades. They have been part of governing coalitions at the municipal, regional, and national level in many states across the continent. The European United Left–Nordic Green Left group within the European Parliament and the Party of the European Left both represent many of these far-left groups within the framework of the EU, including Greece's Syriza and Spain's Podemos (although the latter is not part of the Party of the European Left), whose various electoral successes have alarmed so much of the mainstream press on the continent. The lack of formal leaders, too, in the traditional sense of the term, has been a feature of green parties and politics in Europe for decades.[40] In this sense, ZL is not novel, but its transposition of a model of organizing and thinking about politics that has hitherto not existed in the Balkans is nevertheless hugely significant.

Specifically, one might say that the ZL's party model, and its position within the actually existing Balkan political landscape, anticipate or "prefigure" the broader social changes the party advocates, which, beyond their avowed socialist proclivities, are primarily concerned with substantive democratization – deepening and expanding opportunities for popular governance in Slovenia. In this respect, it is again local rather than international factors which are most important in recognizing the significance of this party in the Balkan context. ZL's "anti-neoliberal" agenda certainly puts it in the company of other far-left groups in Europe and, indeed, the party is a member of the European Left Party. But both the party's origins and its overall programme are difficult to understand without primarily privileging Slovenia's decidedly Balkan history, especially the lack of turnover among the political elite and the accompanying culture of corruption and patrimonialism. This is not to dismiss entirely the progress Slovenia has made in the last two decades, especially in terms of integrating its economy with the global market. After all, it was for this reason that the country was so significantly affected by the 2008 financial crisis in the first place. But, tellingly, in articulating a new political programme in the wake of the global recession, local activists ultimately focused on addressing the structural shortcomings of Slovenia's democratization process within the specific context of the failed post-Yugoslav transition.

In Slovenia we are therefore already witnessing the kinds of grass-roots initiatives necessary to begin a long-term process of bottom-up democratization, especially with respect to establishing a pipeline between civil society agitation and legislative activity. And here, again, the fact that ZL has done little more than emulate existing patterns of left and progressive mobilization, which have a proven track record in the rest of Europe, is an encouraging and important part of the story. It demonstrates that the Balkan polities, although the products of their specific and particular patterns of historical development, are not completely unlike the rest of the nominally democratic world. That is, the modes of social organization, agitation, and participation which have proved successful in other post-authoritarian polities (in which we can reasonably include Greece and Spain, even if their dictatorships collapsed in the mid-1970s) apply here also. Granted, there are significant differences between the emergence of anti-austerity parties in the wake of the global financial crisis and the fall of Europe's right-wing dictatorships in the 1970s (as well as the 1989 revolutions) and, in this respect, ZL has more in common with the former than the latter. Nevertheless, for the purposes of this discussion, what is important is that popular mobilizations have begun to affect Slovenian politics at least, and that street-level activists have shown their capacity to translate momentary insurrections into sustained electoral victories. That is a shift in the structural dynamics of Balkan politics with potentially revolutionary implications.

On the other hand, in the rest of the region socio-political conditions are markedly worse than in Slovenia. This means that more radical efforts are required to reach a comparable level of baseline democratic activism and progress. In this respect, the case of BiH is especially striking, a country where the very concept of citizenship remains contested. And while virtually every aspect of the general Balkan political malaise is especially acute in BiH – whether it is the persistence of corruption, nationalism, or the provincial, ever-mutating authoritarianism of ruling elites – the country is also for that reason the indispensable lynchpin of meaningful reform in the region as a whole. Indeed, it is no exaggeration to state that, as in the 1940s and 1990s, wherever BiH goes, so the Balkans go in their entirety. If and when BiH can be politically transformed, the toughest regional nut will have been cracked and, by the same token, so long as BiH remains the rotten core of the former Yugoslavia, genuine democratization in the Balkans will remain out of reach.

2. Bosnia and Herzegovina

In 2011, the BiH Constitutional Court passed a largely technical decision concerning the harmonization of personal identification documents. The ruling was part of a broader set of decisions necessitated by the country's complex administrative and institutional borders, further complicated by the practice of post-war name changes in various settlements (primarily in the now Serb-dominated eastern half of the country), war-time expulsions, and refugee returns. The central element of the 2011 decision concerned the issuing of the "Unique Master Citizen Number", better known by the local acronym "JMBG", a document akin to the American social security number. The court tasked MPs with drafting a new law and set a final deadline for implementation of February 2013.[41]

Immediately, representatives from the Serb nationalist SNSD (Alliance of Independent Social Democrats) demanded that the new law should designate distinct numerical codes for JMBG cards issued in the RS and Federation of Bosnia and Herzegovina (FBiH). The SDA and SDP (the Social Democratic Party of Bosnia and Herzegovina) rejected this proposal and insisted that the new JMBG should contain no regional or ethnic markers, like the country's licence plates. No agreement was reached in time for the February 2013 deadline. As a result, children born after 28 February 2013 received no JMBGs, without which they were effectively undocumented persons. Specifically, a child born after 28 February 2013 could not receive a passport. And without passports, children in need of medical treatments not available in BiH were essentially left to die in BiH's chronically underfunded and fractured healthcare system.

The protests that broke out in June of that year were peaceful and optimistic. Initially organized by parents of ill children needing documents to leave the country, they soon swelled and became a general social mobilization – quickly dubbed the "Baby Revolution" – comprising students, workers, and pensioners. Thousands gathered in front of the state parliament in Sarajevo and demanded the adoption of a new law. Protesters called for an end to the politics of division and chauvinism, creating a human chain around the building and refusing to allow the dignitaries inside to leave until they passed the appropriate legislation. Opting to use their bodyguards and police to flee the scene instead, the callous and uninterested behaviour of the scurrying politicians left the crowds aghast. Eventually a new law was passed, but BiH's famously loathed leaders had sunk to a new moral low in the eyes of a significant portion of the public. At the time, some observers called the gatherings a sign of a growing "civic consciousness" in post-war BiH.[42] In retrospect, a minor, albeit important, manifestation of still seething discontent would have been a more accurate description. Still, a kind of general social taboo against direct civic action had been broken and it further revealed the explicit contours of the post-war Bosnian political system, one in which even the lives of new-born children were fodder for ethno-partisan feuds.

Eight months later, on 4 February 2014, several hundred workers gathered in front of the seat of the Tuzla canton. In a city that was once one of the leading industrial centres in Yugoslavia, residents of post-war Tuzla now lived in the shadows of cavernous and empty factories and chemical plants. The protest was only the most recent in a years-long confrontation between the workers and local authorities. Shady privatizations had left the factories shuttered and asset-stripped, and the workers destitute. As before, the authorities refused to meet with the workers. The angry confrontations between the crowds and the police that followed were broadcast on national television that night. The protests were nothing new, but their militant tone was distinct from both the optimistic scenes at the JMBG protests and the rehearsed (if deeply sectarian) political discourse in BiH as such. The footage of infuriated workers attempting to push past officers guarding the cantonal buildings suggested that popular discontent in the city had reached fever pitch. Small, peaceful solidarity summits sprang up the next day in Sarajevo but these fizzled out quickly. But in Tuzla itself the crowds continued to grow, and by 6 February there were at least six thousand people in the streets, workers and students, women and men alike. The small cordon of riot police guarding the cantonal building could do little to hold back the crowds. That night, Bosnians and

Herzegovinians watched Tuzla erupt; in the ensuing clashes between the crowds and police, a hundred officers were injured and nearly a dozen cars torched.[43] It was an unprecedented show of popular discontent in post-war BiH and nothing of the sort had been seen in the Western Balkans since at least the initial anti-Milošević protests in Belgrade in 1991.

The next day, 7 February, protests erupted all over the country. In Tuzla, the crowds finally breached the police lines and torched the seat of the canton. The same occurred in Sarajevo, where the crowds went on to sack the state presidency building, torching police cruisers along the way. In Mostar, the newly refurbished cantonal building was torched along with the headquarters of the HDZ and SDA. Similar scenes played out in more a dozen other towns and cities across the country, and in Brčko locals even held the mayor hostage at one point. As the sun set on 7 February and running clashes continued into the night in Tuzla and Sarajevo, it appeared as if BiH was on the brink of a genuine social revolution. Over the next few days, four cantonal premiers resigned amid the chaos, as well as the director of police coordination – essentially the country's top police officer.[44] For the first time since the end of the war, BiH was headline news around the world, and helpfully scrawled on the walls of the burnt-out husks of the government buildings in Tuzla and Sarajevo were the proverbial theses of the events in question; in Tuzla "death to nationalism", in Sarajevo "sow hunger, reap fury".[45]

While the protests occurred primarily (though not exclusively) in the FBiH entity, aggressive pre-emptive policing in the RS was proof enough of the local authorities' fear of wider ramifications. Two years earlier, a small protest movement sprang up in Banja Luka to save one of the city's few remaining green spaces, known informally as Picin Park.[46] The issue started when a local businessman, known for his close association with entity president Milorad Dodik, was granted permission by the city to bulldoze the park and build an office tower. Outraged, locals and activists began organizing weekly "protest walks", insisting that the "park is ours". It was a powerful sight, this display of civic resistance focused on ecological and social concerns, bereft of nationalist rhetoric or symbolism, and contingents of activists from Sarajevo, Zenica, and Tuzla were soon arriving in Banja Luka to aid their neighbours across the "inter-entity boundary line". Everyone involved recognized the broader political significance of the marches, as the organizers noted in a manifesto: "[We] are in a time when the ruling oligarchy confirms that we, the ordinary people, are the biggest losers of the war and the transition. The oligarchy puts profit above people under the banner of national interest, personal interest above justice, and terror in place of equality".[47] They went on to declare their intention to change matters: "We citizens declare that we are not irrelevant, that the authorities are afraid of 'the street!' We are in solidarity on the basis of the differences by which they mean to divide us!"[48] In short, it was the intent of the Banja Luka marchers to disrupt politics as usual in their city and entity and thereby the country as a whole.

In response, the local police initiated a concerted campaign of intimidation and questioning, repeatedly accusing the various organizers of breaching the public peace while rarely formally charging them with any crimes. Minor infractions were met with vicious police assaults while both the city and entity government made it clear that the planned construction project would go ahead regardless of the public outcry.[49] Like the JMBG protests a year later, the manifestations in Banja Luka exposed that the political establishment in BiH, like their peers across the region, was uniform in its commitment to rule by fiat. The sight of armed police officers shoving and threatening mothers with strollers and dreadlocked students was a public relations nightmare for the Dodik administration. Apparently having learned the lesson not to allow matters to get to this point, when news broke of solidarity rallies in the RS in February 2014, the authorities reacted quickly. Attempts at rallies in Banja Luka, Zvornik, and Bijeljina were met with immediate arrests and a sharp increase in police presence in all public squares.[50] Privately, activists and residents reported police encouraging rumours that local hospitals were braced for a rush of casualties, strongly hinting that the police themselves were prepared to brutalize protesters.

BiH's political establishment as a whole had a great deal to fear from the spread of the February protests. Not only had some of the country's primary political institutions been torched by angry crowds but the act was overwhelmingly endorsed by the population at large. A 12 February 2014 poll revealed that 98 per cent of those surveyed in the FBiH and

78 per cent of those polled in the RS supported the demonstrations, and nearly half of those polled across BiH supported violent protest as well.[51] Clearly, the overwhelming majority of the population felt that elections were no longer a credible or plausible means of delivering meaningful political change to the country, and the direct mobilization of citizens was now necessary. To this end, the initial protests were followed by the creation of ad hoc, grassroots, public assemblies, first organized by a small group of students and workers in Tuzla but later expanded to Sarajevo, Zenica, and Mostar and attended by thousands of citizens in each of those cities. Not only had the citizens of BiH turned against their leaders, but they had begun to create new, parallel decision-making institutions: the directly democratic citizen assembly, or what they simply called the plenum. Whereas the Slovenian activists had bridged the street-to-parliament divide through the creation of a populist political party, the Bosnians opted for the creation of their own parliament. The move demonstrated, at once, not only a remarkable degree of popular energy and social solidarity but also the depths of general social disillusionment in BiH. Despite nearly two decades of multiparty electioneering, BiH's democracy remained moribund, unrepresentative, and illegitimate in the eyes of many of its citizens.

Theoretically, two points are worth noting about the emergence of the plenums. First, whether consciously or not on the part of the participants, the tenor of the protests recalls the political scientist James Scott's assessment of the vital role of popular insurrection in the creation of genuine democratic regimes. Scott argues that most "of the great political reforms of the nineteenth and twentieth centuries have been accompanied by massive episodes of civil disobedience … Representative institutions and elections by themselves, sadly, seem to rarely bring about major changes".[52] Even this briefest eruption of popular anger in February 2014 already opened genuinely new paths for democratic organizing as the plenums became the material articulation of Wolin's vision of the political as a "[moment] of commonality when, through public deliberations, collective power is used to promote or protect the well-being of the collectivity".[53] The plenum was the actualization of the political moment or, at the very least, one concerted attempt to establish something close to it. In short, the actions of the Bosnian and Herzegovinian plebes, though dramatic and frightening from the perspective of the international community's "peace implementation" project, were nevertheless deeply rooted in a substantive and legitimate articulation of the democratic tradition.

In the following weeks, citizens who attended the summits not only had an opportunity to air their grievances with the existing authorities, but, more importantly, were invited to participate in the formation of a new kind of political project altogether – an attempt to create a series of institutions that would become the elements of a new political society in which decisions were made collectively and directly through deliberation and debate. In the plenums, people came as individuals, not as representatives of parties or, worse still, of "nations". Everyone had an opportunity to speak, to respond, to share their concerns with the community.[54] The plenum name also obviously and deliberately invoked the memory of the old Yugoslav workers' councils. This was a recognition by the organizers that BiH, like the whole of the former Yugoslavia, did have its own experiences and experiments with democracy, which remained current and relevant in the minds of many ordinary citizens, and which could be usefully drawn upon and reanimated in the struggle to substantively democratize the country from below. But in place of the mere performance of equality, these latter-day assemblies attempted to be "a public space for debate, without prohibition, and without hierarchies ... the plenum will have a working method [but] it will not have leaders".[55] While facilitators were present to teach the rules of engagement in these new forums, the agenda was set by the participants themselves.

While the effort was complex, occasionally chaotic, and involved dozens of organizers and thousands of participants, the motives behind the plenums were eminently simple. In a country in which fourteen different parliaments existed but none of these represented the interests of the public, it was necessary to convene assemblies of the citizens themselves. Accordingly, the agenda and demands that the plenums did produce were of an almost exclusively socio-economic nature: they called for reviews of existing privatizations, annulments of pending privatization schemes, confiscation of illegally obtained properties, the resignation of all local leaders and, often, a wholesale return to workers' self-management.[56] While each set of demands was unique, clear themes emerged which cut across ethnic lines. The demands in Prijedor (RS) were virtually identical to those in Bihać (FBiH); ethnically mixed Mostar was no different from predominantly Bosniak Sarajevo or predominantly Croat Livno. Everywhere, the citizens demanded investigations of what they perceived to be the ill-gotten gains of the country's elites and the ousting of all local governments, the level at which corruption was most readily visible to all concerned parties. In other words, given the opportunity to engage in meaningful, grassroots, participatory political discourse, the citizens demonstrated that the constantly invoked "national question" that supposedly defined BiH and the Western Balkans as a social space melted away. What concerned them, what defined their lives, was not their presumed ethno-nationality but their material deprivation. And in this miserable abyss, there came a genuine epiphany:[57] ordinary Serbs, Croats, Bosniaks, and everyone else could recognize each other as equals and allies.

Much as the citizens formed a united front, so too did the politicians – against the citizens, that is. In the days following 6 and 7 February, the leaders of the SDA, HDZ, and SNSD attempted to spin the protests in virtually identical language. The cause of the protests, they explained, had not been the dissatisfaction of the citizens per se but the involvement of "foreign centres of power", a phrase that was repeated by all three parties. The SDA claimed the protests were an elaborate plot to marginalize the Bosniak people, the HDZ claimed the same in the name of the Croats, and the SNSD echoed it with respect to the Serbs.[58] As usual, each side blamed the other, but the construction was identical, almost word for word. Confronted by social insurrection, the nationalist blocs could only appeal to their usual narratives, exposing in the process the homogeneity of their actual patrimonial interests, as described in Chapter I. As in the nineteenth century, contemporary Bosnian elites, regardless of their presumed sectarian allegiances, were in agreement about their exclusive claims to power. Indeed, the very idea of attempting to blame foreign saboteurs for what was self-evidently a local, social insurrection belied the crux of their shared programme: that their rule was immutable, non-negotiable, and entirely separate from the actual preferences and views of the public. And they revealed in their absurd chorus that the suspicions and claims of the protesters in Tuzla, Sarajevo, and Mostar were correct –

namely, that BiH's existing electoral system did not offer a credible or plausible mechanism for removing these elites from power.

Of course, one should not overstate how transformative those few weeks were in the spring of 2014, but the sense that something had fundamentally changed in BiH was nevertheless strong. An interview with a senior citizen in Sarajevo observing the damage to the cantonal buildings in the days after the protests summed up the mood. Asked by the interviewer whether the torching of the building could be justified, even with the dire socio-economic situation in the country, the man responded without hesitation: "the only mistake [the protesters] made was not to suffocate everyone inside there. There was no point in burning [the building]. Wipe the criminals out, there is no other way".[59] The optimism of the JMBG protests had melted away and its place was now taken by unbridled rage and resentment at the political class as a whole. Even the plenums, though also a move towards discernible moderation and institutionalization on the part of the activists, continued to produce vitriolic indictments of the BiH elite and their disregard for the indignities of everyday life borne by the majority of the population. The country's political discourse and general climate had become polarized between the anger of the many and the vulgar unaccountability of the few. This fact was also recognized across the former Yugoslavia. The rage on display in the streets of Tuzla, Sarajevo, and Mostar sent shock waves throughout the region, with speculation running amok that the "Bosnian Spring"[60] would unleash a "Balkan Spring". Take for instance the remarkable warning issued by the Police Union of Belgrade to the authorities in Serbia:

> A "Bosnian Spring" has begun to spread in Bosnia – a far-reaching front of violent protests of the unemployed, the hungry, the neighbours whose rights have been trampled upon … Before those desperate people stand our professional colleagues, and it's their bodies that will take the anger directed at the incapable and corrupt government. The law of communicating vessels is not just a phenomenon in physics, but also in geopolitics; so that it is quite possible that the river Drina will not be wide enough and deep enough to stop the protests and demonstrations. It is completely reasonable that a similar scenario can be seen in [Serbia], where there are also many destitute, unemployed, or employed people not receiving salaries, with corruption at all levels, and political manipulation of citizens.

And then again, we, the police officers, just like our colleagues ... would find ourselves between a rock and a hard place; [we] would find ourselves in a situation in which we would be defending, with our bodies and our lives, the very institutions that have led us into this hopeless situation that holds for hundreds of thousands of residents in Serbia.[61]

The letter was as noteworthy for the striking anti-government sentiment it illustrated in one of Serbia's most conservative quarters, the historically regime-aligned police, as for the strident regional analysis it advanced. Despite the fragmented political geography of the former Yugoslavia and, in particular, the still-fraught relationship between Sarajevo and Belgrade, ordinary Bosnians and Serbians were still bound together by a shared experience of political marginalization and economic dispossession. And in this respect, the struggle of the Bosnians was also necessarily the struggle of the Serbians.

The plenums persisted until May 2014 and won a number of concrete concessions during their tenure – a novel success for Bosnian civil society and also the first time that such a sustained and autonomous civil society and social movement manifestation, which mixed both rage and policy, had emerged in the entire Western Balkans. This was an initiative that challenged the region's political establishments not through polite NGO panels or even elections but through antagonistic, revolutionary fervour. As a result of this insurrectionary dynamic, aside from an initial wave of government resignations the remaining cantonal authorities in Tuzla, Sarajevo, and Mostar were forced to take immediate measures to scrap the "white bread" policy – essentially golden parachute severance packages that were being paid out years after individuals had left government. And while there has been significant retreat on this issue since 2014, the protests nevertheless succeeded in stirring up sufficient public resentment that the topic has remained an albatross for local elites.[62]

In Tuzla, meanwhile, where the protests first erupted, the plight of the workers at the Dita detergent factory became a focal point for anti-government sentiment across the country. After they had been repeatedly locked out of their factory following numerous botched privatization initiatives, the dogged determination of the workers to return to work bore fruit finally when, with the help of a number of civil society activists, the group was able to resume production themselves.[63] Following the model of the "recovered factories movement" in Argentina,[64] the Dita workers essentially transformed their factory – once one of the largest chemical plants in the former Yugoslavia – into a self-managed enterprise.[65] In the process, Dita became a rare economic success story in the region. Despite (still) unclear legal status and persistent disputes with the nominal factory owners, the workers' effort was buoyed by a grassroots media campaign, urging Bosnians to purchase Dita detergent and dishwashing liquid not only as a gesture of solidarity but as an indication of the kind of paradigmatic socio-economic changes citizens themselves could precipitate.

The broader plenum movement petered out by May through a combination of police pressure and catastrophic flooding, the worst the country had witnessed in nearly a century. But in the case of the floods, as Asim Mujkić argues, it may be said that the plenums simply shifted their focus from political activism to humanitarian aid, much as in Tuzla a labour protest had grown into an insurrection, then morphed into the plenum, and finally returned to the labour struggle.[66] The unleashed creative energies of BiH's activists quickly showed their capacity for adaptability, shifting their focus from one elite-manufactured crisis to the next. With BiH's inept and cynical leaders squabbling over decision-making hierarchies and the distribution (i.e. theft) of aid monies and supplies, it was volunteers from the plenums that provided the first relief efforts in the worst-hit areas. In this, they not only circumvented the relevant authorities but, as the worst flooding was along the inter-entity boundary, activists again challenged the taboo of inter-ethnic solidarity.[67] In the process, as the journalist Gordan Duhaček noted, the floods and the grassroots response to them revealed an essential truth of BiH political life: "[That] that country is not actually divided between its three constituent peoples ... The biggest, and for the future of BiH the most destructive, division has for years been the one between two groups: the political class and all the others".[68] That much remains true of the region in its entirety.

As though to cement Duhaček's observation, in the immediate aftermath of the protests, the plenums, and the floods, the assorted BiH authorities were only able to agree on one major joint initiative: a $12 million spending spree on anti-riot gear and crowd dispersal equipment for the country's myriad police forces.[69] In other words, the

BiH elites recognized that their authoritarian and kleptocratic regime could be challenged by popular mobilizations, as both the Baby Revolution and the Bosnian Spring had shown. But rather than attempt to ameliorate the causes of public dissatisfaction, they opted to double down on violence and, in the intervening years, the politics of division, dispossession, and chauvinism, in a desperate bid to cement their dissolving authority. Their effort has proved successful inasmuch as we have not seen another outbreak of protests in BiH since 2014. Yet the structural conditions for such events remain present, while public trust in the static, sclerotic, and cynical Bosnian political establishment remains low. Thus, rather than having dispelled the spectre of large-scale social revolts, BiH's elites have merely delayed them.[70]

Disturbingly, however, as we saw in the intermission between the Baby Revolution and the February protests, much as with the Orange Revolution and the Euromaidan in Ukraine, the general sense of desperation and disillusionment in BiH is doubtlessly growing worse. And the result of that desperation is that the next time there is an appropriate spark, there may be far more chaos and destruction unleashed than the momentary burst of rage we saw in 2014. The EU's attempt to deal with this situation has been to usher the country through at least the first phase of the candidate process.[71] While this is, at some level, a pragmatic and well-meaning effort to further stabilize BiH's position and political situation through the institutional weight of the EU, the strategy does little to address the underlying crisis of BiH governance and that of the Balkans more broadly – namely, the fundamentally authoritarian and, in the eyes of many, illegitimate nature of the country's governing regimes. If these regimes and their corresponding elites survive the process of EU integration – as they have in Slovenia and Croatia – then, like BiH's own leaders, Brussels is merely postponing the inevitable social reckoning that such elastic patterns of authoritarian rule give rise to. Only then, as the experience of the Greek financial crisis has illustrated, will the ensuing chaos be of genuinely continental consequence.

3. Macedonia

In between the comparative ease of the Slovenian protests and the apparent invention of civil society from the ground up in BiH, there is a third example of an emerging democratic momentum to consider in the contemporary Western Balkans: the case of Macedonia. Like BiH, Macedonia is a country beset by sectarian cleavages, but like Slovenia it is also a polity where street-based civil society mobilizations have translated into parliamentary changes. While each of these phenomena has been somewhat less pronounced in Macedonia than in BiH and Slovenia, on the whole the country's so-called Colourful Revolution is another optimistic sign of the transformative potential of grassroots activism in the Western Balkans. Although the situation remains fluid, Macedonia appears at the time of writing to be on an accelerated path of democratic renewal at the domestic level and also in its relations with its neighbours. And, in both respects, this sudden reanimation of genuine reform efforts in the country is, above all, the result of processes initiated by grassroots, civil society, and social movement activists in the wake of the controversial 2014 elections.

At the heart of Macedonia's post-2014 political crisis was the government of Nikola Gruevski and his VMRO-DPMNE party. Although Macedonia's post-independence development has been a continuous exercise in "competitive authoritarianism",[72] with the centre-right VMRO-DPMNE and centre-left SDSM alternating in power, the origins of the protest movements which are of concern in this section are nevertheless the specific product of the post-2006 administration of the Gruevski government. In the past, each party used its tenure to infringe upon the freedom of the press and civil liberties, using the security apparatus and courts to harass political opponents, while installing their loyalists in assorted ministerial posts to administer the country's economy of favours and patronage. These alternating and duelling tenures between the VMRO-DPMNE and the SDSM have compelled scholars to use the term of competitive authoritarianism, or what I have elsewhere referred to as "fractured authoritarianism",[73] to describe both Macedonia's political system and the political regimes of many of the post-Yugoslav states (as well as the post-Soviet states, including those in central Asia). That is, while there has traditionally been a degree of intra-elite competition in Macedonia, governance as such has remained patrimonial and authoritarian.[74] Thus even in trading pole positions – mandates to govern – both parties have usually oper- ated as sectarian criminal syndicates, focused primarily on plundering the resources of the state and compromising the democratization of the polity, rather than acting as legitimate political movements with ideo- logical principles and objectives beyond their own self-enrichment.

Owing to this zero-sum political culture, fistfights and scuffles have remained a regular feature of Macedonian parliamentary politics,[75] while at the same time opportunistic nationalist politicians, primarily those from VMRO-DPMNE, have consistently sought to reanimate the communal cleavages between the majority (ethnically) Macedonian community and the ethnic Albanian minority.[76] As in BiH, instead of "power-sharing",[77] the experience of conflict and, in particular, the existence of an internationally brokered, ethnically constituted peace agreement as a central aspect of the country's constitutional order have encouraged elites to continue fomenting sectarian grievances as a means of preserving their own power and control. Where Gruevski and the VMRO-DPMNE have "innovated" with this formula is in their attempt to move Macedonia into the realm of one-party rule, perhaps more drastically and overtly than any other government in the region.[78] After the general elections in 2006 and 2009 were each marred by irregularities, the opposition SDSM flatly refused to accept the results of the 2014 elections, which once again saw the VMRO- DPMNE returned as the parliamentary majority under a cloud of fraud allegations.[79] In response to the opposition's complaints, Gruevski accused the SDSM leader, Zoran Zaev, of planning a coup against the "duly" elected government.[80] It is Zaev's response, however, that caused the dispute to reach international headlines. The SDSM leader released evidence that Gruevski's government had illegally wiretapped as many as twenty thousand Macedonian citizens, "including journalists, politicians and religious figures – a larger number than were bugged under communism".[81]

The ensuing crisis precipitated not only direct American and European mediation on a scale not seen since the signing of the Ohrid Agreement of 2001, and the appointment of a special prosecutor to investigate the wiretap claims, but, more importantly, the eruption of sustained civil society mobilizations that all but completely crippled the Gruevski regime's ability to govern.[82] The first protests against the government had begun still earlier, with the organization of student plenums in the fall of 2014, the result of both the dubious election results and Macedonia's broader socio-economic crisis, one which affected the country's youth – and their (lack of) economic prospects – in particular.[83] Clearly inspired, in part, by recent events in BiH, these mobilizations quickly left the bounds of university and high school campuses, growing throughout the spring and summer of 2015, as the full extent of the wiretapping scandal came to light. In response to these protests, the political scientists Florian Bieber and Anastas Vangeli stated the facts of the country's tumult bluntly: "Macedonia's incumbent government has lost its legitimacy at home, it is increasingly unaccountable and erratic, and poses a threat not only to the national, but rather the broader regional stability … Macedonia's government is no longer legitimate and has to resign as a first step for rehabilitation of the country's devastated institutions and economic system".[84]

This analysis was published in June 2015, but the fundamental illegitimacy of the government in Skopje had been clear to Macedonians since at least the time of the 2014 election. Yet even so, the truly frightening, violent ends to which the Gruevski regime would go to preserve its power were only made apparent in May 2015. Labelling the incident an "anti-terrorism" operation, but widely considered an event purposely orchestrated by the government, police stormed the northern (and ethnically mixed) town of Kumanovo in search of purported Albanian militants. The ensuing shootout lasted the better part of 9 and 10 May and caused the deaths of eight police officers and ten suspected militants.[85] Presented by the Gruevski government as a national security crisis, the action was instead quickly recognized by large segments of the public as a deliberate and dangerous attempt to derail an "all Macedonian" insurrection against the regime. In response, the protesters returned to the streets, this time explicitly waving Macedonian, Albanian, and Turkish flags as a sign of the pan-ethnic character of their opposition to the government.[86] As in BiH, where protesters had scrawled "death to nationalism" on the flame-licked walls of the government buildings they had stormed, the Macedonians recognized and rejected the Kumanovo incident as a government ploy to reignite nationalist tensions in order to preserve their administration in power. In a sense, after decades of similar antics, it was a rare instance of elastic authoritarianism caught in the act and summarily rebuffed by popular solidarity.

After a year of protests, with public anger at boiling point, American and EU mediators forced Gruevski to step down in January 2016 and called for fresh elections.[87] The gesture was purely for show, however, as Gruevski clearly remained in charge of the VMRO-DPMNE-led caretaker government. It was in response to this latest half-measure that the Colourful Revolution began in earnest, demonstrating a remarkable and hitherto unseen degree of sustainability on the part of any protest movement in the former Yugoslavia, notwithstanding the shifting priorities of the activists in post-2014 BiH. Focusing their frustrations on the "Skopje 2014"[88] project, a half-a-billion-dollar VMRO-DPMNE initiative to "revitalize" the downtown core of the capital with gaudy statues of Alexander the Great and faux Baroque facades for assorted government ministries, the protesters began pelting these eyesores with paint-filled balloons.[89] Aside from producing striking visuals for front pages all over Europe for weeks on end, the act was a perfect metaphor for the protesters' struggle: the vibrant, energetic release of democratic agency and diversity washing over the false, Potemkin-like facades of the Gruevski regime's claim to legitimacy. And after more than a year of protest behind them already, it was a signal that the Macedonian "indignados" – as some observers had optimistically begun to refer to the protesters – were determined to persist.[90]

During the height of this second wave of protests, thousands gathered in the capital, night after night, squaring off with cordons of riot police, demanding transparent investigations of the surveillance scandal (still obstructed by Gruevski's proxies despite the appointment from outside of a special investigator), public accounts of the slush funds that had financed the Skopje 2014 project, and resolution of the country's paralysing year-old political crisis. Importantly, despite claims to the contrary by the VMRO-DPMNE, the protests were not an SDSM initiative, although the opposition clearly supported and benefited from them. Instead, the protests represented a genuine articulation of civic presence and opposition.[91] If anything, SDSM leaders appeared to realize the need to genuinely associate with and democratize their party through the protests, at least if they wanted a real chance not only to form a government again but to survive as a relevant political entity in the new, post-apathetic Macedonian climate. Whether the SDSM follows through on its apparent democratic turn remains to be seen, of course, yet it is clear already that the party's relationship with the protests was not one of "instrumentalization"[92] but rather transformation. That is, the Macedonian protesters transformed what was politically possible in their country; they created new realities, new options, and new possibilities, and forced elites to react accordingly. Rather than having been the architects of this process, the SDSM were beneficiaries and appendages of this popular turn towards grassroots democratization.

Indeed, no longer content to allow their politics to be polluted by the partisan bickering of the two feuding blocs – while Macedonia's economy continued to stagnate into oblivion, driving one of the highest rates of youth brain drain in the region[93] – the protesters inserted and asserted themselves as the deciding factor in the country's governance and its overall political direction. As in both Slovenia and BiH, when democracy could no longer be reliably conducted through the ballot box, it needed to be demanded in the streets. Civil society, if it was to exist and to matter in the Macedonian polity and the Western Balkans more generally, needed to go through a baptism of disobedience, rancour, and antagonism. In opposing Gruevski, the Macedonian demos had taken a decisive step towards midwifing for themselves, as only they could, a genuine, substantive, participatory democracy, while offering their peers across the region a concrete model for their own mobilization.

After nearly a year of delays and stalling by the VMRO-DPMNE, new elections were held in December 2016. The VMRO-DPMNE lost ten MPs and, while again emerging as the largest bloc in the parliament, it now only had two more than the SDSM. The protests showed then that even stubbornly clientelistic patterns of voting could be disrupted, provided that activists demonstrated, as they had in Macedonia, a genuine critical mass of support for their mobilizations. The politics of the street was therefore not just capable of leading to parliamentary change, as the experience of Slovenia had already shown, but was indeed an intrinsic part of the process. As a result, soon after the election, the VMRO-DPMNE's traditional Albanian coalition partners abandoned the party in favour of the SDSM, repulsed by Gruevski's growing and desperate anti-Albanian chauvinism.[94] A familiar ploy by the party to once again engineer its survival by whipping up nationalist hysteria, the gambit failed as the Albanian bloc decisively moved to back the SDSM. President Gjorge Ivanov, a Gruevski ally, refused to recognize the new parliamentary majority, but his "soft coup", while equal parts dangerous and desperate, was never likely to succeed in the light of the combined pressures of the SDSM, its new Albanian partners, and most importantly, the looming spectre of renewed protests.[95]

Despite the obvious futility of its position, the VMRO-DPMNE orchestrated one last-ditch effort at maintaining power, when the party's supporters (and their enablers in the security and police forces) physically stormed the Macedonian parliament in April 2017.[96] It was yet another attempt to use overt violence to sabotage the democratic process, much as with the Kumanovo shootings. The ugly scenes, in which SDSM and ethnic Albanian MPs were physically assaulted, beaten, and bloodied, illustrated in sharp relief the desperate depths to which Gruevski, and Balkan authoritarians more generally, were prepared to stoop to hang onto their patrimonial regimes. Few seasoned observers, though – with the possible exception of Brussels' tone-deaf technocrats – were surprised by the scenes. After all, as this book has traced, in the nineteenth and early twentieth century, and again in the 1980s and 1990s, Western Balkan and Yugoslav elites had conspired to plunge the whole region into war and genocide rather than allow for the peaceful evolution of democratic politics. Since the underlying dynamic (i.e. the persistence of elastic authoritarian norms) has continued into the post-Yugoslav period, it was entirely expected that Macedonia's elites would revert to form when they were seriously challenged by the demands of the emerging demos. What remains unknown is how similar future scenarios in, say, BiH[97] or Serbia[98] – whose occurrence, as previously noted, is inevitable – will turn out. Much will depend on whether the Europeans, in particular, will be any more prepared to assist the efforts of local civil societies in confronting their entrenched and recalcitrant authoritarian elites. As Macedonia's experience has shown, constructive and determined international involvement can facilitate genuine democratic transition, whereas dithering, as in the 1990s, can result in disaster.

Throughout the duration of the Macedonian crisis, and especially in its final weeks, the Europeans and Americans released scathing diplomatic missives, urging Ivanov to respect the constitution and allow the SDSM to form a new parliamentary majority.[99] Curiously, the Austrian government largely stayed quiet on these developments, despite the then foreign minister, Sebastian Kurz, stumping for the VMRO-DPMNE in 2016. But as Gruevski grew more desperate, he increasingly leaned on the spectre of Russian assistance rather than his former associates in Vienna.[100] Like other Balkan authoritarians before him, in his moment of panic Gruevski attempted to turn from cajoling and cavorting with the Westerners to threatening them. And even though the Kremlin was unable to save his regime from what Moscow's media labelled a "Soros-funded" revolution,[101] they nevertheless gave him the diplomatic and political framework to further destabilize the region. Indeed, Macedonia's experience revealed how deeply committed Russia was to ensuring the "neutrality" of the region's EU and NATO candidate states, which, of course, in practice means the preservation of their authoritarian regimes. There is every reason to believe that Moscow will continue to closely monitor the activities of the new government in Skopje, and given the slightest opportunity, the Kremlin will sabotage – by virtually any means necessary – its efforts to move Macedonia decisively out of Russia's orbit and to break out of the familiar pattern of authoritarian reconsolidation.

All the same, Gruevski's government was not removed by Brussels or Washington and the fate of his successor will not be determined by Moscow. His removal and, ultimately, the future of Macedonian democracy depended on, and will depend still, on his continued suppression by the combined efforts of democratic forces within the parliament and in the streets of Macedonia itself. With his claim to power now seemingly definitely dissolved, the task remaining will be for the country's newly awakened civil society to sustain its energy and ensure that the new SDSM-led government does not succumb to its own authoritarian and kleptocratic ghosts. Macedonia's demos have acted as a social wedge and opened up space for themselves to conduct genuine experiments with the political. The next step, the one that will need to be repeated again and again, is to ensure that this space for democratic experimentation grows and that civil society remains central to all future political discourse and conduct in the country. In managing so adeptly the transition between the politics of the street and parliamentary procedure, Macedonia has melded the best and most optimistic aspects of the democratic eruptions in Slovenia and BiH. For that reason, the country's recent experiences stand out as a model and blueprint for the whole of the Western Balkans, a path to be followed if elastic authoritarianism is to be replaced with participatory democracy.

Conclusions

These three case studies of recent and emerging post-Yugoslav social insurrections and revolts are not an exhaustive treatment of the subject. I am aware that I have given short shrift to a number of important struggles currently developing in the region, especially those in Serbia[102] and Kosovo, where the situation appears to share some early similarities with what we have recently witnessed in Macedonia.[103] Nevertheless, the events in Slovenia, BiH, and Macedonia are the paradigmatic exemplars for the cause of grassroots democratic renewal in the Western Balkans. Only in these three polities have we seen the full articulation of the kinds of mobilizations necessary to effect genuine change in Balkan society, which remains deeply stuck in the muck of institutional and societal authoritarianism. To that end, it is worth stating clearly the lessons of these upheavals and what they suggest to us about the future of democratization as both a bottom-up and top-down enterprise in the former Yugoslavia.

First, it is true that conceptualizing these revolts as having already driven, and continuing to drive in the years to come, the region's democratization is a generous and optimistic reading of the events in question. However, it is an argument rooted in the broader history of democracy and democratization as a social phenomenon. Ultimately, democracy is a form of social administration and governance that can only take root through sustained local efforts and popular agitation. As in post-war Germany, outside actors can help craft basic constitutional arrangements, ensure the absence of active warfare, and prosecute war criminals. However flawed it may be, and such flaws have been discussed at length in this book, the international response in this region has proved that a process similar to the one that took place in post-war Germany has likewise occurred in the Western Balkans. This means that while a role still exists for a robust international presence in the Western Balkans (the Obama administration's decision to sanction Milorad Dodik in 2016 being one important and positive example), aside from the broader process of Euro-Atlantic integration, the era of grand international engagement in the region is over. Democratic consolidation, if it is ever to occur, must come from within and from the grassroots.

Because of both the long-term patterns of socio-political development in the region (i.e. elastic authoritarianism) and the particular fragmentation that has followed the Yugoslav Wars, we should not expect the existing elite establishment in the Western Balkans to assist such civil society initiatives. Yet we should also not be so banal as to believe that it is, or that it has ever been, the role of the state or the elite to bestow on the demos and the plebes substantive democratic regimes. Democratic regimes emerge when the citizens force concessions from the dominant power structures and power-holders in a society, when they win for themselves the franchise, and, through both this franchise and frequent resort to protest and disobedience, discipline these elites to genuinely represent and articulate their interests and demands. In short, no democracy has ever emerged or long survived without a vibrant, active, and autonomous civil society.

In the meantime, local Balkan elites are clearly engaged in a deliberate effort to detach themselves from the network of global liberal democratic institutions and norms with which they only begrudgingly associated themselves in the first place. The resurgence of authoritarianism and nationalist populism across the West has given them a new lease on life. But while they have lived to see perhaps the end of Western interest and intervention in the Balkans, local elites have not yet squared the circle of domestic discontent. Of course, this has been obvious for the better part of the decade. Although it was in the particular context of BiH, already in 2012 I wrote that a "groundswell of discontent" was as palpable in the Balkans as it had been in the pre-Arab Spring Middle East. Looking ahead, I argued that a "new social order which will ensure participation and protection for all peoples is the only option left … because all other alternatives have been exhausted … As neither the local nor international political establishment seems to have any meaningful intention of creating such a society, the task has fallen to ordinary Bosnians themselves. The time for a Bosnian, a Balkan Spring is long, long overdue".[104] The Slovenian protests began only a few months after that essay was published; BiH's JMBG protests occurred the next year; and by 2014, the "Bosnian Spring" showed that patient civility and apathy had run its course even in the region's most fractured and complicated polity. Though still evolving and still very much at risk of possible authoritarian resurgence, the situation in Macedonia has likewise cemented the essential validity of this claim.

Unless one is willing to accept ignorant and Orientalist accounts about the inherent backwardness of Balkan society, as static and shrouded in a perpetual fog of tribal resentments and superstitions, then the prevailing social conditions in the region are obviously unsustainable. Moreover, these social conditions should be the cause of significant critical scrutiny and analysis. Indeed, it is precisely because the dominant patterns of accumulation and governance in the region have remained primitive, which is again to say rooted in violence, coercion, and dispossession, that enduring stability in the Western Balkans has proved elusive. Yet the way out of the morass of the former Yugoslavia's persistent, elite-engineered elastic authoritarianism has never been complex. It has simply required the emergence and articulation of a genuine civil society in the region, demanding meaningful inclusion in the process of governance both through the ballot box and in the public square.

This claim is not merely glib sloganeering. To achieve such a democracy, truly generational social struggles are necessary. By way of comparison, consider that for all the claims of American democratic and republican exceptionalism, the full franchise in the US was not won until the passage of the Civil Rights Act in 1964. In other words, the legal right of African Americans to participate fully in the electoral politics of the US required, at least, the Civil War, Reconstruction, and the Civil Rights Movement – nearly two centuries of social struggle, above all, by African Americans to have their basic humanity recognized by the American state. And as recent manifestations like the "Black

Lives Matter" movement have shown, much work remains to be done. In the Western Balkans, meanwhile, where segregated schools remain common, where minorities like the Roma are almost completely socially marginalized, and "truth and reconciliation" remains aspirational rather than actual, these generational processes have only recently begun.

Democracy is not, however, guaranteed. The arc of the moral universe does not in and of itself bend towards justice, as the Rev. Martin Luther King Jr. famously declared – at least, not by itself, as King himself of course knew. Instead, the history of democratic government is the history of struggle, of the demos and the plebes, asserting their right to participate fully in the administration of common affairs. The process of genuine democratization, the process of establishing a regime characterized by participation and inclusion, is not defined by instituting and maintaining multiparty elections. This is but one shape, one version of democratic administration. Truly free and fair elections are, however, only possible when there exists a free civil society, independent and autonomous of any parliament or legislative body, a civil society that ensures the integrity and obedience of its representatives or delegates through continuous agitation and participation.

As noted at the outset, the argument of this book, in short, is one stated far more eloquently and pointedly by the great American abolitionist Frederick Douglass:

> Those who profess to favor freedom and yet depreciate agitation, are people who want crops without ploughing the ground; they want rain without thunder and lightning; they want the ocean without the roar of its many waters. The struggle may be a moral one, or it may be a physical one, or it may be both. But it must be a struggle. Power concedes nothing without a demand. It never did and it never will.[105]

What is most important to take from Douglass and the broader canon of radical democratic theorists who, as suggested at the beginning, ought to inform our views of the nature of democracy and democratization is the need for constant, continuous participation. Indeed, what the theoretical treatises cited in the first quarter of this book all suggest is that it is the process of social mobilization itself that is emancipatory. The protests in Macedonia, like the plenums in BiH and the mobilizations in Slovenia, have confirmed as much already. The social bonds and basic organizing skills that are developed during such episodes are critical for informing and shaping future initiatives. Thus, regardless of whether particular instances or episodes of social revolt fail to precipitate larger, structural changes in a society, these episodes still leave behind the ideological DNA for freer societies.

Democracy is a practice, a practice of the demos that, while perhaps only fully possible in episodic bursts, as Wolin suggests, must nevertheless be strung together into a coherent tradition if a society is ever to resemble anything akin to an ideal polis. And even in little lands, nestled between empires and hegemons, there are practices of revolt and dissent which we can call upon to inspire and inform future democratic movements. We need only to have the eyes and courage to see and realize the politics and polities that might yet be.

CONCLUSIONS

This book has advanced two broad arguments. Firstly, that the parliamentary democracies of the Western Balkans are in a crisis whose origins are rooted in two phenomena: the elastically authoritarian political-economic development of the state in the region since the nineteenth century, and the failure of US and EU state-building and democratization efforts to confront local elites who have reanimated and perpetuated these patterns and norms since the end of the Yugoslav Wars, despite the importation of liberal democratic institutional arrangements. Secondly, that following the Trump election and the UK's departure from the EU, the Euro-Atlantic project in the region is on its last legs. Accordingly, the future of the Western Balkans will depend on the outcome of a clash between patrimonial local elites and the region's emerging civil society and social movements. While the former are certain to be buttressed by a constellation of new authoritarian benefactors, it remains to be seen whether the latter will enjoy the support of what remains of the liberal international community.

In short, is the future of the Western Balkans democratic or authoritarian? Although the choice is stark, ultimately the essential thesis of this book is a hopeful one. Namely, if the future of the region is to be democratic, then it will require the activation and agency of millions of ordinary people working together to draft a new social contract for themselves and their peers. Therefore, the future of democracy in the

Balkans depends necessarily on the emergence of a politics that is participatory and emancipatory. In other words, the emergence of genuine democratic activism and politics in the region will be an end in itself and the act of creating such politics will present us with hitherto unknown social possibilities. In rejecting the arbitrary and larcenous rule of the few, we could unleash the creative possibilities of the many.

Yet if one were to judge the matter by international headlines, the only question worth asking about the Balkans is whether there will be another war. This seems to be the dominant concern in both Brussels[1] and much of the region itself.[2] Granted, this has been a consistent mantra for the better part of two decades, but since the premise of this book has been to examine the structural factors driving politics in the Balkans, this perennial question must be dealt with – not to answer it, but to ask why it persists. Namely, why is this the only question being asked about the future of the Western Balkans and, by extension, what other questions are therefore not being asked?

The Prussian military theorist and general Carl von Clausewitz famously explained that "war is a mere continuation of policy by other means".[3] What Yugoslavia's dissolution suggests is that while this is technically true, in that the question of "who gets what, when, and how"[4] is still being decided during periods of conflict, the only salient portion of this formulation in times of war is the "who". Who are the parties in society with the agency and power to determine the distribution of rights and goods? In this respect, we must recognize that war is necessarily an exercise in authoritarianism. In war it is those with the superiority of arms who decide all of these questions, including whether those without arms are permitted the right to life. Moreover, wars are in almost every case the product of decisions taken exclusively among elites, and their consequences disproportionately affect the lives and wellbeing of those who have the least say in the commencement of such "policy by other means". Wars may therefore represent the continuation of policy and politics of one sort or another, but they universally signify the extinguishing of the political.

None of this means that democratic regimes are incapable of dissolving into armed conflict. But it is indeed a process of dissolution that takes place in such scenarios. Once partisan disputes within a society can no longer be resolved through democratic means, then that polity has, by definition, ceased to be a democracy. What generally keeps democracies from unravelling in this manner, however, is that these regimes radically redistribute power in society, making the kind of elite manipulation and domination necessary for armed conflict less likely. By fragmenting the amount of power any one person or group of people can wield at one time, genuinely democratic systems increase both opportunities for power-sharing and opportunities for conflict resolution.

This claim should not, however, be confused for what has been the fashion in the Western Balkans, as practised by both local and international elites, since at least 1974: fragmentation without democratization. The claim that ethnic partition or homogeneity leads to democratization and stability is as ignorant as it is dangerous. If these claims were true, North Korea, one of the most ethnically homogeneous societies on the planet, would not be the last remaining totalitarian regime on earth. Similarly, Hungary, Belarus, Azerbaijan, and Saudi Arabia, each remarkably ethnically homogeneous states, run the gamut from illiberal democracy to reactionary theocracy with not a single stable constitutional regime in any of them. In contrast, Canada, Brazil, and South Africa are some of the most diverse and multicultural societies in the world. Yet, according to Freedom House, they are also some of the most democratic, notwithstanding significant variation in the quality of democracy within this bloc.[5]

Moreover, ethnic, communal, confessional, and racial identities are inherently fluid and are, for the most part, determined by rather than being the determinants of broader socio-political confrontations.[6] This makes policymaking on the assumption of static identity a fool's errand of the highest order. The absurdity is only heightened further when we recall that, traditionally, the biggest proponents of ethnic politics in the Balkans (and the world more generally) have been some of history's most prolific mass murderers. And while arguments for partition in the Balkans, Ukraine, Syria, Iraq and so on are not necessarily arguments for genocide and ethnic cleansing, they are certainly arguments for authoritarianism, despite claims of the best of intentions by advocates. After all, whether a polity is democratic depends not on demographics but on the extent of substantive opportunities for participation, advocacy, and agency afforded to the people in that society. Claiming otherwise is to give cover to those who use nationalist politics as a veneer for authoritarianism and all of its accompanying political and economic ills. Furthermore, if ethnic majoritarianism were a guarantee of (or requirement for) democracy, the large-scale remaking of regional demographics during the 1990s[7] should have resulted in stable, prosperous, and democratic polities after the war. Instead, as this book has shown, the post-Yugoslav statelets of the Western Balkans, much like their post-Ottoman and post-Austro-Hungarian predecessors, are little more than glorified Bantustans.[8]

Actually existing democracies too, can be sabotaged and undone in this manner. As all societies are replete with diversities which in times of crisis may be reframed as cleavages, segments of the demos and the plebes can become a mob and opportunistic demagogues can easily direct these mobs to truly horrific ends. Political theorists have known as much for generations, which is why the mob and the demagogue are ever-present spectres from Plato to James Madison, from Emma Goldman to Hannah Arendt. And yet their respective answers about how to protect the polis from these threats have differed markedly. Plato rejected democracy outright, favouring instead the despotism of enlightened philosopher-kings; Madison favoured a constitutional republic with regular elections; Goldman rejected the state and opted for radical direct democracy; and Arendt contained multitudes but was above all a critic of totalitarianism and fascism, seeing in these manifestations the darkest abyss to which even the most enlightened societies could succumb in the right circumstances.

Each of these theorists represents philosophical traditions which have, to various degrees and at various times, influenced our thinking about the nature of democratic governance. As the liberal democratic world order is consumed by disputes and factionalism, as all around the forces of authoritarianism and chauvinism appear ascendant, the mutual contradictions and disagreements of our philosophical predecessors appear to confirm that true democracy is, as Sheldon Wolin suggests, fugitive and possible only in episodic and momentary bursts. To conclude, however, that democracy is therefore destined to be continuously extinguished, even if it is likewise continuously reborn, is to fundamentally misunderstand both Wolin and the notion of participatory democracy as a whole.

CONCLUSIONS

Wolin's conception of democracy is not fugitive because it is only possible in episodic bursts of popular energy per se, but because these moments are necessary for the demos and the plebes to reclaim and reassert the participatory and insurrectionary character of democracy. To this end, James Scott argues compellingly that "most revolutions are not the work of revolutionary parties but the precipitate of spontaneous and improvised action ... the great emancipatory gains for human freedom have not been the result of orderly, institutional procedures but of disorderly, unpredictable, spontaneous action cracking open the social order from below".[9] In other words, democracy is a process even when it consists of protest and tumult, and its vitality ebbs and flows depending on the degree and quality of popular participation, regardless of its form. To the extent that it is possible to found republics on the rule of law and constitutional procedure, such arrangements, both Wolin and Scott caution us, must continue to allow for the full participation of all persons in a multiplicity of forms and the expansion of our definition of who is and may become a democratic agent.

These theories may appear like self-important theoretical ruminations but they are the essential principles of democracy as a social experience, on which both parliaments and free societies depend. And they are, more importantly, the kinds of discussions that are foreclosed by the constant, immobilizing chorus that asks when there will be another war in the Balkans. It is not an exaggeration to say that it is an act of psychological terror to hang this rhetorical sword constantly over the heads of the peoples of the Western Balkans. In fact, it is precisely why local elites encourage this question in the first place: to terrorize and thus pacify the impoverished and traumatized masses over which they rule. But American and European policymakers and journalists are not innocent in this regard either. After nearly three decades of international presence in the region, countless newspaper and academic articles, books and documentaries, policy summits and cultural exchanges, how is it possible that war (and not even the actually existing wars of the past, but some future, imagined wars) is all that any of them can articulate as a relevant concern for the future?

Obviously, as this book itself has shown, real and urgent concerns exist about the political stability of the Western Balkans. But to think about these issues strictly through the lens of war and conflict is not actually to address them, and amounts instead to a failure of imagination. The same might be said of those who can only imagine and speak of policy and politics in connection with war. The international community has tried to pacify the Western Balkans for nearly three decades, and in the process it has traded every value, every norm, and every procedure for the privilege of vague promises from local elites that they will not revert to conflict as a means of securing their claims to power. Unsurprisingly, we have talked of virtually nothing but war during this entire period. Brussels and Washington may be frustrated as a result, but the people of the Balkans are desperate – desperate for a new politics.

We can be sure that in the coming years, this desperation will transform into fury. After all, too many promises have been betrayed by both the West and the local elites for anyone to seriously believe in any truly new agenda that will not have as its fundamental starting point the washing away of the old order in the Balkans. As a result, this fury will be terrifying and it will rip open the social terrain of the Western Balkans. But this storm will also have been a long time coming and, if we allow it to, it will leave in its wake fresh soil from which genuinely reformed societies may emerge. Indeed, it is the only way that a substantive shift from authoritarianism to democracy has ever occurred.

NOTES

INTRODUCTION

1 Hirschfeld, Katherine, *Gangster States: Organized Crime, Kleptocracy and Political Collapse*, New York: Palgrave Macmillan, 2015.

2 I am aware of the vagueness of "the West" as a conceptual category. Aside from Edward Said's seminal deconstruction of the categories of both "the East" ("the Orient") and "the West", Liah Greenfeld, in her classic *Nationalism: Five Roads to Modernity*, also convincingly argues that Western modernity was initially a localized, English phenomenon that can be traced to that country's social and political transformation in the seventeenth century. Only later did France, Germany, and other European states join the political and cultural space of what would later become known as "the West," as each followed its own paths to "modernity". While both Said's and Greenfeld's insistence on the historically contingent nature of the term is well taken, it is also no doubt the case that to speak of the West today is to definitively gesture at a relatively coherent collection of societies. Accordingly, I use the term to refer to the western European states, plus the settler-colonial states founded by British imperialists – specifically, the US, Canada, Australia, and New Zealand – in other words, the prosperous, stable parliamentary democratic regimes that dominate both the world's economy and geopolitics. See: Greenfeld, Liah, *Nationalism: Five Roads to Modernity*, Cambridge and London: Harvard University Press, 1993.

3 A recent neologism, the term "Western Balkans" is primarily employed by policy wonks within the EU and US foreign policy establishments. It is a term meant to avoid the (supposed) anachronism of consistently referring to the region as "the former Yugoslavia" while also including Albania in all future EU (and NATO) negotiations. Yet in practice the Western Balkans is a term simply for the non-EU states of southeastern Europe: BiH, Montenegro, Serbia, Kosovo, Macedonia, and Albania – but not Turkey. The term generally does not include Slovenia or Croatia for no reason other than their (quite recent) EU membership. Nor does any relevant Euro-Atlantic institution or body refer to the existence of an "Eastern Balkans", although Bulgaria

is occasionally considered part of the "Eastern Mediterranean", which also includes Greece and Turkey. These peculiar distinctions, of course, reflect a broader and older ambiguity, if not outright hostility, towards the whole notion of "the Balkans" as a distinct social and historical space. While this book will occasionally refer to the Western Balkans, I should stress from the onset that for my purposes, the Balkans are a distinct region of Europe, with a rich and inexorably intertwined history (and future). I understand the Balkans to include Slovenia, Croatia, BiH, Montenegro, Serbia, Kosovo, Macedonia, Bulgaria, Romania, Greece, and Turkey, while a strong case could also be made for the historic (if not geographic) connectedness of Austria and Hungary to the region as well. For the standard introduction to anti-Balkan sentiments in the West, interested readers should consult: Todorova, Maria, *Imagining the Balkans*, Oxford: Oxford University Press, 2009.

4 The most noteworthy exception here is the anti-Milošević Otpor movement in Serbia in the late 1990s and early 2000s. I will deal with this movement in more detail in Chapter III.

5 Kenney, Padraic, *A Carnival of Revolution: Central Europe 1989*, Princeton: Princeton University Press, 2002.

6 Kaplan, Robert D., *Balkan Ghosts: A Journey Through History*, New York: Picador, St. Martin's Press, 2005.

7 Štiks, Igor and Jo Shaw, *Citizenship after Yugoslavia*, London and New York: Routledge, 2013.

8 Breaugh, Martin, *The Plebeian Experience: A Discontinuous History of Political Freedom*, New York: Columbia University Press, 2013, p. xv.

9 Ibid., p. xviiii.

10 Ibid., p. xix.

11 Silber, Laura and Allan Little, *The Death of Yugoslavia*, London and New York: Penguin Books, 1995; Andjelic, Neven, *Bosnia-Herzegovina: The End of a Legacy*, London: Frank Cass Publishers, 2003; Glaurdić, Josip, *The Hour of Europe: Western Powers and the Breakup of Yugoslavia*, New Haven & London: Yale University Press, 2011.

12 Campbell, David, *National Deconstruction: Violence, Identity, and Justice in Bosnia*, Minneapolis and London: University of Minnesota Press, 1998; Wilmer, Franke, *The Social Construction of Man, the State and War: Identity, Conflict, and Violence in Former Yugoslavia*, New York and London: Routledge, 2002; Žarkov, Dubravka, *The Body of War: Media, Ethnicity, and Gender in the Break-up of Yugoslavia*, Durham and London: Duke University Press, 2007; Todorova, Maria, *Imagining the Balkans*, Oxford and New York: Oxford University Press, 2009.

13 The political is a concept appearing in virtually all of modern political and democratic theory. I emphasize Wolin's contribution and the contributions of other radical democratic thinkers because theirs is ultimately the conception that most

readily makes sense to me within the context of the Balkans. I specifically steer clear of Carl Schmitt's conceptualization of the state and the political, especially as it concerns the "friend–enemy" distinction and notions of "sovereign dictatorship", as these lead us down the path of insisting on more autocratic state authority and more virulent nationalism, when the aim here is to distil the deeply problematic facets of both in the first place.

14 Wolin, Sheldon, "Fugitive Democracy" in Seyla Benhabib, *Democracy and Difference: Contesting the Boundaries of the Political,* New Jersey: Princeton University Press, 1996, p. 31.

15 Manin, Bernard, *The Principles of Representative Government*, Cambridge, UK: Cambridge University Press, 1997, p. 1.

16 Wolin, 1996, p. 42.

17 Marx, Karl and Friedrich Engels, *The Communist Manifesto*, New York, London, Toronto, Sydney: Pocket Books, 1964, p. 61.

18 Mujanović, Jasmin, "The Baja Class and the Politics of Participation" in Damir Arsenijević, *Unbribable Bosnia and Herzegovina: The Fight for the Commons*, Baden-Baden: Nomos, 2014.

19 Eyal, Gil, Iván Szelényi and Eleanor R. Townsley, *Making Capitalism without Capitalists: Class Formation and Elite Struggles in Post-Communist Central Europe*, London and New York: Verso, 1998; Volkov, Vadim, *Violent Entrepreneurs: The Use of Force in the Making of Russian Capitalism*, Ithaca, New York: Cornell University Press, 2002.

20 Mujkić, Asim, "We, the Citizens of Ethnopolis", *Constellations: An International Journal of Critical and Democratic Theory*, Vol. 14, No. 1, 2007, p. 122.

21 In this respect, this work is most influenced by the *longue durée* approach of the Annales School and the so-called "Political Marxist" view of social transformation. It borrows from the Annales School the rejection of "histoire événementielle", that is, of history as seen as a series of dramatic events or as dominated by particular individuals and their associates. In order to fully grasp their social and historical relevance, even the specific decisions of particular leaders need to be understood in the context of broader patterns of development. Indeed, as Fernand Braudel's pioneering work on the Mediterranean suggests, in this respect, even the environment can play a defining role in the evolution of particular societies. Admittedly, Braudel has occasionally been accused of a kind of "environmental determinism" in his work. Such accounts, however, do a disservice to the intricate and complex network of social, political, and geographic relations and factors Braudel depends on to inform his view of the Mediterranean region, the most relevant of his studies for the purposes of this work. Nevertheless, environmental determinist accounts do exist, especially in the popular literature on the Balkans. And although Chapter I, in particular, makes reference to certain environmental factors in the social development of the

region, it is not where the explanatory stress of this text rests. Assisting the use of Braudel's macro-historical approach is also the work of Political Marxist scholars like Benno Teschke and Ellen Meiksins Wood. Teschke's critical assessment of the role of the Peace of Westphalia in the development of the modern state system is important for considering the peculiar mutations of the state form in southeastern Europe. Wood's critique of the traditional accounts of the emergence of capitalism ("question-begging [assumptions] that it has always existed in embryo, just needing to be liberated from its natural constraints") parallels the attempt here to dislodge nationalism from the centre of Balkan historiography. Such question-begging, exclusionary ethno-nationalist theses dominated popular accounts of the region in the 1990s and, although most scholarship since then has challenged notions of "ancient ethnic hatreds" as catalysts of southeast European history, comparatively little work has been done in examining the phenomenon according to the parameters of something like the Political Marxist or Annales School approach. Thus there is still a need to examine the region as a space of vibrant and on-going political and social contestation, a region that is not only benefited by a critical theoretical examination but that in turn also enriches our theories of the varieties of state and social formation. This book is an attempt to undertake such an examination. Since nationalism persists as the dominant analytical lens for the Western Balkans – even when it is rejected as a relevant category by informed scholars – understanding the phenomenon as a social form, with both political and socio-economic functions, rather than merely a cultural trait, must be part of the foundation for a new critical approach. See: Braudel, Fernand, *The Mediterranean and the Mediterranean World in the Age of Philip II, Volume 1*, Berkeley, Los Angeles, London: University of California Press, 1995; Teschke, Benno, *The Myth of 1648: Class, Geopolitics and the Making of Modern International Relations*, London and New York: Verso, 2003; Wood, Ellen Meiksins, *The Origins of Capitalism: A Longer View*, London and New York: Verso, 2003, p. 97.

22 Kanin, David B., "Big Men, Corruption, and Crime", *International Politics*, Vol. 40, Issue 4, 2003, pp. 491-526.

23 Levine, Robert S., John Stauffer and John R. McKivigan, *Frederick Douglass: The Heroic Slave, A Cultural and Critical Edition*, New Haven and London: Yale University Press, 2015, pp. 133-134.

1. CLIENTS AND BRIGANDS

1 Max Weber's *Economy and Society* is the standard referential text on patrimonialism. Weber distinguishes between bureaucracy as a "precision instrument" and patrimonialism, a system in which the "political realm as a whole is approximately identical with a huge princely manor". Of course, bureaucratic regimes are not necessarily democratic, and while the origins of the patrimonial model are patriarchal, its logic is clearly capable of expanding far beyond the family or clan. Its essential character-

istics and thus contemporary salience remain the manner in which power is wielded autocratically, discretionally, and clientelistically. See: Weber, Max, *Economy and Society: An Outline of Interpretative Sociology*, Berkeley, Los Angeles, London: University of California Press, 1978, p. 1013.

2 Vulliamy, Ed, "Bosnia's survivors gather and grieve as the soil endlessly gives up its dead", *The Guardian*, https://www.theguardian.com/world/2015/aug/08/bosnias-agony-continues-as-the-earth-endlessly-gives-up-its-dead-srebrenica, last accessed 11 March 2017.

3 "Constitution Acts, 1867 to 1982 – Section 91", *Justice Laws Website*, http://laws-lois.justice.gc.ca/eng/Const/section-91.html, last accessed 11 March 2017.

4 Horvat, Srećko and Igor Štiks, *Welcome to the Desert of Post-Socialism: Radical Politics after Yugoslavia*, London: Verso, 2015.

5 Though deploying Harvey's use of the term "accumulation through dispossession", my view of the phenomenon is informed primarily by Marx's original usage: primitive (cf. original, previous) accumulation of capital through the use of extra-economic violence. Still, the former concept is important to make explicit that the political economy of the Balkans remains in this form but that it is not some "previous" epoch of development. Indeed, Harvey astutely argues that accumulation through dispossession is a lasting quality of capitalism. Yet as Marx originally claimed, it is also a process of accumulation constitutive of pre- or non-capitalist social relations. In this respect, the absence of bourgeois political institutions in the Western Balkans cannot be divorced from the absence of capitalist property relations. Therefore, while contemporary dispossession practices in the Balkans are to a small extent part of global patterns of neoliberal dispossession, they are primarily a local phenomenon, the result of local class dynamics.

6 Barkey, Karen, *Bandits and Bureaucrats: The Ottoman Route to State Centralization*, Ithaca: Cornell University Press, 1994; Mazower, pp. 20-36.

7 One need only take the examples of the *kapetanije*, an Ottoman administrative system not exclusive to BiH but, perhaps, most fully autonomous there. It was a "peculiar local military and administrative structure [that] evolved in Bosnia … In the border zones, mainly in and around the military forts, officials known as *kapetans* or *kapudans* (captains) performed a mix of military, administrative, and border police duties. They also went to war when the sultan called upon them. While at the end of the 17th century there were 12 of such districts, all of them along the border, a hundred years later there were 39 *kapetanije* throughout [BiH]". The author continues: "Because the imperial center was so formidable, the *kapetans* were successfully kept in check. During the 16th and 17th centuries, however, the *kapetans* were able to convert the land into private holdings, make their office hereditary, treat the local peasants as they pleased, diminish the power of the governor … and make Bosnia a state within the state". The legacy of the captains is most readily visible today in certain (often, prominent) family names in BiH such as Kapetanović and Gavrankapetanović

(literally "Raven Captain"). See: Čuvalo, Ante, *The A to Z of Bosnia and Herzegovina*, Lanham, Toronto, and Plymouth: The Scarecrow Press, 2010, p. xxxiv.

8 Kitromilides, Paschalis M., "'Imagined Communities' and the Origins of the National Question in the Balkans", *European History Quarterly*, Vol. 19, Issue 2, 1989, pp. 149-194. See also: Hroch, Miroslav, *European Nations: Explaining Their Formation*, London and Brooklyn: Verso, 2015.

9 Despite nationalism dominating popular accounts of the region, little has been written on the subject of the socially constructed, elite-driven project in the Balkans even though works by Benedict Anderson and Eugen Weber are classics in the field of nationalism studies. While there is a robust literature on the phenomenon in the context of the dissolution of Yugoslavia, its origins in the nineteenth century are either glossed over or ignored. As a result, in considering the period, one is left with the impression that while the "nationalist awakenings" of the nineteenth century were morally good and represented the "authentic" communal identities of the Balkan peoples, their subsequent inability to "evolve" beyond these programmes meant that these societies could not turn into proper democratic and multicultural regimes. The obvious implication here is that Western societies, on the other hand, managed to do exactly this. Aside from ignoring the contradictory tensions within the emergence of representative democracy in the West (cf. Manin, Wolin, etc.), and its spread throughout the world largely though the extermination and colonization projects of European imperial powers, this narrative ignores also the continued assumptions of white power and privilege that underpin contemporary multiculturalism in the West. All of which is to say, ignoring the constructed nature of the nation (ethnicity, race) and the class dynamics driving these processes has served to obscure the origins of the state not merely in the Balkans but also in the West. See: Anderson, Benedict, *Imagined Communities: Reflections on the Origin and Spread of Nationalism*, revised edn, London and New York: Verso, 1991; Weber, Eugen, *Peasants into Frenchmen: The Modernization of Rural France, 1870–1914*, Stanford, California: Stanford University Press, 1974; Gagnon, V.P., *The Myth of Ethnic War: Serbia and Croatia in the 1990s*, Ithaca and London: Cornell University Press, 2004; Hage, Ghassan, *White Nation: Fantasies of White Supremacy in a Multicultural Society*, New York and London: Routledge, 2000; Banac, Ivo, *The National Question in Yugoslavia: Origins, History, Politics*, London and Ithaca: Cornell University Press, 1988; Hajdarpasic, Edin, *Whose Bosnia? Nationalism and Political Imagination in the Balkans, 1840–1914,* Ithaca: Cornell University Press, 2015.

10 Anderson, Perry, *Lineages of the Absolutist State,* London and New York: Verso, 1979, p. 387.

11 Hobsbawm, Eric, *Bandits*, New York: Pantheon Books, 1981, p. 71.

12 Hassiotis, Loukianos, "The Ideal of Balkan Unity from a European Perspective (1789–1945)", *Balcanica*, Vol. XLI, 2010/2011, pp. 209-229.

13 Andreas, Peter, *Blue Helmets, Black Markets: The Business of Survival in the Siege of Sara-*

jevo, Ithaca and London: Cornell University Press, 2008.

14 Barkey, p. 21.

15 Ibid.

16 Ibid., p. 16.

17 Ibid., p. 18.

18 Ibid., p. 92.

19 Ibid., p. 95.

20 Lampe, John R. and Marvin R. Jackson, *Balkan Economic History, 1550–1950: From Imperial Borderlands to Developing Nations*, Bloomington: University of Indiana Press, 1982, p. 23.

21 Ibid., p. 24.

22 Ibid., p. 25.

23 Ibid.

24 Mazower, p. 19.

25 Lampe and Jackson, p. 26.

26 Ibid.

27 Hoffmann, Clemens, *The Eastern Question and the Fallacy of Modernity: On the Pre-Modern Origins of the Modern Inter-State Order in Southeastern Europe*, Sussex: University of Sussex, 2010, p. 108.

28 Anderson, pp. 375-376.

29 The *ayans* were the landlords of the *chiflik* system.

30 An honorific akin to governor, which tellingly in popular (Bosnian, especially) parlance remains a term of affection or respect.

31 An administrative system whereby individual legal codes existed for the various religious communities in the empire and into which all individuals were classed.

32 Velikonja, Mitja, *Religious Separation and Political Intolerance in Bosnia-Herzegovina*, College Station: Texas A&M University Press, 2003, p. 59.

33 Toal, Gerard and Carl T. Dahlman, *Bosnia Remade: Ethnic Cleansing and Its Reversal*, Oxford: Oxford University Press, 2011, p. 117.

34 Kanin, p. 521.

35 Bracewell, Wendy, "'The Proud Name of Hajduks' Bandits as Ambiguous Heroes in Balkan Politics and Culture" in Norman M. Naimark and Holly Case, *Yugoslavia and Its Historians: Understanding the Balkan Wars of the 1990s*, Stanford: Stanford University

Press, p. 27.

36 Carmichael, Cathie, *Ethnic Cleansing in the Balkans: Nationalism and the Destruction of Tradition*, London: Routledge, 2002, p. 41.

37 Hajdarpasić, Edin, "Out of the Ruins of the Ottoman Empire: Reflections on the Ottoman Legacy in Southeastern Europe", *Middle Eastern Studies*, Vol. 44, Issue 5, 2008, p. 719.

38 Ibid., p. 718.

39 Glenny, Misha, *The Balkans: Nationalism, War, and the Great Powers, 1804–1999*, New York: Penguin Books, pp. 167-168.

40 Ibid.

41 Garašanin, Ilija, "Naćertanije Program spoljašne i nacionalne politike Srbije na koncu 1844. Godine", *Projekat Rastko*, http://www.rastko.rs/istorija/garasanin_nacertanije.html, last accessed 13 March 2017.

42 Garašanin nevertheless distinguishes between "Serbs" and "Bosniaks". The former are strictly the inhabitants of Serbia, while the latter are all of the inhabitants of BiH, including the Orthodox Christians. This is an important historical aside, as since the 1990s the term "Bosniak" has come to be the preferred ethnic moniker of the Muslim community in BiH. Well into the twentieth century, however, the term was synonymous with "Bosnian", meaning anyone from Bosnia, regardless of ethnic or confessional origin. Hence, Bosniak is a common last name in Croatia, evidence that earlier generations had migrated from Bosnia; by the same token, Horvat (i.e. *Hrvat* meaning Croat) is a common last name in BiH. In any case, while Garašanin repeatedly gestures towards nineteenth-century Bosniaks as supposedly "natural Serbs", his insistence on the necessity of national education is nevertheless striking. It suggests clearly that one had to be initiated into nationalist perspectives, thus that the whole project was consciously and deliberately socially constructed by opportunistic elites.

43 Sells, Michael A., *The Bridge Betrayed: Religion and Genocide in Bosnia*, Berkeley and Los Angeles: University of California Press, 1998, p. 41.

44 In standard Serb nationalist accounts, all Southern Slavs are, in reality, Serbs of various religious persuasions. Thus Croats and Bosniaks are but Catholic and Muslim Serbs, respectively, rather than distinct ethnic or cultural communities.

45 Bakunin, Mikhail in Sam Dolgoff, *Bakunin on Anarchy: Selected Works by the Activist-Founder of World Anarchism*, New York: Vintage Books, 1972, p. 344.

46 Stojanović, Dubravka, "Unfinished Capital – Unfinished State: How the Modernization of Belgrade Was Prevented, 1890–1914", *Nationalities Papers*, Vol. 41, Issue 1, 2013.

47 Ćirković, Sima M., *The Serbs*, Malden, MA, and Oxford, UK: Blackwell Publishing, 2004, pp. 256-257.

48 Mouzelis, Nicos P., *Politics in the Semi-Periphery: Early Parliamentarianism and Late Industrialization in the Balkans and Latin America*, New York: St. Martin's Press, 1986, p. xvii.

49 As with the Russian Bolsheviks, Tucović's use of the "bourgeois" label was propagandist expediency rather than careful analysis. Both Tsarist Russia and the Kingdom of Serbia lacked developed bourgeois social formations and were essentially agrarian societies.

50 Trotsky would write of Tucović's death: "How many harbingers of the Balkan Federation have fallen in the wars of the last years! The heaviest blow for Serbian and all Balkan social-democracy in the war was the fate of Dimitrije Tucovic who was one of the noblest and most heroic figures of the Serbian workers' movement". See: Trotsky, Leon, "Rakovsky and Kolarov", *Marxist Internet Archive*, https://www.marxists.org/archive/trotsky/profiles/rakovsky.htm, last accessed 13 March 2017.

51 Zeman, Z.A.B., "The Balkans and the Coming of War" in Hartmut Pogge von Strandmann and R.J.W. Evans, *The Coming of the First World War*, Oxford: Oxford University Press, 1990.

52 Palairet, Michael R., *The Balkan Economies c.1800–1914: Evolution without Development*, Cambridge and New York: Cambridge University Press, 1997, pp. 34-39.

53 Sakib Korkut was one of the founders of the Yugoslavian Muslim Organization (JMO), the first Muslim political party in the region.

54 As noted below, anti-Muslim pogroms largely centred on the expropriation of property. The reference here to "other people's property" concerned the efforts of dispossessed Muslims to win some restitution for lands taken by the new Yugoslav authorities in Belgrade. See: Banac, p. 368.

55 Incidentally, these debates remain popular among contemporary nationalists in the region, for whom the "real" nationality of the likes of Nikola Tesla and Ivo Andrić is a far more pressing concern than their actual accomplishments.

56 This logic is today best encapsulated by far-right Serb and Bosniak organizations like Obraz (literally, cheek; figuratively, honour) and the Bosnian Movement for National Pride (BPNP). While they insist on propagating the "true" extent of the genocide against their people (in the 1940s and 1990s, respectively), they happily celebrate the genocide of the other (in the 1990s and 1940s, respectively). However, what both Obraz and the BPNP agree on is that left-wingers and LGBT people are the real threat to national self-preservation precisely because they explode the zero-sum dichotomy of Serbs and Bosniaks by introducing questions of class, performance, identity and gender.

57 Magaš, Branka, "On Bosnianness", *Nations and Nationalism*, Vol. 9, Issue 1, 2003.

58 Hoare, Marko Attila, *The History of Bosnia: From the Middle Ages to the Present Day*, London: Saqi Books, 2007, p. 59.

59 With regards to Benedict Anderson's point about the relationship between the spread of the printing press and the rise of nationalism, it is interesting to note that the first printing presses in Croatia and Serbia were in operation by 1493 and 1507, respectively. Meanwhile, the first Ottoman press operated by a Muslim, rather than one of the "commercial minorities", was not opened until 1727 and was not fully legally established until considerably later in the eighteenth century. Clearly, the formation of Muslim national identities lagged behind those of their Christian peers. See: *Incunabula Short Title Catalogue: The International Database of 15th-century European Printing*, http://data.cerl.org/istc/_search, last accessed 13 March 2017; Sabev, Orlin, "Waiting for Godot: The Formation of Ottoman Print Culture" in Geoffrey Roper, *Historical Aspects of Printing and Publishing in Languages of the Middle East: Papers from the Symposium at the University of Leipzig, September 2008*, Leiden and Boston: Brill, 2014.

60 Ljiljak, Aleksandar and Miroslava Miljanović, *Ivan Franjo Jukić: Dokumentarna građa*, Sarajevo: Muzej književnosti Bosne i Hercegovine, 1970, p. 54.

61 Magaš, p. 20.

62 Banac, p. 362.

63 Ottoman title, akin to "lord" or "governor" of an administrative unit.

64 Palmer, Alan, *The Decline and Fall of the Ottoman Empire*, London: John Murray Press, 1992, p. 114.

65 Lampe and Jackson, p. 286.

66 Ibid., p. 284.

67 Ibid.

68 Banac, p. 367.

69 Ibid.

70 Casid, Jill H., *Sowing Empire: Landscape and Colonization*, Minneapolis: University of Minnesota Press, 2005, p. 49.

71 Donia, Robert, "The Proximate Colony: Bosnia-Herzegovina in the Twilight of Empire", *Godišnjak: Centar za balkanološka ispitivanja Akademije nauka i umjetnosti Bosne i Hercegovine*, Vol. 42, 2013, p. 197.

72 Biondich, Mark, *Stjepan Radić, the Croat Peasant Party, and the Politics of Mass Mobilization, 1904–1928*, Toronto: University of Toronto Press, 2000, p. 16.

73 Trouton, Ruth, *Peasant Renaissance in Yugoslavia 1900–1950: A Study of Development of*

Yugoslavia as Affected by Education, Milton Park, Abingdon, Oxford: Routledge, 2007, p. 50.

74 Ibid., pp. 51-52.

75 Alexander, R.S., *Europe's Uncertain Path: 1814–1914 – State Formation and Civil Society*, Malden and Oxford: Wiley-Blackwell, 2012, p. 217.

76 Banac, p. 368.

77 Velikonja, p. 145.

78 Banac, p. 368.

79 Semiz, Dzenana Efendia, "Serbian Land Reform and Colonization in 1918" in Ante Beljo and Aleksander Ravlic, *Southeastern Europe 1918–1995: An International Symposium*, Zagreb: Hrvatski informativni centar, 1996.

80 Stephen Schwartz even suggests that the ultimate dissolution of the SFRJ had its roots in the specific "backwardness" of Serbia in contrast to all the other former Yugoslav republics, BiH included, beginning with the post-Ottoman transition. He argues that a realization dawned on the Serbian elite in the late 1980s with the dimming of the Cold War: "Aside from the superficial cultural sophistication of Belgrade, Serbia had very little to offer the new world. While Slovenia was producing computer peripherals and the Croats were planning resort hotels and the Bosnians were getting rich by exporting agricultural products, Serbia's economy rested on the major assets it had possessed since the beginning of monarchist Yugoslavia at the end of World War I: the Yugoslav state bureaucracy, the army, and the police ... It was raw fear for the future of a statist, centralist Serbia in a free-market world that transformed the Serbian communist organization into an agency of ultranationalist incitement to violence. The Slovene communists thoroughly and effectively remade themselves as free-marketeers, and the Croat and Bosnian Muslim communists were prepared to surrender power to elected non-communist parties, because they all knew they had professional, economic, and political options other than as communist bureaucrats. That is, they were willing to exchange power for property; but for the Serb communists, loss of power meant loss of everything. There was no economic buffer to make the transition easier for them". Schwartz's point is somewhat polemical but largely concurs with the one made by Gagnon. Namely, that the violently engineered dismantling of the SFRJ was a transitional strategy for the Belgrade elite to prevent a popular push for democratization. Both Schwartz and Gagnon implicitly draw attention to the coercive, autocratic character of the state in Serbia, a characterization I argue, in turn, applies to the region as a whole. See: Schwartz, Stephen, "Beyond 'Ancient Hatreds'", *Hoover Institution*, http://www.hoover.org/research/beyond-ancient-hatreds, last accessed 13 March 2017.

81 Bokovoy, Melissa K., *Peasants and Communists: Politics and Ideology in the Yugoslav Countryside, 1941–1953*, Pittsburgh: University of Pittsburgh Press, 1998.

82 Curtis, G.E., "Introduction of Socialist Self-Management" in G.E. Curtis, *Yugoslavia: A Country Study*, Washington, DC: Federal Research Division, Library of Congress, 1990.

83 Mazower, p. 14.

84 Djokić, Dejan, *Elusive Compromise: A History of Interwar Yugoslavia*, New York: Columbia University Press, 2007.

2. THE WARLORDS' PEACE

1 Bassuener, Kurt, "The EU Is Paying a Protection Racket in Bosnia", *BIRN*, http:// www.democratizationpolicy.org/pdf/BDaily_The%20Eu%20is%20paying%20a%20 protection%20racket%20in%20Bosnia_p.12-13.12-13.pdf, last accessed 15 March 2017.

2 Manin, pp. 132-160.

3 Manning, Carrie, "Political Elites and Democratic State-building Efforts in Bosnia and Iraq" in *Democratization*, Vol. 13, Issue 5, 2006, p. 725.

4 Glaurdić, Josip, *The Hour of Europe: Western Powers and the Breakup of Yugoslavia*, New Haven and London: Yale University Press, 2011, p. 41.

5 Ibid., pp. 1-2.

6 Liotta, P.H., *The Wreckage Reconsidered: Five Oxymorons from Balkan Deconstruction*, Lanham, Boulder, New York and Oxford: Lexington Books, 1999, p. 56.

7 Bush, George H.W., "A Europe Whole and Free", *The U.S. Diplomatic Mission to Germany*, http://usa.usembassy.de/etexts/ga6-890531.htm, last accessed 13 March 2017.

8 "Transitional Justice in the Former Yugoslavia", *International Center for Transitional Justice*, https://www.ictj.org/sites/default/files/ICTJ-FormerYugoslavia-Justice-Facts-2009-English.pdf, last accessed 13 March 2017.

9 Bećirević, Edina, *Genocide on the Drina River*, New Haven and London: Yale University Press, 2014, pp. 50-143.

10 See: Silber and Little; Gagnon; Hoare, 2007; Glaurdić.

11 Djokić, pp. 223-268.

12 Hoare, Marko Attila, *The Bosnian Muslims in the Second World War: A History*, London: Hurst Publishers, 2013.

13 Obradović, Marija, "From Revolutionary to Clientelistic Party: The Communist Party of Yugoslavia, 1945–1952", *East European Politics and Societies*, Vol. 27, Issue 3, 2013, p. 379.

14 Ibid., pp. 387-388.

15 Ibid., p. 379.

16 Despite the significant peasant influx into the ranks of the partisans during the war, anti-fascist organizing remained robust and sophisticated in the cities as well. The four-volume collection *Sarajevo u Revoluciji* ("Sarajevo in the Revolution") provides a series of fascinating first-person accounts by many of the organizers themselves in one such urban setting. Among these, Munira Karahasanović-Serdarević's text describes in detail the evolution of the movement from pre-war underground activities to war-time organizing, the role of young intellectuals and, in particular, the role of women in the movement from her own first-hand experiences. Incidentally, Ms Karahasanović-Serdarević is my grandmother. See: Karahasanović-Serdarević, Munira, "Za Narodnooslobodilaćki Pokret" in Nisim Albahari, Miodrag Ćanković, Mehmed Džinić, Dane Olbina, *Sarajevo u Revoluciji: Komunistićka partija Jugoslavije u pripremama i organizaciji ustanka, No. 2*, Sarajevo: Istoriski Arhiv Sarajevo, 1977.

17 Ibid., p. 380.

18 Banac, p. 18.

19 Suvin, Darko, "Splendours and Miseries of the Communist Party of Yugoslavia (1945-74)", *Socialism and Democracy*, Vol. 27, No. 1, 2013, p. 173.

20 Rusinow, Dennison I., *The Yugoslav Experiment 1948–1974*, Berkeley and Los Angeles: University of California Press, 1977, p. 61.

21 Bokovoy, pp. 101-125.

22 Glenny, pp. 545-550.

23 Despite the ethnically charged nature of much of the war-time fighting in BiH, as Glenny notes, the uprising was a multi-ethnic affair of Bosniak and Serb peasants against local authorities. Relatedly, Srđan Šušnica provides an achingly beautiful account of the proud tradition of multi-ethnic anti-fascist organizing in the Bosnian Karjina, in particular among the region's Bosnian Serbs; a tradition that was violently dismantled, in the words of his grandmother, by "bearded *ćetniks* and priests" in the 1990s. Her words recall vividly the images of "patriotic bandits" at the end of the nineteenth century discussed at length in Chapter I. See: Šušnica, Srđan, "Banja Luka: The City of Oblivion and Disdain", *Balkanist*, http://balkanist.net/banja-luka-amnesia/ last accessed 13 March 2017.

24 Suvin, pp. 173-174.

25 Yugoslavia's chief ideologue, Edvard Kardelj, acknowledged as much explicitly: "Self-management in Yugoslavia was born during the National Liberation War and has since the very beginning been one of the factors in and forms of the socialist revolution". See: Kardelj, Edvard, "Socialist Self-Management in Yugoslavia", *International Review of Administrative Sciences*, Vol. 42, Issue 2, 1976, pg. 103.

26 Suvin, p. 173.

27 Ibid.

28 Unkovski-Korica, Vladimir, "Workers' Councils in the Service of the Market: New Archival Evidence on the Origins of Self-Management in Yugoslavia 1948-1950", *Europe-Asia Studies*, Vol. 66, Issue 1, 2013, p. 117.

29 Rajak, Svetozar, *Yugoslavia and the Soviet Union in the Early Cold War: Reconciliation, Comradeship, Confrontation, 1953–1957*, New York: Routledge, 2011.

30 Cvetković, Srćan, "Kradljivci tućih leća', Obraćun sa anarholiberalistićkim grupama u SFRJ posle 1968", *Istorija 20 Veka*, Issue 3, 2011.

31 Pribechevich, Stoyan (trans.), *Yugoslavia's Way: The Program of the League of the Communists of Yugoslavia*, New York: All Nations Press, p. 120.

32 Ibid., p. 116.

33 Unkovski-Korica, p. 119.

34 "Territorial communities" is a striking term to avoiding making reference to the Yugoslav state, the respective republics or the various nations and peoples that composed the new Yugoslav federation. It is demonstrative of a continuous attempt on the part of Kardelj and his cohorts to keep thinking beyond the state and to engage in thorough ideological examinations of the problem of coercive state power for a socialist society. Moreover, it proves that such theoretical debates were viewed as important and imminent tasks. Accordingly, it also makes Tito's and Kardelj's actual crushing of democratic dissent all the more startling and tragic.

35 Pribechevich, p. 117.

36 Bockman, Johanna, *Markets in the Name of Socialism: The Left-Wing Origins of Neoliberalism*, Stanford: Stanford University Press, 2011, p. 82.

37 Pribechevich, pp. 117-118.

38 Rusinow, p. 111.

39 Ibid., pp. 81-87.

40 The Praxis School was a group of Marxist humanist scholars from Belgrade and Zagreb, primarily, whose 1964–1974 journal *Praxis* was the leading voice of left-democratic critiques of the Yugoslav regime. The Praxis-organized Korćula Summer School (1963–1974) attracted leading international scholars, from Marcuse to Habermas and Fromm, to engage in what (to the authorities) were thinly veiled attacks on the legitimacy of the LCY's leadership and, moreover, for the "Praxists" to continue these activities at their various teaching engagements in western Europe and the US was for Kardelj clear evidence of their inherently anti-socialist leanings. After the purges of the late 1960s and early 1970s, the group, along with virtually the entirety of the left opposition, all but disappeared from Yugoslav public life.

Many of those that later reappeared, like Mihailo Marković, did so as nationalists of the most virulent sort. How exactly the transition from Marxist humanism to vulgar nationalism took place among these individuals is a process that would require a degree of speculative psychoanalysis I am not prepared to engage in at this time.

41 Kardelj, Edvard, *Pravci razvoja političkog sistema socijalističkog samoupravljanja*. Beograd: Izadavćki Centar "Komunist", 1977, p. 72.

42 It has never been definitely established what Ranković did to be purged from the ruling apparatus in 1966, though it is widely speculated that he had had Tito's private quarters bugged and was, presumably, interested in politically blackmailing the marshal. This story itself, however, may have masked Tito's ulterior desire to curb the growing influence of the Yugoslav secret services, a network with which Ranković was closely aligned.

43 Kardelj, 1976, p. 104.

44 Despite his loathing for the "ultra-left", Kardelj is here all but plagiarizing Peter Kropotkin's writing on anarchist federalism and mutual aid, among other prominent anarchist theorists of whom Kardelj was certainly aware. Rather than being a source of confusion, the rhizomatic network of partisan cells that marked the war years was precisely the model that ensured the success and popularity of the communist war effort. Yet the LCY's leadership made its first post-war task the dismantling of these proto-democratic structures, a process they had to reverse yet again after the Tito–Stalin split. The result of these confused policies was an essentially schizophrenic and fundamentally unsustainable conception of the state in Yugoslav political life.

45 Ibid.

46 Curtis.

47 Comisso, Ellen T., "The Logic of (Non)Participation in Yugoslav Self-Management", *Review of Radical Political Economics*, Vol. 13, Issue 2, 1981.

48 Ibid., p. 21.

49 Ibid.

50 Bockman, p. 80.

51 Sell, pp. 187-189.

52 Cohen, Philip J., "The Complicity of Serbian Intellectuals in Genocide of the 1990s" in Thomas Cushman and Stjepan Meštrović, *This Time We Knew: Western Responses to Genocide in Bosnia*, New York City: New York University Press, 1996, p. 49.

53 Andjelic, p. 55.

54 Pedrotty, Kate Meehan, "Yugoslav Unity and Olympic Ideology at the 1984 Sarajevo Winter Olympic Games" in Hannes Grandits and Karin Taylor, *In Yugoslavia's Sunny*

Side: A History of Tourism in Socialism (1950s-1980s), Budapest: Central European Press, 2010, pg. 340.

55　Miller, Nick, *The Nonconformists: Culture, Politics, and Nationalism in a Serbian Intellectual Circle, 1944–1991*, Budapest: Central European Press, 2007, pp. 96-97.

56　Zukin, Sharon, *Beyond Marx and Tito: Theory and Practice in Yugoslav Socialism*, Cambridge: Cambridge University Press, 1975, p. 257.

57　Narayanswamy, Ramnath, "Yugoslavia: Self-Management or Mismanagement?", *Economic and Political Weekly*, Vol. 23, No. 4, 1988, p. 2054.

58　Ibid.

59　Ibid.

60　Ibid.

61　Vodovnik, Žiga, "Democracy as Verb: New Mediations on the Yugoslav Praxis Philosophy", *Journal of Balkan and Near Eastern Studies*, Vol. 14, Issue 4, 2012, p. 449.

62　Ibid., p. 441.

63　Perlman, Fredy, "Birth of a Revolutionary Movement in Yugoslavia", *Marxist Internet Archive*, https://www.marxists.org/reference/archive/perlman-fredy/1969/revolutionary-movement-yugoslavia.htm, last accessed 14 March 2017.

64　Ibid.

65　Job, Cvijeto, *Yugoslavia's Ruin: The Bloody Lessons of Nationalism*, Oxford: Rowman and Littlefield Publishers, 2002, p. 75.

66　There are useful comparisons to be drawn between the MASPOK period in Croatia and the Quiet Revolution in Quebec, Canada. In both instances, there was the perception of marginalization on the part of a regional majority in the context of a larger federal state in which they were a minority. In both instances, the protest against this perceived marginalization was asserted through a spectrum of political options. Moreover, in both instances, the essential critique of the marginalized group was eventually accepted by the federal authorities. The difference is in the treatment of the proponents of these respective projects. In Canada, while extremist groups like the Front de libération du Québec (FLQ) were actively dismantled, legitimate opposition groups like the Parti Québécois (PQ) were allowed to persist, indeed, flourish, the events of the October Crisis notwithstanding. In Croatia, as in Serbia and much of the rest of the SFRJ, a determined conservative reaction destroyed a generation of progressive leaders, as a result of which the entire political system underwent a rapid period of stagnation and corruption from which it never recovered. In short, the destruction of democratic opposition in Yugoslavia once again proved paradigmatic to the region's further development.

67　Dejan Guzina observes that only one republic, Slovenia, managed to avoid the purging of its reform-minded leadership. "In the case of Slovenia, only the top echelon of the 'liberal' party was replaced. On the other hand, Tito thoroughly overhauled the party structure in Serbia and Croatia, presumably because he saw obedient party leadership in these regions as vital to the stability of the country. His sparing treatment of Slovenia gave it 20 years of uninterrupted political development, which helps explain its high level of political culture and tact during the crisis of the 1980s, and its relatively smooth transition from communism to a more democratic regime. The same period will be remembered in a totally different light in Croatia and Serbia. While constant internal political frictions characterized political life in Serbia, Croatia witnessed a full re-bureaucratization of social life. In both cases, communist as well as post-communist leaders were totally unprepared for the challenges that the collapse of the system posed". See: Guzina, Dejan, "The Self-Destruction of Yugoslavia", *Canadian Review of Studies in Nationalism*, Vol. 27, No. 1/2, 2000, p. 31.

68 Irvine, Jill, "The Croatian Spring and the Dissolution of Yugoslavia" in Lenard J. Cohen and Jasna Dragović-Soso, *State Collapse in South-Eastern Europe: New Perspectives on Yugoslavia's Disintegration*, West Lafayette, Indiana: Purdue University Press, 2011, p. 169.

69 Campbell, David, "Apartheid Cartography: The Political Anthropology and Spatial Effects of International Diplomacy in Bosnia", *Political Geography*, Vol. 18, 1999, p. 404.

70 Glaurdić, p. 290.

71 Crampton, Jeremy, "Bordering on Bosnia", *GeoJournal*, Vol. 39, No. 4, 1999, p. 359.

72 Zimmerman, Warren, *Origins of a Catastrophe: Yugoslavia and Its Destroyers*, New York: Times Books, 1996.

73 Holbrooke, Richard, *To End a War*, New York: Random House, 1998, p. 21.

74 Ibid., pp. 28-29.

75 Glaurdić, p. 22.

76 Conversi, Daniele, *Ethnonationalism in the Contemporary World: Walker Connor and the Study of Nationalism*, London and New York: Routledge, 2004, pp. 274-275.

77 Simms, Brendan, *Unfinest Hour: Britain and the Destruction of Bosnia*, London and New York: Penguin Books, 2002.

78 Ajami, Fouad, "The Mark of Bosnia: Boutros-Ghali's Reign of Indifference", *Foreign Affairs*, May/June 1996.

79 A portion of my analysis in this section appears also in my article "Princip, Valter, Pejić and the Raja: Elite Domination and Betrayal in Bosnia-Herzegovina", *South-East European Journal of Political Science*, Vol. I, No. 3, 2013.

80 Wolin, 1996, p. 38.

81 Ibid., p. 37.

82 Pejic, Nenad, "How I Failed to Stop the War in Bosnia", *Radio Free Europe - Radio Liberty*, http://www.rferl.org/a/how_i_failed_to_stop_the_war_in_bosnia/24537627.html, last accessed 15 March 2017.

83 Ibid.

84 Ibid.

85 Ibid.

86 "Sjećanje na početak rata u Sarajevu", *Al Jazeera Balkans*, https://www.youtube.com/watch?v=N-FiMz0FM7c, last accessed 15 March 2017.

87 Gagnon, p. 91.

88 Glaurdić, p. 88.

89 Stojanović, Nenad, "When non-nationalist voters support ethno-nationalist parties: the 1990 elections in Bosnia and Herzegovina as a prisoner's dilemma game", *Southeast European and Black Sea Studies*, Vol. 14, Issue 4, 2014.

90 Glaurdić, p. 88.

91 Gagnon, pp. 131-177.

92 Pejanović, Mirko, *Država Bosna i Hercegovina i Demokratija*, Sarajevo: University Press Sarajevo, 2015, p. 57.

93 Manning, p. 725.

94 Magyar, Bálint, *Post-Communist Mafia State:The Case of Hungary*, Budapest: Central European Press, 2016; Krasztev, Peter and Jon Van Til (eds.), *The Hungarian Patient: Social Opposition to an Illiberal Democracy*, Budapest and New York: Central European Press, 2015.

95 Jacobsson, Kerstin and Steven Saxonberg (eds.), *Social Movements in Post-Communist Europe and Russia*, Milton Park and New York: Routledge, 2015.

96 Knaus, Gerald and Felix Martin, "Lessons from Bosnia and Herzegovina:Travails of the European Raj", *Journal of Democracy*, Vol. 14, Issue 3, 2003.

97 Mujanović, Jasmin, "Elections and ethnic cleansing in Bosnia-Herzegovina", *openDemocracy*, https://www.opendemocracy.net/5050/jasmin-mujanovi%C4%87/elections-and-ethnic-cleansing-in-bosniaherzegovina, last accessed 15 March 2017.

98 Merdzanovic, Adis, *Democracy by Decree: Prospects and Limits of Imposed Consociational Democracy in Bosnia and Herzegovina*, Stuttgart: Ibidem, 2015, pp. 225-350.

99 Divjak, Boris and Michael Pugh, "The Political Economy of Corruption in Bosnia

and Herzegovina", *International Peacekeeping*, Vol. 15, Issue 3, 2008; Pugh, Michael and Neil Cooper with Jonathan Goodhand, *War Economies in a Regional Context*, London and Boulder: Lynn Rienner Publishers, 2004, pp. 143-194; Bideleux, Robert and Ian Jeffries, *The Balkans: A Post-communist History*, London and New York: Routledge, 2007.

100 Volkov; Hignett, Kelly, "The Changing Face of Organized Crime in Post-Communist Central and Eastern Europe", *Journal of Contemporary Central and Eastern Europe*, Vol. 18, Issue 2008.

101 Transparency International – Bosnia and Herzegovina, "Privatizacija državnog kapitala u Bosni i Hercegovini", https://ti-bih.org/wp-content/uploads/2011/03/PRIVATIZACIJA_DRZAVNOG_KAPITALA_U_BiH.pdf, last accessed 16 March 2017; Komšić, Ivo, "The Washington Agreement", *Spirit of Bosnia*, http://www.spiritofbosnia.org/volume-11-no-1-2016january/the-washington-agreement/, last accessed 16 March 2017; Radaljac, Danko, "Mutne devedesete: Privatizacijske muljaže amenovali hrvatski graćani", *Novi list*, http://www.novilist.hr/Vijesti/Hrvatska/Mutne-devedesete-Privatizacijske-muljaze-amenovali-hrvatski-gradani, last accessed 16 March 2017.

102 Donais, Timothy, *The Political Economy of Peacebuilding in Post-Dayton Bosnia*, London and New York: Routledge, 2005, pp. 16-46.

103 Wampler, Brian, *Participatory Budgeting in Brazil: Contestation, Cooperation, and Accountability*, University Park: Pennsylvania State University Press, 2007.

104 Greer, Patrick, Anne Murphy and Morten Øgård (eds.), *Guide to Participatory Democracy in Bosnia and Herzegovina and in Serbia and Montenegro*, Strasbourg: Council of Europe Publishing, 2005.

105 Bidey, Tim, "Time for real democracy in Bosnia?", *Insight on Conflict*, https://www.insightonconflict.org/blog/2014/10/bosnia-constitution-reform/, last accessed 15 March 2017.

106 Vulliamy, Ed, *The War Is Dead, Long Live the War: Bosnia – The Reckoning*, New York: Random House, 2014.

107 World Bank Group, *South East Europe Regular Economic Report – No. 10*, http://pubdocs.worldbank.org/en/521981474898709744/SEE-RER-Report-Fall-2016.pdf, last accessed 15 March 2017.

108 Filipović, Miroslav, "Kodna i kobna riječ jest – egzodus", *Al Jazeera Balkans*, http://balkans.aljazeera.net/vijesti/kodna-i-kobna-rijec-jest-egzodus, last accessed 15 March 2017.

109 Zelenika, Pero, "Svaki treći zaposlenik u BiH radi u javnoj upravi", *Večernji list*, http://www.vecernji.ba/svaki-treci-zaposlenik-u-bih-radi-u-javnoj-upravi-954862, last accessed 15 March 2017.

110 Veselinović, Gojko, "Kako smanjiti broj zaposlenih u državnoj administraciji u BiH?", *Radio Slobodna Evropa*, http://www.slobodnaevropa.org/a/kako-smanjiti-broj-zapo-slenih-u-adminsitraciji-u-bih/25185541.html, last accessed 15 March, 2017.

111 Gordy, Eric, "From Antipolitics to Alterpolitics: Subverting Ethnokleptocracy in Bosnia and Herzegovina" in Damir Arsenijević, *Unbribable Bosnia and Herzegovina: The Fight for the Commons*, Baden-Baden: Nomos, 2014, p. 111.

3. GEOPOLITICS AND THE CRISIS OF DEMOCRACY IN THE WESTERN BALKANS

1 European Commission, "Connectivity Agenda: Co-financing of Investment Projects in the Western Balkans in 2016", https://ec.europa.eu/neighbourhood-enlarge-ment/sites/near/files/pdf/western_balkans/20160704_paris_package.pdf, last accessed 16 March 2017.

2 Balkans in Europe Policy Advisory Group, "The Crisis of Democracy in the Western Balkans. Authoritarianism and EU Stabilitocracy", http://www.biepag.eu/wp-con-tent/uploads/2017/03/BIEPAG-The-Crisis-of-Democracy-in-the-Western-Balkans.-Authoritarianism-and-EU-Stabilitocracy-web.pdf, last accessed 3 July 2017.

3 Pargan, Benjamin, "Bosnia is still Europe's black-hole of corruption", *Deutsche Welle*, http://www.dw.de/opinion-bosnia-is-still-europes-black-hole-of-corruption/a-18114406, last accessed 16 March 2017.

4 Marusic, Sinisa Jakov, "Ousted Macedonian PM Risks Years behind Bars", *Balkan Insight*, http://www.balkaninsight.com/en/article/ousted-macedonian-pm-risks-years-behind-bars-06-30-2017, last accessed 3 July 2017.

5 Rettman, Adrews, "Survey: Croatia and Slovenia most corrupt in EU", *EUobserver*, https://euobserver.com/justice/120064, last accessed 16 March 2017.

6 Milekic, Sven, "Croatia Urged to Tackle Rampant Culture of Plagiarism", *Balkan Insight*, http://www.balkaninsight.com/en/article/academic-plagiarism-not-sanc-tioned-properly-in-croatia-12-02-2016, last accessed 16 March 2017.

7 Freedom House, "Freedom of the Press – Croatia", https://freedomhouse.org/report/freedom-press/2015/croatia, last accessed 16 March 2017.

8 IFEX, "'Obvious interference' ahead of Croatia election", https://www.ifex.org/croatia/2016/08/10/obvious_interference/, last accessed 16 March 2017.

9 "Slovenia: Worries about freedom of the press", *The Economist*, http://www.econo-mist.com/blogs/easternapproaches/2014/04/slovenia, last accessed 16 March 2017.

10 Sakurai, Joji, "Make Croatia great again: how fascism emerged in the EU's young-est state", *New Statesman*, http://www.newstatesman.com/culture/observa-

tions/2016/05/make-croatia-great-again-how-fascism-emerged-eu-s-youngest-state, last accessed 16 March 2017.

11 "Slovenia: 20 Years Later – Issue of the Erased Remains Unresolved", *Amnesty International*, https://www.amnesty.org/en/press-releases/2012/02/slovenia-20-years-later-issue-erased-remains-unresolved/, last accessed 16 March 2017.

12 The Erased: Information and documents, "About erasure", http://www.mirovni-institut.si/izbrisani/en/about-erasure/, last accessed 16 March 2017.

13 Kohn, Sebastian, "Victory for Slovenia's 'erased citizens' at the European Court of Human Rights", *European Network on Statelessness*, http://www.statelessness.eu/blog/victory-slovenias-erased-citizens-european-court-human-rights, last accessed 16 March 2017.

14 Kauffman, Sylvie, "Europe's Illiberal Democracies", *New York Times*, https://www.nytimes.com/2016/03/10/opinion/europes-illiberal-democracies.html, last accessed 17 March 2017; Shekhovtsov, "Tit for Tat: Illiberal Tendencies and the Far Right in Visegrad", *The Aspen Institute*, http://www.aspeninstitutece.org/en/article/2-2016-tit-for-tat-illiberal-tendencies-and-the-far-right-in-the-visegrad/, last accessed 17 March, 2017; "Illiberal central Europe: Big, bad Visegrad", *The Economist*, http://www.economist.com/news/europe/21689629-migration-crisis-has-given-unsettling-new-direction-old-alliance-big-bad-visegrad, last accessed 17 March 2017.

15 Aligica, Paul Dragos and Anthony John Evan, *The Neoliberal Revolution in Eastern Europe: Economic Ideas in the Transition from Communism*, Cheltenham and Northampton: Edward Elgar, 2009.

16 Sachs, Jeffery, *Poland's Jump to the Market Economy*, Cambridge, MA: The MIT Press, 1994; Ramet, Sabrina P., *The Liberal Project and the Transformation of Democracy: The Case of East Central Europe*, College Station: Texas A&M University Press, 2007; Epstein, Rachel A., *In Pursuit of Liberalism: International Institutions in Postcommunist Europe*, Baltimore: Johns Hopkins University Press, 2008.

17 Kopeček, Michal and Wciślik, Piotr (eds.), *Liberal Democracy, Authoritarian Pasts, and Intellectual History in East Central Europe after 1989*, Budapest: CEU Press, 2015; Dawson, James and Seán Hanley, "Poland Was Never as Democratic as It Looked", *Foreign Policy*, http://foreignpolicy.com/2017/01/03/poland-was-never-as-democratic-as-it-looked-law-and-justice-hungary-orban/, last accessed 17 March 2017.

18 Wolff, Stefan, Ana-Maria Anghelea and Ivana Djuric, "Minority Rights in the Western Balkans", *European Parliament – Directorate of General External Policies of the Union*, http://www.europarl.europa.eu/RegData/etudes/etudes/join/2008/385559/EXPO-DROI_ET(2008)385559_EN.pdf, last accessed 17 March 2017.

19 Bush, George W., "Text of Bush's Speech at West Point", *New York Times*, http://www.nytimes.com/2002/06/01/international/text-of-bushs-speech-at-west-point.html, last accessed 18 March 2017.

20 Peterson, John, "The US and Europe in the Balkans" in John Peterson and Mark A. Pollack (eds.), *Europe, America, Bush: Transatlantic Relations in the Twenty-First Century*, London and New York: Routledge, 2003, pp. 94-97.

21 Vesnic-Alujevic, Lucia, *European Integration of Western Balkans: From Reconciliation to European Future*, Brussels: Centre for European Studies, 2012, pp. 25-39.

22 Karasavvoglou, Anastasios and Persefoni Polychronidou (eds.), *Economic Crisis in Europe and the Balkans: Problems and Prospects*, Cham, Heidelberg, New York, Dordrecht, and London: Springer, 2014.

23 De Borja Lasheras, Francisco with Vessela Tcherneva and Fredrik Wesslau, *Return to Instability: How Migration and Great Power Politics Threaten the Western Balkans*, London: European Council on Foreign Relations, 2016.

24 Pula, Besnik, "The Budding Autocrats of the Balkans", *Foreign Policy*, http://foreignpolicy.com/2016/04/15/the-budding-autocrats-of-the-balkans-serbia-macedonia-montenegro/, last accessed 17 March 2016.

25 Mappes-Niediek, Norbert, "'Europe is the powder keg – the Balkans are the fuse'", *Deutsche Welle*, http://www.dw.com/en/europe-is-the-powder-keg-the-balkans-are-the-fuse/a-37605628, last accessed 17 March 2017.

26 Bieber, Florian, "EWB Interview, Florian Bieber: The EU Should Put More Focus on the State of Democracy in the Western Balkans", *European Western Balkans*, https://europeanwesternbalkans.com/2016/11/17/ewb-interview-florian-bieber-the-eu-should-put-more-focus-on-the-state-of-democracy-in-the-western-balkans/, last accessed 17 March 2017.

27 Jakov Marusic, Sinisa, "Austrian FM Defends Decision to Back Macedonia Ruling Party", *Balkan Insight*, http://www.balkaninsight.com/en/article/critics-slam-kurz-s-support-for-macedonia-s-ruling-party-11-28-2016, last accessed 17 March 2017.

28 Vurušić, Vlado, "Stigao novi jaki saveznik, Putin spleo mrežu u EU: Ruski lider okupio čak 15 radikalno desnih stranaka s kojima kreće rušiti Bruxelles", *Jutarnji Vijesti*, http://www.jutarnji.hr/vijesti/svijet/stigao-novi-jaki-saveznik-putin-spleo-mrezu-u-eu-ruski-lider-okupio-cak-15-radikalno-desnih-stranaka-s-kojima-krece-rusiti-bruxelles/5733251/, last accessed 17 March, 2017; Sasso, Alfredo, "The ethnic question comes to the European Parliament", *Vox Europ*, http://www.voxeurop.eu/en/2017/bosnia-herzegovina-5120772, last accessed 17 March 2017.

29 Collett, Elizabeth, "The Paradox of the EU-Turkey Refugee Deal", *Migration Policy Institute*, http://www.migrationpolicy.org/news/paradox-eu-turkey-refugee-deal, last accessed 17 March 2017.

30 Cunningham, Erin, "U.N. slams Turkey for 'alarming' reports of human rights abuses", *Washington Post*, https://www.washingtonpost.com/world/middle_east/turkey-under-fire-from-un-for-alarming-reports-of-rights-

abuses/2016/05/10/0f9eccb7-45cd-4685-9483-181fdfd2cadf_story.html?utm_
term=.07e732318b81, last accessed 17 March 2017.

31 Shaheen, Kareem, Patrick Wintour and Jennifer Rankin, "Turkey threatens to end
refugee deal in row over EU accession", *The Guardian*, https://www.theguardian.
com/world/2016/nov/25/turkey-threatens-end-refugee-deal-row-eu-accession-
erdogan, last accessed 17 March 2017.

32 Bajekal, Naina, "The 5 Big Questions about Europe's Migrant Crisis", *Time*, http://
time.com/4026380/europe-migrant-crisis-questions-refugees/, last accessed 17
March 2017.

33 Ezrow, Natasha M. and Erica Frantz, *Dictators and Dictatorships: Understanding Authoritarian Regimes and Their Leaders*, New York and London: Continuum International
Publishing Group, 2011, pp. 54-80.

34 Walt, Stephen M., "The Collapse of the Liberal World Order", *Foreign Policy*,
http://foreignpolicy.com/2016/06/26/the-collapse-of-the-liberal-world-order-
european-union-brexit-donald-trump/, last accessed 17 March 2017.

35 Hamid, Shadi, "Islamism and Trumpism: The search for a politics of meaning",
Brookings, https://www.brookings.edu/blog/markaz/2016/11/17/islamism-and-
trumpism-the-search-for-a-politics-of-meaning/, last accessed 17 March 2017.

36 Krastev, Ivan, "EU goes back to the future in the Balkans", *Financial Times*, https://
www.ft.com/content/620509da-0968-11e7-ac5a-903b21361b43, last accessed 17
March 2017.

37 Osnos, Evan, David Remnick and Joshua Yaffa, "Trump, Putin, and the New Cold
War", *New Yorker*, http://www.newyorker.com/magazine/2017/03/06/trump-pu-
tin-and-the-new-cold-war, last accessed 17 March 2017; Kasparov, Garry, *Winter Is
Coming: Why Vladimir Putin and the Enemies of the Free World Must Be Stopped*, New York:
Public Affairs, 2015; Judah, Ben, *Fragile Empire: How Russia Fell In and Out of Love with
Vladimir Putin*, New Haven and London: Yale University Press, 2013.

38 Dempsey, Judy, "The Western Balkans Are Becoming Russia's New Playground",
Carnegie Europe, http://carnegieeurope.eu/strategiceurope/57301, last accessed
17 March 2017; Wićniewski, Jarosław, "Russia has a years-long plot to influence
Balkan politics. The U.S. can learn a lot from it", *Washington Post*, https://www.
washingtonpost.com/news/monkey-cage/wp/2016/09/19/heres-how-russias-
trying-to-sway-opinion-in-serbia-and-the-balkans/?utm_term=.cdf2548d5e90,
last accessed 17 March 2017; Tanner, Marcus, "Russia Never Went Away from the
Balkans", *Balkan Insight*, http://www.balkaninsight.com/en/article/russia-never-
went-away-from-the-balkans-01-18-2017, last accessed 17 March 2017.

39 Bechev, Dimitar, "Russia in the Balkans: Conference Report Back", *London
School of Economics*, http://www.lse.ac.uk/europeanInstitute/research/LSEE/
Events/2014-2015/Russia-in-the-Balkans/merged-document.pdf, last accessed 17,

March 2017.

40 Cameron-Rice, John, "Eurasianism Is the New Fascism: Understanding and Confronting Russia", *Stanford Political Journal*, https://stanfordpolitics.com/eurasian-
ism-is-the-new-fascism-understanding-and-confronting-russia-7e0c2eef6288#.sl-
wiapc6u, last accessed 17 March 2017; Klump, Sarah Dixon, "Russian Eurasianism:
An Ideology of Empire", *Wilson Center – Kennan Institute*, https://www.wilsoncen-
ter.org/publication/russian-eurasianism-ideology-empire, last accessed 17 March
2017; Clover, Charles, "The Unlikely Origins of Russia's Manifest Destiny", *Foreign
Policy*, http://foreignpolicy.com/2016/07/27/geopolitics-russia-mackinder-
eurasia-heartland-dugin-ukraine-eurasianism-manifest-destiny-putin/, last accessed
17 March 2017.

41 Knezevic, Gordana, "Krastev: The Balkans are key to Russia's policy of divide and
rule", *Radio Free Europe – Radio Liberty*, https://www.slobodnaevropa.org/a/
krastev-the-balkans-are-key-to-russias-policy-of-divide-and-rule/26837407.html,
last accessed 5 July 2017.

42 Mujanović, Jasmin, "Moscow's man in Banja Luka", *openDemocracy*, https://www.
opendemocracy.net/od-russia/jasmin-mujanovi%C4%87/moscow%E2%80%99s-
man-in-banja-luka, last accessed 17 March 2017.

43 Knezevic, Gordana, "Serbia, Beware Russians Bearing Gifts", *Radio Free Europe – Radio Liberty*, http://www.rferl.org/a/serbia-beware-russians-bearing-
gifts/28188904.html, last accessed 17 March 2017.

44 Petsinis, Vassilis, "From pro-American to pro-Russian? Nikola Gruevski as a political
chameleon", *openDemocracy*, https://www.opendemocracy.net/can-europe-make-
it/vassilis-petsinis/from-proamerican-to-prorussian-nikola-gruevski-as-political-
cha, last accessed 17 March 2017.

45 Knezevic, Gordana, "Serbia and Self-Fulfilling Russian Prophecies", *Radio Free
Europe – Radio Liberty*, http://www.rferl.org/a/serbia-self-fulfilling-russia-
prophecies/27707245.html, last accessed 17 March 2017; Braw, Elisabeth, "Putin
Seeks to Influence Radical Parties in Bid to Destabilise Europe", *Newsweek*, http://
www.newsweek.com/2015/01/16/putins-envoys-seek-influence-european-radi-
cals-297769.html, last accessed 17 March 2017.

46 "Russia, Serbia, Belarus Hold 'Slavic Brotherhood' Military Drills", *Radio Free Europe
– Radio Liberty*, https://www.rferl.org/a/slavic-brotherhood-military-drills-russia-
serbia-belarus/28531473.html, last accessed 5 July 2017.

47 Belford, Aubrey, Saska Cvetkovska, Biljana Sekulovska and Stevan Dojćinović,
"Leaked Documents Show Russian, Serbian Attempts to Meddle in Macedonia", *OC-
CRP*, https://www.occrp.org/en/spooksandspin/leaked-documents-show-russian-
serbian-attempts-to-meddle-in-macedonia/, last accessed 5 July 2017.

48 Higgins, Andrew, "Finger Pointed at Russians in Alleged Coup Plot in Montene-

gro", *New York Times*, https://www.nytimes.com/2016/11/26/world/europe/
finger-pointed-at-russians-in-alleged-coup-plot-in-montenegro.html, last accessed
17 March 2017; Tanner, Marcus, "Why Britain Won't Shut Up about Montenegro",
Balkan Insight, http://www.balkaninsight.com/en/article/why-britain-won-
t-shut-up-about-montenegro-03-16-2017, last accessed 17 March 2017; Ellis,
Glenn and Katerina Barushka, "A Very Montenegrin Coup", *Al Jazeera*, http://
www.aljazeera.com/programmes/peopleandpower/2017/03/montenegrin-
coup-170302060130440.html, last accessed 17 March 2017.

49 Latal, Srecko, "Bosnia Clinches New €550m Deal with IMF", *Balkan Insight*, http://
www.balkaninsight.com/en/article/bosnia-to-get-new-550-million-program-
from-imf-05-25-2016, last accessed 17 March 2017.

50 Latal, Srecko, "Bosnian Serb Leader Fishes for Funds in Moscow", *Balkan Insight*,
http://www.balkaninsight.com/en/article/bosnian-serb-leader-fishes-for-budget-
support-in-moscow-10-14-2015, last accessed 17 March 2017.

51 Karabeg, Omer, "Serbia: Sitting between Russia and NATO", *Radio Free Europe – Radio Liberty*, http://www.slobodnaevropa.org/a/serbia-sitting-between-russia-and-
nato/27316179.html, last accessed 17 March 2017.

52 Dragojlo, Sasa, "Serbia to Host Two Military Drills with Russia", *Balkan Insight*,
http://www.balkaninsight.com/en/article/serbia-s-hosting-two-joint-military-
exercises-with-russia-08-17-2016, last accessed 17 March 2017.

53 "Serbia to Help Russian Aid Operation in Syria", *Balkan Insight*, http://www.
balkaninsight.com/en/article/serbia-to-help-moscow-military-operations-in-
syria-08-09-2016, last accessed 17 March 2017.

54 Pantovic, Milivoje, "Serbia Arms Experts Query Value of Russia's 'Gifts'", *Balkan
Insight*, http://www.balkaninsight.com/en/article/serbian-arms-deal-with-russia-
may-be-too-expensive-12-22-2016, last accessed 17 March 2017.

55 "Macedonia: Ex-PM threatens foreign ambassadors, NGOs", *Deutsche Welle*,
http://www.dw.com/en/macedonia-ex-pm-threatens-foreign-ambassadors-
ngos/a-36833009, last accessed 17 March 2017.

56 Hinshaw, Drew, "Former U.S. Ally in Bosnia Turns His Back", *Wall Street Journal*, https://www.wsj.com/articles/former-u-s-ally-in-bosnia-turns-his-
back-1477992604, last accessed 17 March 2017.

57 Erlanger, Steven, "Montenegro Leaders Balk at Taking on Milosevic", *New York Times*,
http://www.nytimes.com/2000/09/12/world/montenegro-leaders-balk-at-
taking-on-milosevic.html, last accessed 17 March 2017.

58 Patrucić, Miranda, Mirsad Brkić, and Svjetlana Ćelić, "Đukanović's Montenegro a
Family Business", *OCCRP*, https://www.reportingproject.net/underground/in-
dex.php?option=com_content&view=article&id=6&Itemid=19, last accessed 17
March 2017.

59 Morrison, Kenneth, "Montenegro's Great Survivor Returns to Mixed Applause", *Balkan Insight*, http://www.balkaninsight.com/en/article/montenegro-s-great-survivor-returns-to-mixed-applause, last accessed 17 March 2017.

60 Lees, Lorraine M., *Keeping Tito Afloat: The United States, Yugoslavia, and the Cold War, 1945–1960*, University Park: Pennsylvania State University Press, 2010.

61 Gow, James, *Triumph of the Lack of Will: International Diplomacy and the Yugoslav War*, New York: Columbia University Press, 1997.

62 Diehl, Jackson, "Putin's hope to ignite a Eurasia-style protest in the United States", *Washington Post*, https://www.washingtonpost.com/opinions/global-opinions/putins-hope-to-ignite-a-eurasia-style-protest-in-the-united-states/2016/10/16/0f271a60-90a4-11e6-9c85-ac42097b8cc0_story.html?utm_term=.f6123de1b1c7, last accessed 17 March 2017.

63 Holland, Steve and Jeff Mason, "Obama, in dig at Putin, calls Russia 'regional power'", *Reuters*, http://www.reuters.com/article/us-ukraine-crisis-russia-weakness-idUSBREA2O19J20140325, last accessed 17 March 2017.

64 Tonchev, Plamen, "China's Road: Into the Western Balkans", *European Union Institute for Security Studies Brief*, No. 3, 2017.

65 Poulain, Loïc, "China's New Balkan Strategy", *Center for Strategic and International Studies – Central Europe Watch*, Vol. 1, No. 2, 2011.

66 "Data: Chinese Contracts and Workers in Africa", *Johns Hopkins School of Advanced International Studies – China-Africa Research Initiative*, http://www.sais-cari.org/data-chinese-workers-in-africa/, last accessed 19 March 2017.

67 "Kinezi grade veliki kulturni centar u Beogradu", *N1 Srbija*, http://rs.n1info.com/a131290/Biznis/Kinezi-grade-veliki-kulturni-centar-u-Beogradu.html, last accessed 19 March 2017.

68 Zeneli, Valbona, "China's Balkan Gamble", *The Diplomat*, http://thediplomat.com/2014/12/chinas-balkan-gamble/, last accessed 19 March 2017.

69 "Kineska nova godina obilježena u Sarajevu uz bogat program i vatromet", *Klix*, https://www.klix.ba/vijesti/bih/kineska-nova-godina-obiljezena-u-sarajevu-uz-bogat-program-i-vatromet/170118147#21, last accessed 5 July 2017.

70 Tubilewicz, Czeslaw, *Taiwan and Post-Communist Europe: Shopping for Allies*, London and New York: Routledge, 2007, pp. 124-155.

71 Wen, Wang and Chen Xiaochen, "Who Supports China in the South China Sea and Why", *The Diplomat*, http://thediplomat.com/2016/07/who-supports-china-in-the-south-china-sea-and-why/, last accessed 19 March 2017; "Who Is Taking Sides after the South China Sea Ruling?", *Asia Maritime Transparency Initiative*, https://amti.csis.org/sides-in-south-china-sea/, last accessed 19 March 2017.

72 Gotev, Georgi, "EU unable to adopt statement upholding South China Sea ruling", *Euractiv*, http://www.euractiv.com/section/global-europe/news/eu-unable-to-adopt-statement-upholding-south-china-sea-ruling/, last accessed 19 March 2017.

73 Michel, Casey, "2 Years On, Eurasian Economic Union Falls Flat", *The Diplomat*, http://thediplomat.com/2017/01/2-years-on-eurasian-economic-union-falls-flat/, last accessed 19 March 2017.

74 Wertime, David, "China Quietly Abandoning Bid for 'New Model of Great Power Relations' with U.S.", *Foreign Policy*, http://foreignpolicy.com/2017/03/02/china-quietly-abandoning-bid-for-new-model-of-great-power-relations-with-u-s/, last accessed 19 March 2017.

75 Cooley, Alexander, *Great Games, Local Rules: The New Power Contest in Central Asia*, Oxford and New York: Oxford University Press, 2012.

76 Boduszyćski, Mieczysław P., "The Gulf and the Balkans: Islam, Investment, and Influence", *Gulf State Analytics Monthly Monitor*, January 2015, pp. 5-8.

77 Sito-Sucic, Daria, "Gulf tourism frenzy in Bosnia delights business, polarizes locals", *Reuters*, http://www.reuters.com/article/us-bosnia-arabs-investment-idUSKC-N10W08L, last accessed 19 March 2017.

78 Ljubas, Zdravko, "One Arab project could change Bosnia-Herzegovina", *Deutsche Welle*, http://www.dw.com/en/one-arab-project-could-change-bosnia-herzegovina/a-18790892, last accessed 19 March 2017.

79 Shepard, Wade, "A Look at Abu Dhabi's 'Bad Joke': The Belgrade Waterfront Project", *Forbes*, https://www.forbes.com/sites/wadeshepard/2016/12/08/inside-abu-dhabis-bad-joke-the-belgrade-waterfront-project/#19ba4e966c12, last accessed 19 March 2017.

80 Sekularac, Ivana, "UAE's Etihad to buy 49 percent stake in Serbian airline", *Reuters*, http://www.reuters.com/article/us-etihad-jat-idUSBRE9700EX20130801, last accessed 19 March 2017.

81 Rose, Eleanor, "Bosnia, Serbia Launch Joint Trade Offensive in Saudi Arabia", *Balkan Insight*, http://www.balkaninsight.com/en/article/bosnian-serbian-delegation-launches-charm-offensive-in-saudi-arabia-01-30-2017, last accessed 19 March 2017.

82 Marzouk, Lawrence, "Croatia Approved €101 Million of Saudi Arms Exports", *Balkan Insight*, http://www.balkaninsight.com/en/article/croatia-approved-101-million-of-saudi-arms-exports-03-26-2017, last accessed 27 March 2017.

83 Cosic, Jelena, "Serbia PM Defends Lucrative Saudi Arms Sales", *Balkan Insight*, http://www.balkaninsight.com/en/article/serbia-pm-defends-lucrative-saudi-arms-sales-08-02-2016-1, last accessed 27 March 2017.

84 Tomovic, Dusica, "Montenegro Probes Controversial Saudi Arms Sales", *Balkan*

Insight, http://www.balkaninsight.com/en/article/montenegro-probes-controversial-saudi-arms-sales-03-20-2017, last accessed 27 March 2017.

85 Marzouk, Lawrence, Anuska Delic and Pavla Holcova, "Slovenian Ammunition Link to ISIS Suspected", *Balkan Insight*, http://www.balkaninsight.com/en/article/slovenian-ammunition-link-to-isis-suspected-11-28-2016, last accessed 27 March 2017.

86 "The Balkan arms trade: Ask not from whom the AK-47s flow", *The Economist*, http://www.economist.com/news/europe/21697019-answer-often-serbia-croatia-or-bulgaria-ask-not-whom-ak-47s-flow, last accessed 27 March 2017.

87 Jukic, Elvira, "Bosnia Presidency Condemns Arms Sales to Ukraine", *Balkan Insight*, http://www.balkaninsight.com/en/article/bosnia-presidency-stands-against-ammunition-sales-to-ukraine, last accessed 27 March 2017.

88 "Saudijska Arabija najveći arapski investitor u BiH", *Klix*, https://www.klix.ba/biznis/investicije/saudijska-arabija-najveci-arapski-investitor-u-bih/170302098, last accessed 19 March 2017.

89 Karasik, Theodore, "Gate to the Balkans: UAE and Serbia strengthen ties", *Al Arabiya English*, https://english.alarabiya.net/en/views/news/world/2013/12/18/Gate-to-the-Balkans-the-growing-relationship-between-the-UAE-and-Serbia.html, last accessed 19 March 2017.

90 "European Union, Trade in goods with Western Balkans 6", *European Commission – Directorate General for Trade*, http://trade.ec.europa.eu/doclib/docs/2006/september/tradoc_111477.pdf, last accessed 19 March 2017.

91 Cappello, John, "Russian Information Operations in the Western Balkans", *Real Clear – Defense*, http://www.realcleardefense.com/articles/2017/02/02/russian_information_operations_in_the_western_balkans_110732.html, last accessed 27 March 2017.

92 Ilić, Velimir, "Arapske investicije u Srbiji: Više euforije nego ekonomije", *Al Jazeera Balkans*, http://balkans.aljazeera.net/vijesti/arapske-investicije-u-srbiji-vise-euforije-nego-ekonomije, last accessed 19 March 2017.

93 Jehl, Douglas, "U.S. Looks Away as Iran Arms Bosnia", *New York Times*, http://www.nytimes.com/1995/04/15/world/us-looks-away-as-iran-arms-bosnia.html, last accessed 19 March 2017.

94 Pomfret, John and David B. Ottaway, "U.S. Allies Fed Covert Pipeline of Arms to Bosnia", *Washington Post*, https://www.washingtonpost.com/archive/politics/1996/05/12/us-allies-fed-pipeline-of-covert-arms-to-bosnia/9d2d9f71-c191-490a-b1cc-c468c0a8468a/?utm_term=.b1697f1e754a, last accessed 19 March 2017.

95 Hoare, Marko Attila, *How Bosnia Armed*, London: Saqi Books, 2004, pp. 131-135.

96 Hoare, Marko Attila, "Christopher Deliso, John R. Schindler and Shaul Shay on al-Qaeda in Bosnia", *Greater Surbiton*, https://greatersurbiton.wordpress.com/2008/06/02/al-qaida-in-bosnia/, last accessed 19 March 2017.

97 Qirezi, Arben, "Kosovo Arrests 19 Suspected of Terror Attacks", *Balkan Insight*, http://www.balkaninsight.com/en/article/kosovo-arrests-19-on-suspicion-of-planning-is-attacks-11-17-2016, last accessed 19 March 2017.

98 Toe, Rodolfo, "Bosnia Police Swoop on 11 ISIS Suspects", *Balkan Insight*, http://www.balkaninsight.com/en/article/bosnian-police-arrests-15-persons-suspected-of-connections-with-isis-12-22-2015, last accessed 19 March 2017.

99 "Kosovo police say terror attack on Israeli team prevented", *Associated Press*, https://apnews.com/133a2151d0a549d6913392b7e7708dc1/kosovo-police-say-terror-attack-israeli-team-prevented, last accessed 5 July 2017.

100 Toe, Rodolfo, "Bosnia Ends Abu Hamza's Seven-Year Ordeal", *Balkan Insight*, http://www.balkaninsight.com/en/article/bosnia-releases-abu-hamza-02-18-2016, last accessed 19 March 2017.

101 Rose, Eleanor, "Experts Scorn Claim That Bosnia Is 'Terrorist Haven'", *Balkan Insight*, http://www.balkaninsight.com/en/article/bosnian-authorities-have-responded-to-terrorism-threats-says-expert-02-03-2017, last accessed 19 March 2017.

102 "Foreign Fighters in Iraq and Syria: Where do they come from?", *Radio Free Europe – Radio Liberty*, http://www.rferl.org/a/foreign-fighters-syria-iraq-is-isis-isil-infographic/26584940.html, last accessed 19 March 2017.

103 Kovacevic, Danijel, "Bosnian Serbs Halt Cooperation with State Police, Court", *Balkan Insight*, http://www.balkaninsight.com/en/article/bosnian-serb-entity-halts-all-cooperation-with-state-institutions-12-10-2015-1, last accessed 19 March 2017.

104 Rose, Eleanor, "US Sanctions Dodik for Obstructing Dayton Agreement", *Balkan Insight*, http://www.balkaninsight.com/en/article/us-sanctions-dodik-for-obstructing-dayton-agreement-01-17-2017, last accessed 19 March 2017.

105 Zuvela, Maja, "Biggest Serb party in Bosnia threatens 2018 secession", *Reuters*, http://www.reuters.com/article/us-bosnia-serbs-secession-idUSKBN0NG-0NB20150425, last accessed 19 March 2017.

106 Bringa, Tone, *Being Muslim the Bosnian Way: Identity and Community in a Central Bosnian Village*, Princeton: Princeton University Press, 1995; Merdjanova, Ina, *Rediscovering the* Umma*: Muslims in the Balkans between Nationalism and Transnationalism*, Oxford and New York: Oxford University Press, 2013.

107 Puhalo, Srđan (ed.), *Selefije u Bosni i Hercegovini: Ko su oni, kako ih drugi vide i kako se izvještava o njima*, Banja Luka: Pro Educa Centar za Edukaciju, 2016.

108 Simkus, Albert and Kirsten Ringdal (eds.), *The Aftermath of War: Experiences and Social Attitudes in the Western Balkans*, London and New York: Routledge, 2012.

109 Huseinovic, Samir and Marina Martinovic, "Turkey's Gulen crackdown comes to Bosnia", *Deutsche Welle*, http://www.dw.com/en/turkeys-gulen-crackdown-comes-to-bosnia/a-19490024, last accessed 19 March 2017; Marusic, Sinisa Jakov, "Macedonia May Shut Gulen-Linked Turkish Schools", *Balkan Insight*, http://www.balkaninsight.com/en/article/macedonia-hints-closing-gulen-organizations-upon-turkish-request-08-25-2016, last accessed 19 March 2017; Mejdini, Fatjona, "Albania Weighs Turkey's Claim to Be Gulenist Hub", *Balkan Insight*, http://www.balkaninsight.com/en/article/in-gulen-erdogan-fight-albania-should-put-its-interests-first-expert-11-02-2016, last accessed 19 March 2017; Bytyci, Fatos, "Turkey asks Kosovo to punish journalist over coup comments", *Reuters*, http://www.reuters.com/article/us-kosovo-turkey-journalist-idUSKCN1061A1, last accessed 19 March 2017.

110 Birnbaum, Michael, "Turkey brings a gentle version of the Ottoman empire back to the Balkans", *The Guardian*, https://www.theguardian.com/world/2013/apr/02/bosnia-turkey-ottoman-influence-balkans-sarajevo, last accessed 19 March 2017; Somun, Hajrudin, "Turkish Foreign Policy in the Balkans and 'Neo-Ottomanism': A Personal Account", *Insight Turkey*, Vol. 13, No. 3, 2011, pp. 33-41.

111 Bechev, Dimitar, "What's behind the Turkey-Russia reset?", *Al Jazeera*, http://www.aljazeera.com/indepth/opinion/2016/08/turkey-russia-reset-160808103350290.html, last accessed 19 March 2017.

4. THE COMING UPHEAVALS IN THE WESTERN BALKANS

1 Mujanović, Jasmin, "Democracy blooming at the margins: Bosnia-Herzegovina, Ukraine and Taiwan", *openDemocracy*, https://www.opendemocracy.net/jasmin-mujanovi%C4%87/democracy-blooming-at-margins-bosniaherzegovina-ukraine-and-taiwan, last accessed 20 March 2017.

2 Anscombe, Frederick F., "The Balkan Revolutionary Age", *Journal of Modern History*, Vol. 84, No. 3, 2012; Stavrianos, L.S., *Balkan Federation: A History of the Movement toward Balkan Unity in Modern Times*, Hamden: Archon Books, 1964.

3 Onuch, Olga, "Miadans Past and Present: Comparing the Orange Revolution and the Euromaidan" in David R. Marples and Frederick V. Mills, *Ukraine's Euromaidan: Analysis of a Civil Revolution*, Stuttgart: Ibidem, 2015, pp. 27-56.

4 Gana, Nouri (ed.), *The Making of the Tunisian Revolution: Contexts, Architects, Prospects*, Edinburgh: Edinburgh University Press, 2013.

5 Dzihic, Vedran, "Democracy and Democratic Values in the Balkans", *idee*, No. 6, 2011, pp. 13-16.

6 Spoerri, Marlene, *Engineering Revolution: The Paradox of Democracy Promotion in Serbia*, Philadelphia: University of Pennsylvania Press, 2015.

7 Henley, Jon, "Meet Srdja Popovic, the secret architect of global revolution", *The Guardian*, https://www.theguardian.com/world/2015/mar/08/srdja-popovic-revolution-serbian-activist-protest, last accessed 21 March 2017.

8 Torov, Ivan, "The Resistance in Serbia" in Jasminka Udovićki and James Ridgeway, *Burn This House: The Making and Unmaking of Yugoslavia*, Durham and London: Duke University Press, 2000, pp. 247-266.

9 Stevanovic, Vidosav, *Milosevic: The People's Tyrant*, London and New York: I.B. Tauris, 2004, pp. 176-182.

10 Spoerri, pp. 55-120.

11 Bujosevic, Dragan and Ivan Radovanovic, *The Fall of Milosevic: The October 5th Revolution*, New York: Palgrave Macmillan, 2003.

12 Grodsky, Brian, *The Democratization Disconnect: How Recent Democratic Revolutions Threaten the Future of Democracy*, Lanham, Boulder, New York and London: Rowman and Littlefield, 2016, pp. 153-154.

13 Gordy, Eric, *Guilt, Responsibility, and Denial: The Past at Stake in Post-Milosevic Serbia*, Philadelphia: University of Pennsylvania Press, 2013, pp. 69-86.

14 Ibid., pp. 151-156.

15 Krstić, Nikola, "Balkan model of authoritarianism: 6 similarities between the regimes in Macedonia and Serbia", *European Western Balkans*, https://europeanwest-ernbalkans.com/2016/04/21/balkan-model-of-authoritarianism-6-similarities-between-the-political-regimes-in-macedonia-and-serbia/, last accessed 21 March 2017.

16 "Study: PTSD Haunts Bosnian War Survivors", *Balkan Insight*, http://www.balka-ninsight.com/en/article/study-ptsd-haunts-bosnian-war-survivors, last accessed 21 March 2017.

17 Less, Timothy, "Dysfunction in the Balkans", *Foreign Affairs*, https://www.foreignaf-fairs.com/articles/bosnia-herzegovina/2016-12-20/dysfunction-balkans, last accessed 21 March 2017.

18 As my friend Damir Imamović once observed, despite the widespread perception of constant war in the Balkans, the broader Yugoslav conflict is the only one referred to colloquially as "*naš rat*" or "our war".

19 Biermann, Rafael, André Härtel, Andreas Kaiser and Johann Zajaczkowski, "Ukrainian Civil Society after the Maidan: Potentials and Challenges on the Way to Sustainable Democratization and Europeanization", *Deutschland und Europastudien – Friedrich-Schiller-Universität Jena*, http://www.des.uni-jena.de/maeuropamedia/Fi

nal+Conference+Report+_+Civil+Society+after+Maidan+_+2015+.pdf, last accessed 21 March 2017.

20 "Romanian Protests Inspire Activists across Balkans", *Balkan Insight*, http://www. balkaninsight.com/en/article/balkan-politicians-call-for-romania-inspired-protests-02-06-2017, last accessed 21 March 2017.

21 Knezevic, Gorana, "Milosevic 'Exonerated'? War-Crime Deniers Feed Receptive Audience", *Radio Free Europe – Radio Liberty*, https://www.rferl.org/a/milosevic-war-crime-deniers-feed-receptive-audience/27910664.html, last accessed 7 July 2017.

22 Da Silva, Chantal, "Serbian protesters accuse media of turning blind eye, as anti-corruption rallies continue", *The Independent*, http://www.independent.co.uk/news/world/europe/serbia-protests-media-aleksandar-vucic-prime-minister-police-a7673532.html, last accessed 7 July 2017.

23 Stavljanin, Dragan, "Serbian Elections: The Ghost of Milosevic Haunts Serbia's European Path", *Radio Free Europe – Radio Liberty*, https://www.slobodnaevropa.org/a/serbian-elections-the-ghost-of-milosevic-haunts-serbias-europen-path/27704322.html, last accessed 7 July 2017.

24 Vasovic, Aleksandar, "Thousands protest against Serb government and flagship project", *Reuters*, http://www.reuters.com/article/us-serbia-protests-idUSKBN-17R2L6, last accessed 7 July 2017.

25 Kljajic, Sanja, "Young Serbians protest Vucic victory", *DeutscheWelle*, http://www.dw.com/en/young-serbians-protest-vucic-victory/a-38315174, last accessed 7 July 2017.

26 Mujanović, Jasmin (ed.), *The Democratic Potential of Emerging Social Movements in Southeastern Europe*, Sarajevo: Friedrich Ebert Stiftung – Dialogue Southeast Europe, 2017.

27 Djankov, Simeon, *Inside the Euro Crisis: An Eyewitness Account*, Washington, DC: Peterson Institute for International Economics, 2014, pp. 153-155.

28 Tomšić, Samo, "The people returns: a footnote to protests in Slovenia", *Critical Legal Thinking*, http://criticallegalthinking.com/2013/01/16/the-people-returns-a-footnote-to-protests-in-slovenia/, last accessed 21 March 2017.

29 Ibid.

30 Hacler, Tina and Andrej Ćebokli, "Največja vseslovenska vstaja do zdaj. Protestiralo 20.000 ljudi", *MMC*, http://www.rtvslo.si/slovenija/foto-najvecja-vseslovenska-vstaja-do-zdaj-protestiralo-20-000-ljudi/302017, last accessed 21 March 2017.

31 "Slovenia's election: A new man for the job", *The Economist*, http://www.economist.com/news/europe/21607863-dissatisfied-slovenes-vote-heavily-political-newcomer-new-man-job, last accessed 21 March 2017.

32 Bieber, Florian, "Revisiting New Universities in the Balkans: European Visions, UFOs and Megatrends", *Balkanist*, http://balkanist.net/revisiting-new-universities-balkans-european-visions-ufos-megatrends/, last accessed 21 March 2017.

33 Bilefsky, Dan, "17,000 Migrants Stranded in Croatia by Border Crackdown", *New York Times*, https://www.nytimes.com/2015/09/19/world/europe/refugee-migrant-crisis-europe.html, last accessed 21 March 2017.

34 In June 2017, the party reorganized and formally renamed itself Levica (The Left). In the process, one of their six MPs left the party to sit as an independent. As this is still a very recent development at the time of writing, for the sake of clarity I will continue to refer to the group as ZL.

35 Toplišek, Alen, "The Slovenian United Left: from protest to movement, and from movement to party", *openDemocracy*, https://www.opendemocracy.net/can-europe-make-it/alen-topli-ek/slovenian-united-left-from-protest-to-movement-and-from-movement-to, last accessed 21 March 2017.

36 Zerofsky, Elisabeth, "The Counterparty", *Harper's Magazine*, http://harpers.org/archive/2015/12/the-counterparty/, last accessed 21 March 2017.

37 Toplišek.

38 Zivulovic, Srdjan, "Same-Sex Marriage Referendum Fails in Slovenia", *Newsweek*, http://www.newsweek.com/same-sex-marriage-referendum-fails-slovenia-407499, last accessed 21 March 2017.

39 Brown, Archie, *The Myth of the Strong Leader: Political Leadership in the Modern Age*, New York: Basic Books, 2014.

40 Frankland, E. Gene, Paul Lucardie and Benoît Rihoux (eds.), *Green Parties in Transition: The End of Grass-roots Democracy?*, Surrey and Burlington: Ashgate, 2008.

41 "Pravni haos: Zakon o JMBG nije u skladu sa Ustavom BiH", *Vaša prava BiH*, http://www.vasaprava.org/?p=1669, last accessed 21 March 2017.

42 Maksimovic, Maja and Ioannis Armakolas, "'Babylution': A Civic Awakening in Bosnia and Herzegovina?", *Hellenic Foundation for European and Foreign Policy*, http://www.eliamep.gr/wp-content/uploads/2013/08/34_2013_-WORKING-PA-PER-_Armakolas-12.pdf, last accessed 21 March 2017.

43 Dzidic, Denis, "Bosnia-Herzegovina hit by wave of violent protests", *The Guardian*, https://www.theguardian.com/world/2014/feb/07/bosnia-herzegovina-wave-violent-protests, last accessed 21 March 2017.

44 Domi, Tanya L. and Jasmin Mujanović, "Bosnian Spring Signals New Possibilities for Bosnia-Herzegovina", *Harriman Magazine*, Summer 2014, pp. 22-25.

45 Kurtović, Larisa, "'Who sows hunger, reaps rage': on protest, indignation and redistributive justice in post-Dayton Bosnia-Herzegovina", *Southeast European and Black*

Sea Studies, Vol. 15, Issue 4, 2015.

46 Fagan, Adam and Indraneel Sircar, *Europeanization of the Western Balkans: Environmental Governance in Bosnia-Herzegovina and Serbia*, New York: Palgrave Macmillan, 2015, pp. 160-161.

47 Mujanović, Jasmin, "Institutionalizing Crisis: The Case of Dayton Bosnia-Herzegovi-na" in Deric Shannon (ed.), *The End of the World as We Know It? Crisis, Resistance, and the Age of Austerity*, Oakland: AK Press, 2014, p. 159.

48 Ibid.

49 Isović, Maja, "Dogaćaj 2012. godine: Borba za park u Banjaluci", *Buka*, http://www.6yka.com/novost/32405/dogadaj-2012.-godine-borba-za-park-u-banjaluci, last accessed 21 March 2017.

50 "Graćani RS o protestima u FBiH", *RTVBN*, https://www.youtube.com/watch?v=OBJDsq6JWWg, last accessed 21 March 2017.

51 "Većina graćana podržava proteste, a nasilje predstavlja preveliku cijenu promjena", *Klix*, https://www.klix.ba/vijesti/bih/vecina-gradjana-podrzava-proteste-a-nasilje-predstavlja-preveliku-cijenu-promjena/140212119, last accessed 21 March 2017.

52 Scott, James, *Two Cheers for Anarchism*, Princeton: Princeton University Press, 2014, pp. 16-17.

53 Wolin, 1996, p. 31.

54 The similarities to the organizational and participatory methods used by the "Occupy Wall Street" activists here are not accidental. Central to creating a more participatory political culture is challenging hierarchies and challenging the fetishization of leadership. I have explained on numerous occasions now, to various audiences, that the eventual "failure" of the plenums was not due to their "lack of leadership". Quite on the contrary, the lack of leadership was a critical element in educating ordinary citizens in the basic praxis of social movement organizing. The point of the plenums was not to lift up "new leaders" but to illustrate how collective action could intervene and perhaps even replace top-down modes of organization (e.g. parties). Moreover, the plenums aimed to allow citizens to imagine themselves as the agents of change in BiH, rather than "their leaders".

55 "Tuzla: Održan drugi Plenum graćana", *Tuzlanski TV*, https://www.youtube.com/watch?v=xY0fprvijxw, last accessed 21 March 2017.

56 Kilibarda, Konstantin, Amila Jašarević, Marina Antić, and Jasmin Mujanović (trans.), "The Demands of the People of Bosnia and Herzegovina", http://www.jasminmuja-novic.com/blog/the-demands-of-the-people-of-tuzla-sarajevo-english, last accessed 21 March 2017.

57 De Noni, Andrea, "Bosnia and Herzegovina: the Plenums' legacy", *Osservatorio Balcani e Caucaso*, http://www.balcanicaucaso.org/eng/Areas/Bosnia-Herzegovina/Bosnia-and-Herzegovina-the-Plenums-legacy-155351, last accessed 21 March 2017.

58 Sijah, Dalio, "Uspjeh protesta u BiH: Ipak je 'i srpska i hrvatska i bošnjaćka'", *Istinomjer*, http://istinomjer.ba/uspjeh-protesta-u-bih-ipak-je-srpska-hrvatska-bosnjacka/, last accessed 21 March 2017.

59 Jašarević, Amila (trans.), "A senior citizen on protests in BiH – with subtitles", *Hayatt TV*, https://www.youtube.com/watch?v=oX_7aax7AEg, last accessed 21 March 2017.

60 Mujanović, Jasmin, "It's spring at last in Bosnia and Herzegovina", *Al Jazeera*, http://www.aljazeera.com/indepth/opinion/2014/02/it-spring-at-last-bosnia-herze-gov-2014296537898443.html, last accessed 21 March 2017.

61 Kilibarda, Konstantin (trans.), "Statement by the Belgrade Police Union", *BH Protest Files*, https://bhprotestfiles.wordpress.com/2014/02/09/statement-by-the-bel-grade-police-union-belgrade-1/, last accessed 21 March 2017.

62 Padalović, Elvir, "Sramotna rastrošnost bh političara: Ponovo uvode bijeli hljeb, a narodu se smiju u facu!", *Buka*, http://www.6yka.com/novost/116465/sramotna-rastrosnost-bh-politicara-ponovo-uvode-bijeli-hljeb-a-narodu-se-smiju-u-facu, last accessed 21 March 2017.

63 Gallo, Mattia, "Reflections on the Bosnian Spring. An interview with Emin Emi-nagic", *LeftEast*, http://www.criticatac.ro/lefteast/bosnian-spring/, last accessed 21 March 2017.

64 Kennard, Matt and Ana Caistor-Arendar, "Occupy Buenos Aires: the workers' movement that transformed a city, and inspired the world", *The Guardian*, https://www.theguardian.com/cities/2016/mar/10/occupy-buenos-aires-argentina-workers-cooperative-movement, last accessed 21 March 2017.

65 Šakanović, Dino, "Teta Minka protiv pljaćkaškog kapitalizma: Dita pobjećuje", *Prometej*, http://www.prometej.ba/clanak/vijesti/teta-minka-protiv-pljackaskog-kapitalizma-dita-pobjedjuje-2915, last accessed 21 March 2017.

66 Mujkić, Asim, "In search of a democratic counter-power in Bosnia–Herzegovina", *Southeast European and Black Sea Studies*, Vol. 4, Issue 15, 2015.

67 Ibid.

68 Duhaćek, Gordan, "Politićari u BiH opet dosljedni - baš ih briga za narod!", *tportal*, https://www.tportal.hr/vijesti/clanak/politicari-u-bih-opet-dosljedni-bas-ih-briga-za-narod-20140521, last accessed 21 March 2017.

69 Mujkić, Semir, "Vlasti u strahu: Za gušenje graćanskih nemira policiji kupljena op-rema vrijedna 23 miliona KM!", http://www.zurnal.info/novost/18625/vlasti-u-strahu-za-gusenje-gradanskih-nemira-policiji-kupljena-oprema-vrijedna-23-miliona-km, last accessed 21 March 2017.

70 Vućetić, Milica, "Mujkić: Protesta će opet biti u BiH", *N1 BiH*, http://ba.n1info.com/a136004/Vijesti/Vijesti/Mujkic-Protesta-ce-opet-biti-u-BiH.html, last ac-

cessed 21 March 2017.

71 Mujanović, Jasmin, "Bosnia-Herzegovina's EU Candidacy: Symbolic or Substantive?", *European Council on Foreign Relations*, http://www.ecfr.eu/article/commentary_bosnia_herzegovinas_eu_candidacy_symbolic_or_substantive_6011, last accessed 11 July 2017.

72 Levitsky, Steven and Lucan A. Way, *Competitive Authoritarianism: Hybrid Regimes after the Cold War*, Cambridge and New York: Cambridge University Press, 2010, pp. 125-129.

73 Mujanović, Jasmin, "Fractured Authoritarianism in Bosnia-Herzegovina", *Religion and Society in East and West*, Vol. 44, Issue 9-10, 2016.

74 Mattioli, Fabio, "Authoritarianism in Macedonia", *Foreign Affairs*, https://www.foreignaffairs.com/articles/southeastern-europe/2017-01-12/authoritarianism-macedonia, last accessed 21 March 2017.

75 Marusic, Sinisa Jakov, "Ethnic Albanian MPs Brawl in Macedonian Parliament", *Balkan Insight*, http://www.balkaninsight.com/en/article/fist-fight-breaks-out-in-macedonian-parliament, last accessed 22 March 2017.

76 Jordanovska, Meri and Sinisa Jakov Marusic, "Pro-Govt Media Inflame Nationalist Hysteria in Macedonia", *Balkan Insight*, http://www.balkaninsight.com/en/article/macedonia-s-propaganda-war-spreads-nationalist-hysteria-03-15-2017, last accessed 22 March 2017.

77 McEvoy, Joanne, *Power-Sharing Executives: Governing in Bosnia, Macedonia, and Northern Ireland*, Philadelphia: University of Pennsylvania Press, 2015.

78 Petkovski, Ljupcho and Bojan Marichikj, "Macedonia at the Crossroads – Is Peaceful Transfer of Power Possible in Authoritarianism?", *Balkans in Europe Policy Blog*, http://www.suedosteuropa.uni-graz.at/biepag/node/243, last accessed 22 March 2017.

79 "Macedonian elections – is a crisis going to follow? Reactions from our experts", *LSE – Research on South Eastern Europe*, http://blogs.lse.ac.uk/lsee/2014/04/29/macedonia-2014-elections-experts-react/, last accessed 22 March 2017.

80 Taleski, Dane, "An Authoritarian Regime Fighting to Survive - A more likely view of the 'spy drama' in Macedonia", *Balkans in Europe Policy Blog*, http://www.suedosteuropa.uni-graz.at/biepag/node/146, last accessed 21 March 2017.

81 MacDowall, Andrew, "Fears for Macedonia's fragile democracy amid 'coup' and wiretap claims", *The Guardian*, https://www.theguardian.com/world/2015/feb/27/fears-macedonias-fragile-democracy-amid-coup-wiretap-claims, last accessed 21 March 2017.

82 Staletović, Branimir, "A reflection on the emerging politics of resistance in Macedonia", *Balkans in Europe Policy Blog*, http://www.suedosteuropa.uni-graz.at/biepag/

node/148, last accessed 21 March 2017.

83 Fouere, Erwan, "Macedonian Students' Plenum - A Cry for Respect", *Balkan Insight*, http://www.balkaninsight.com/en/blog/macedonian-student-s-plenum-a-cry-for-respect, last accessed 22 March 2017.

84 Bieber, Florian and Anastas Vangeli, "Gruevski Does Not Deserve Any More Chances", *Balkan Insight*, http://www.balkaninsight.com/en/blog/gruevski-does-not-deserve-any-more-chances, last accessed 21 March 2017.

85 Mejdini, Fatjona, "Macedonia's Kumanovo Shootout Still Raising Suspicions", *Balkan Insight*, http://www.balkaninsight.com/en/article/macedonia-s-kumanovo-shootout-still-raising-suspicions-05-10-2016, last accessed 22 March 2017.

86 Robinson, Matt and Kole Casule, "Wire-tap scandal brings thousands out against Macedonian leader", *Reuters*, http://www.reuters.com/article/us-macedonia-crisis-idUSKBN0O20A420150517?feedName=worldNews&feedType=RSS, last accessed 22 March 2017.

87 Dimishkovski, Aleksandar, "Macedonian Prime Minister Steps Down, but Tensions over Vote Linger", *The New York Times*, https://www.nytimes.com/2016/01/16/world/europe/nikola-gruevski-macedonia.html, last accessed 22 March 2017.

88 Jakov Marusic, Sinisa, "Cost of Macedonian Capital Revamp Soars Again", *Balkan Insight*, http://www.balkaninsight.com/en/article/macedonian-capital-revamp-cost-soars-again-12-09-2015, last accessed 22 March 2017.

89 O'Sullivan, Feargus, "How Paint Became a Weapon in Macedonia's 'Colorful Revolution'", *CityLab*, http://www.citylab.com/politics/2016/05/macedonia-colorful-revolution-paint/481833/, last accessed 22 March 2017.

90 Lasheras, Francisco de Borja, "The Balkan Indignados", *Prishtina Insight*, http://prishtinainsight.com/the-balkan-indignados/, last accessed 22 March 2017.

91 "Insights on the current protests in Macedonia: An interview with two leading civil society activists", *Civicus*, http://www.civicus.org/index.php/media-resources/news/964-insights-on-the-current-protests-in-macedonia-an-interview-with-two-leading-civil-society-activists, last accessed 22 March 2017.

92 Gjorgjioska, Adela and Anastas Vangeli, "Macedonia in Crisis", *Jacobin*, https://www.jacobinmag.com/2017/02/macedonia-corruption-ethnic-politics-levica-protests/, last accessed 22 March 2017.

93 Volkanovska, Elena, "Macedonia's Brain Drain: A Problem That Won't Go Away", *Kosovo 2.0*, http://archive.kosovotwopointzero.com/en/article/1837/zbrazje-e-trurit-te-maqedonise-problem-qe-nuk-po-iken, last accessed 22 March 2017.

94 Marusic, Sinisa Jakov, "Macedonia's Albanians Urged to Reject Gruevski Coalition", *Balkan Insight*, http://www.balkaninsight.com/en/article/ramadani-macedonia-albanians-must-resist-gruevski-s-tricks-01-17-2017, last accessed 22 March 2017.

95 Fouéré, Erwan, "Gruevski's Party Has Left Macedonia in Limbo", *Balkan Insight*, http://www.balkaninsight.com/en/article/gruevski-s-party-has-left-macedonia-in-limbo-03-20-2017, last accessed 22 March 2017.

96 Bryne, Andrew, "Masked men storm Macedonia parliament and attack MPs", *Financial Times*, https://www.ft.com/content/af17531e-2b7c-11e7-bc4b-5528796fe35c?mhq5j=e3, last accessed 12 July 2017.

97 Mujanović, Jasmin, "Stagnant Bosnia Awaits its 'Macedonian Moment'", *Balkan Insight*, http://www.balkaninsight.com/en/article/stagnant-bosnia-awaits-its-macedonian-moment--06-20-2017-1 last accessed 12 July 2017.

98 Mujanović, Jasmin, "Vucic's Brand of 'Stability' Will be Short-lived", *Balkan Insight*, http://www.balkaninsight.com/en/article/vucic-s-brand-of-stability-will-be-short-lived-04-18-2017 last accessed 12 July 2017.

99 Marusic, Sinisa Jakov, "EU's Hahn Urges Speedy Formation of Macedonia Govt", *Balkan Insight*, http://www.balkaninsight.com/en/article/eu-s-hahn-urges-for-speedy-formation-of-macedonia-s-govt--03-22-2017, last accessed 22 March 2017.

100 McLaughlin, Dan, "Russian Propaganda Exploits Ethnic Tensions to Keep Macedonia Looking Inward, Not Westward", *Coda*, https://codastory.com/disinformation-crisis/information-war/russian-propaganda-exploits-ethnic-tensions-to-keep-macedonia-looking-inward-not-westward, last accessed 22 March 2017.

101 Arnsdorf, Isaac, Andrew Hanna and Kenneth P. Vogel, "GOP Takes Up Russia-Aligned Attack on Soros", *Politico*, http://www.politico.com/magazine/story/2017/03/george-soros-russia-republicans-214938, last accessed 22 March 2017.

102 Moraća, Tijana, "Between defiance and compliance: a new civil society in the post-Yugoslav space?", *Osservatorio Balcani e Caucaso*, http://www.balcanicaucaso.org/eng/Areas/Serbia/Between-defiance-and-compliance-a-new-civil-society-in-the-post-Yugoslav-space-173290, last accessed 22 March 2017.

103 Crosby, Alan and Amra Zejneli, "'Self-Determination' Party Capitalizes on Kosovars' Desire to Punish Governing Parties", *Radio Free Europe – Radio Liberty*, https://www.rferl.org/a/kosovo-vetevendosje-capitalizes-on-desire-for-change/28559391.html last accessed 12 July 2017.

104 Mujanović, Jasmin, "A new narrative – why a 'Bosnian Spring' is Bosnia's only hope", *TransConflict*, http://www.transconflict.com/2012/05/a-new-narrative-why-a-bosnian-spring-is-bosnias-only-hope-305/, last accessed 22 March 2017.

105 Levine, Robert S., John Stauffer and John R. McKivigan, *Frederick Douglass: The Heroic Slave, A Cultural and Critical Edition*, New Haven and London: Yale University Press, 2015, pp. 133-134.

CONCLUSIONS

1 Barber, Lionel, "Juncker warns Trump to stop 'annoying' praise for Brexit", *Financial Times*, https://www.ft.com/content/938452b6-1072-11e7-a88c-50ba212dce4d, last accessed 24 March 2017.

2 Wallace, Joe, "The West Balkans: 'A pan full of oil'", *The World Weekly*, https://www.theworldweekly.com/reader/view/magazine/2017-03-16/the-west-balkans-a-pan-full-of-oil/9809, last accessed 24 March 2017.

3 Clausewitz, Carl von and J.J. Graham (ed.), *On War: Volume 1*, New York: Routledge, 2005, p. 23.

4 Lasswell, Harold D., *Politics: Who Gets What, When and How*, New York: McGraw-Hill, 1936.

5 "Freedom in the World 2017: Populists and Autocrats: The Dual Threat to Global Democracy", *Freedom House*, https://freedomhouse.org/report/freedom-world/freedom-world-2017, last accessed 24 March 2017.

6 Jenkins, Richard, *Rethinking Ethnicity: Arguments and Explorations*, 2nd edn, London, Thousand Oaks, New Delhi, Singapore: Sage Publications, 2008.

7 Toal and Dahlman.

8 Nixon, Rob, "Of Balkans and 'Bantustans': 'Ethnic Cleansing' and the Crisis of National Legitimation", *Transitions*, No. 60, 1993.

9 Scott, p. 141.

INDEX

INDEX

INDEX

INDEX

INDEX

INDEX

modernization, 29, 40
non-Muslims, 27, 28, 40
patrimonialism, 22, 23, 26, 46
patronage, 22, 25
Serbian Uprising, First (1804–
  13), 30, 31
Serbian–Ottoman War (1876–
  78), 33
timar system, 26–7, 40
Our Party (Naša stranka), 142

Pargan, Benjamin, 99
participation, 10, 11, 23, 24, 36,
  48, 59
partition, 72, 76, 138, 171
Party of Democratic Action (SDA),
  78, 145, 147, 151
Party of the European Left, 143
pashas, 29, 37
patrimonialism, 17, 19, 29, 30, 48,
  52, 87, 97, 127, 129, 130, 169
  Austria-Hungary, 42
  Croatia, 101
  Kingdom of Serbs, Croats and
    Slovenes, 43
  Macedonia, 157, 161
  Ottoman Empire, 22, 23, 26, 46
  privatization, 91
  Slovenia, 101, 143
  Socialist Federal Republic of
    Yugoslavia, 65, 66
patronage, 22, 25, 99, 156
Pejaković, Josip, 78
Pejić, Nenad, 77–8
People's Radical Party (NRS), 35
Perić, Vladimir 'Valter', 76
Perlman, Fredy, 68–9
Perović, Latinka, 71
Petar II Petrović-Njegoš, Prince-
  Bishop of Montenegro, 33
Picin Park, Banja Luka, 147–8
Plato, 172

Plavšić, Biljana, 65
plebes, 4–5, 6, 10, 17, 21, 102,
  131, 149, 164
Podemos, 143
Poland, 87, 102, 103
Police Union of Belgrade, 152
polis, 4, 20, 21
political agency, 134
Poos, Jacques, 50
Porto Alegre, Brazil, 90
Portugal, 96
Pozderac, Hamdija, 65
Praxis group, 61, 71, 188
Prijedor, Republika Srpska, 151
printing press, 184
privatization, 30, 47, 89, 90, 91,
  150
*Programme of the League of
  Communists of Yugoslavia* (1958),
  59, 60, 68
protection rackets, 19, 46, 48, 91
PTSD (post-traumatic stress disor-
  der), 125
Putin, Vladimir, 111–12, 116, 126

al-Qaeda, 123
Qatar, 122
Quebec, 190

Radio Televizija Sarajevo (RTS),
  77–8
Ranković, Aleksandar, 62, 189
recovered factories movement, 154
refugee/migrant crisis (2015–),
  106–9, 142
Republic of Užice (1941), 57
Republika Srpska, 86, 113–15,
  124, 128, 145, 147–8, 151, 164
Roma people, 166
Romania, 34, 36, 37, 103, 138
Romanov dynasty (1613–1917), 32
Rusinow, Dennison, 61

INDEX